# Bill Mauldin
# A Life Up Front

*"Just gimme th' aspirin. I already got a Purple Heart."*

# Bill Mauldin
# A Life Up Front

## Todd DePastino

W. W. Norton & Company

New York  London

For information about permission to reproduce
selections from this book, write to Permissions,
W. W. Norton & Company, Inc.,
500 Fifth Avenue, New York, NY 10110

For information about special discounts for bulk purchases, please contact
W. W. Norton Special Sales at specialsales@wwnorton.com or 800-233-4830

Manufacturing by RR Donnelley, Harrisonburg
Book design by Lovedog Studio
Production manager: Julia Druskin

Library of Congress Cataloging-in-Publication Data

DePastino, Todd.
Bill Mauldin : a life up front / Todd DePastino. — 1st ed.
p. cm.
Includes bibliographical references and index.
ISBN 978-0-393-06183-3 (hardcover)
1. Mauldin, Bill, 1921–2003.
2. Cartoonist—United States—Biography.
I. Title.
NC1429.M428D47 2008
741.5092—dc22
[B]

2007040494

W. W. Norton & Company, Inc.
500 Fifth Avenue, New York, N.Y. 10110
www.wwnorton.com

W. W. Norton & Company Ltd.
Castle House, 75/76 Wells Street, London W1T 3QT

1 2 3 4 5 6 7 8 9 0

For the real
Willies and Joes,

with gratitude

# Contents

**Bill Mauldin**
**A Life Up Front**

## Prologue

# "He Was Our Champion"

*It doesn't go away. It sleeps sometimes, but then it awakens again. . . . It's an enormity of an experience. And everything after that has been a footnote.*

—ED STEWART, FORMER SERGEANT,
84TH INFANTRY[1]

ALMOST EVERY DAY in the summer and fall of 2002 they came to Park Superior nursing home in Newport Beach, California, to honor Army Sergeant, Technician Third Grade, Bill Mauldin. They came bearing relics of their youth: medals, insignia, photographs, and carefully folded newspaper clippings. Some wore old garrison caps. Others arrived resplendent in uniforms over a half century old. Almost all of them wept as they filed down the corridor like pilgrims fulfilling some long-neglected obligation.

Sergeant Mauldin had never led men in battle. Only once during World War II had he discharged his weapon, to kill a diseased bull to feed starving Italian peasants.

He had instead fought the war with an ink brush, and now the eighty-year-old cartoonist was dying. Mauldin had barely survived a scalding received in a bathtub months earlier. His body had been ravaged by rounds of subsequent infection, and his mind by Alzheimer's disease. Surrounded by family, friends, and nursing home staff, he remained locked in his own oblivion, staring vacantly out the window. Only occasionally did his dark eyes and broad face hint at his captivating passion and charisma.

The first old soldier at Bill's bedside was Jay Gruenfeld, a seventy-seven-year-old veteran of the 43rd Division who had been wounded five times in the Philippines. The last bullet had almost severed his spine. By that time, his platoon of forty men had been whittled down to eight. He was lying in an army hospital in 1945, a scared, lonely twenty-one-year-old, when his father sent him Mauldin's bestselling book of text and cartoons, *Up Front*.[2]

The book, featuring Mauldin's signature characters Willie and Joe, spoke to Gruenfeld like nothing else had. More important, it spoke *for* him, expressing his grief, exhaustion, and flickering hope. Bill Mauldin, a rifleman himself, knew those feelings. He had read them in other soldiers' eyes, eyes that "were just too old for those young bodies."[3]

Fifty-seven years after finding comfort in these words, Jay Gruenfeld wanted to pay Bill Mauldin back by sending him a copy of his own self-published memoirs.

In April of 2002, Gruenfeld tracked down David Mauldin, Bill's son, in Santa Fe, New Mexico.

"When he called," David said, "I had to tell him Dad was not doing well."

"Well, I have to go see him," Gruenfeld replied. A few days later, he drove two hundred miles to Newport Beach and spent a day with Bill, showing him old cartoons and telling stories from the war. Bill just stared vacantly. Then, before he left, Gruenfeld pinned a replica of the Combat Infantryman Badge onto Bill's pajamas. This simple gesture broke the spell. Bill still did not talk, but his face beamed. "He had the biggest, most beautiful smile on his face," Gruenfeld said. "You have to understand, Mauldin was just a paragon for us. . . . He needed to know he wasn't forgotten."[4]

Upon returning to his home, Gruenfeld wrote to newspapers and veterans' organizations urging other old soldiers to visit. Gordon Dillow, a journalist with the *Orange County Register,* took up Gruenfeld's call. On July 30, Dillow wrote a column for those "too young to remember" about the forgotten greatness of Bill Mauldin. He also asked his older readers, those who had manned foxholes over a half century ago, to visit the cartoonist and boost his spirits the way Willie and Joe had buoyed theirs during the war.[5]

The response was immediate and overwhelming. Within a week Dillow had received hundreds of calls. Hundreds more cards and letters addressed to Bill came from those too infirm to make the trip. In shaky handwriting, veterans told Mauldin that his cartoons "saved my soul in that war" and "kept my humanity alive" amid the slaughter. One man sent a pair of socks, in reference to Willie's gesture during the war (see figure 1). Widows thanked the cartoonist for comforting their husbands before they were killed in battle.[6]

When Bob Greene of the *Chicago Tribune* echoed Dillow's call in a syndicated column on August 11, 2002, thousands more reached out. Mail arrived by the sackful, topping ten thousand letters by autumn. Countrywide, so many World War II veterans leapt at the chance to reach Bill's bedside that the nursing home had to turn most of them away. Bill was not expected to live long enough to see them all.

When reporters caught wind of the grassroots campaign, veterans struggled to explain their devotion. "He was one of us," said John Pellegren, a veteran of Omaha Beach. "He supported the enlisted man. I was an enlisted man. Period. He was our champion, Mauldin was."

"You would have to be part of a combat infantry unit to appreciate what moments of relief Bill gave us," another veteran told Bob Greene. "You had to be reading a soaking wet *Stars and Stripes* in a water-filled foxhole and then see one of his cartoons."[7]

*"Joe, yestiddy ya saved my life an' I swore I'd pay ya back. Here's my last pair o' dry socks."*

**FIGURE 1** This cartoon first appeared in *Stars and Stripes* (Mediterranean edition) on March 2, 1944.

Some who visited and wrote to Bill *did* understand and appreciate the cartoons, even though they had not been there. "My grandfather had been on a destroyer in WWII and to a young boy, that was heady stuff," wrote a thirty-one-year-old man from North Carolina. "However, my mother strictly forbade me from ever asking him about it. . . . One summer, I discovered a copy of your book *Up Front* on my grandparents' bookshelf and read it cover to cover in an afternoon. I must admit it was the cartoons that attracted me at first, but once I read the text, I felt like I understood a little of what my grandfather had been through."[8]

It's a discovery other readers have been making for decades. They find in Mauldin's cartoons a hidden transcript not only of war but of a generation shaped by trauma and endowed with premature wisdom and responsibility. As Bill's troubled friend Audie Murphy, the most decorated combat soldier of World War II, said at the age of thirty-two, "I can't ever remember being young in my life."

Bill Mauldin and those who sat bedside by him in his last months might have spoken the same words. But perhaps when they were there with him, at Park Superior, the old soldiers became young again for a moment. Perhaps after reading aloud the caption from a yellowed cartoon clipping, they saw in Bill not a dying old man, but the kid cartoonist forever young.

# Chapter One

# Roughing It

*(1921–1940)*

CALLIE BEMIS CALLED HIM the angriest baby she had ever seen. He had survived a difficult birth, and so had his eighteen-year-old mother. Now, the baby was slowly starving because he couldn't keep down his mother's milk. With medical help scarce in the mountains of southern New Mexico, sick babies like Billy Mauldin depended on the folk wisdom of such women as Callie Bemis, Billy's grandmother, who had settled on a neighboring farm years before.

"Nana" Bemis struggled unsuccessfully for weeks to find a concoction her grandson could keep down. Though deprived of food, the boy, strangely, never languished. Face twisted, fists clenched, legs curled up, Billy wailed so loudly his cries echoed off the canyon walls. "It probably shaped my whole life," Bill mused in old age. "There are sinkers and there are swimmers. Apparently, I decided to thrash around."

Nana eventually hit upon a formula that kept Billy thrashing, though it lacked the calcium, phosphorous, and vitamin D necessary for bone growth. As a consequence, Billy grew slowly. His mother, Katrina Mauldin, tended to coddle her sick boy indoors, inadvertently shielding him from the ultraviolet light that might have helped his body generate vitamin D and absorb calcium into his bones. As a result, Billy Mauldin became perhaps the first child in the desert Southwest ever to acquire rickets, a bone disease associated more with sooty urban slums than mountain apple farms.

The softened bones and stunted growth left Billy with an odd, almost comical, physique. Short and skinny, he was not a uniformly scrawny child, but carried a pot belly beneath a constricted rib cage and a normal-sized head that appeared large atop narrow shoulders. His ears were also normal-sized, only turned outward, like open doors on a taxicab. They, too, looked large, especially framing such a baby face. Billy always appeared younger than he was. In second or third grade, his teacher thought him so cute she cast him in the role of bridesmaid—complete with makeup, flowered hat, and hooped skirt—in a school production of *A Tom Thumb Wedding*.[1]

Billy was, in fact, what the farmers, ranchers, and lumberjacks around the Sacramento Mountains called a "runt," someone nobody expected to compete in the rough arena of rural enterprise. The contrast with his older brother Sid could hardly have been greater. Born just a year earlier than Billy, Sid towered over his little brother, both in stature and ability. Trusted with heavy farm chores from an early age, Sid could outfight just about any kid on the mountain, and also, remarkably, dismantle and rebuild car and truck engines before he could even drive, which in southern New Mexico meant around the age of nine or ten. By age fourteen, Sid stood six feet tall and outweighed Billy by at least fifty pounds. Strikingly handsome, he looked the part of a Hollywood cowboy, so much so that later on strangers thought him related to Gregory Peck.[2]

"I, on the other hand," recalled Bill, "had no talents at all." As a child, Billy could not be trusted with even the simplest chores. When the woodstove needed just a few armfuls of kindling, Billy would hide until his frustrated parents filled the stove themselves. The one time Billy showed initiative and poured what he thought was kerosene into the farmhouse's lamps and heaters, he smoked the family out into the cold by dousing the flames with water.

"It's a good thing Billy didn't find the kerosene can or we wouldn't have no house left," observed Sid.[3]

Rather than tending to the orchard, animals, and machines that kept the family living just above subsistence level, Billy spent most of his mountain years on the sleeping porch, in Nana's darkened sitting room, or in a pasture somewhere with the books, pencils, and paper his mother kept in constant supply. Fantasies of worldly achievement consumed him, nurturing his growing suspicion that he did indeed have talents. In his daydreams, often sketched in pencil, Billy led soldiers to victory, flew solo around the world, healed the sick with lifesaving surgery, and held audiences spellbound with inspiring rhetoric. Billy also fantasized about the revenge he would visit upon those who failed to see his worth.

Sensitive about his size, looks, and presumed lack of ability, Billy flew into a rage at any perceived slight. He earned the distinction early on, as he put it, of "starting more fights than anybody else and winning none of them." He counted almost every kid and adult on the mountain as his enemy.

Once, when he was ten, Billy walked past a familiar gathering spot for local men, a well-whittled bench outside a general store close to the Mauldin farm. As Billy passed by, he heard one of the regulars, a nearby cattle rancher, remark to the storekeeper: "If that wuz my kid, I'd drown 'im."

For the next several nights Billy lay awake imagining the rancher flailing and choking in one of the stream-fed pools tucked away in a nearby canyon. As the rancher comes up for one more breath and disappears under the water for the third time, Billy stands at the pool's edge and laughs.[4]

WILLIAM HENRY MAULDIN was born in Mountain Park, New Mexico, on October 29, 1921, just after the apple harvest. The place has changed little since. Seated in the Sacramento Mountains 7,000 feet above sea level, ten miles from the desert floor, the loosely knit community of a few dozen families is still conducive to daydreaming. Amid the ponderosa pine and outcroppings of sedimentary rock deposited by ancient seas, occasional clearings reveal a panorama of desert scrub extending sixty miles west across the Tularosa Basin to the foothills of the San Andres Mountains. Halfway across the basin appears an odd patch of white, the ever-growing gypsum dunes known as White Sands. Even the hardiest plants and animals struggle to survive in the dune fields, and a visit there makes one appreciate the shading trees and life-giving springs of the mountains.

Up in the mountains, an arid climate preserves things long abandoned, such as the squat two-bedroom farmhouse built by Billy's grandfather at the turn of the century. The gnarled apple trees, crowded by wild sweet peas, also remain, still producing enough fruit to feed a large herd of wild elk. The logging train, which in Billy's childhood made six round-trips a day through Mountain Park, stopped running in 1948. The track, once the steepest standard-gauge incline in the world, was dismantled and sold to a Mexican railroad, leaving behind a skeleton of spectacular canyon trestles. With the help of an old map, one can even trace the remains of the treacherous La Luz Canyon Road that once connected the Mauldin farm both to the desert town of Alamogordo, situated eighteen miles by switchback road and 4,500 feet in elevation below, and to the summit resort of Cloudcroft, six miles and 2,000 feet above.[5]

Such measurements are crucial in the Sacramento Mountains, where life is meted out in a patchwork of microclimates. The evening breezes that still slough down from the ridges above Mountain Park descend to the desert floor through six of the world's seven "life zones," distinct belts of flora and fauna adapted to elevation. Indeed, the very concept of the life zone, developed by the biologist C. Hart Merriam in 1889, was inspired by the climatic and ecological diversity of the southern reaches of the Rocky Mountains. While on an expedition in the Southwest, Merriam noted how dramatic variations in temperature, precipitation, and slope in the mountains gave rise to numerous distinct ecosystems that normally stretched across thousands of miles of latitude. Desert turns to grassland, grassland to forest, and forest to tundra within a few thousand feet. Residents of the Sacramento Mountains still live among biotic communities similar to those found in Sonora, Mexico, on the Arctic coast of Canada, and everywhere in between.[6]

The transitions between life zones are so rapid and complete that the 120-acre Mauldin farm itself straddles two separate ecological systems, with scrub oak, piñon, and juniper on the lower end and spruce, ponderosa pine, and Douglas fir bordering the upper end. Thinking of himself as trapped between the more glamorous life zones of desert scrub below and subalpine forest above, Billy played at being both the dusty plainsman and the grizzled mountaineer without ever leaving his property. Rattlesnakes abide these demarcation points, for while they thrive just below the Mauldin farm in Box Canyon, none has ever been found on the property itself. To survive in such an ever-shifting environment, all creatures must follow the rules governing each life zone.[7]

For thousands of years before the Europeans arrived, successive groups of Native Americans adapted to these rules. The last Native Americans to claim the Sacramento Mountains as their homeland were the bison-hunting Plains Indians known as the Mescalero Apache. For almost two centuries the Mescalero used the mountain canyons as a sanctuary from which to launch hunting and raiding expeditions. Their control over the region was so complete that Anglos stayed out of it until the 1880s, when the United States Army defeated the last renegade Apache bands and confined the Mescalero to a reservation straddling the Sacramento Mountains just north of Mountain Park.[8]

An obscure foot soldier in this final act of the Plains Indian Wars and one of the first Anglo settlers to cross the Pecos River was Billy's grandfather and namesake, William Henry Mauldin. A short, trim man with a bushy gray mustache and piercing eyes, William Henry Mauldin the elder was known by all in Billy's childhood as the venerable "Uncle Billy."

When Uncle Billy was born in 1856, not a single town or road existed in southern New Mexico. The region, known as the "empty quarter," was still the most sparsely inhabited place in America, truly the nation's final frontier, when Uncle Billy first passed through in 1882. At his death in 1956, just short of his hundredth birthday, the horse-and-wagon route Uncle Billy took through the Tularosa Basin as a young man had seen the world's first nuclear explosion, the Trinity Test, and become part of the largest military installation in the Western Hemisphere.[9]

The Mauldins had followed the frontier for over two hundred years, scratching out livings in territories still contested by Native Americans. Beginning with Henry Laban Mauldin, born in Cecil County, Maryland, in 1732, each generation of the clan moved southwestward, as if slowly drawn to the empty quarter of New Mexico. By the mid-nineteenth century, Mauldins had made it as far as Burleson County, Texas, where Uncle Billy was born. Cast adrift when his mother died in childbirth and his father went off to fight for the Confederacy, Uncle Billy worked on various farms and sheep ranches until he was old enough to strike out on his own, signing on with the great Texas cattle drives as a cowpuncher in 1879. In so doing, Uncle Billy joined that first generation of southern white Americans to make themselves over as westerners, trading cotton fields for cattle ranches, southern drawls for western twangs.[10]

In a nation overrun with ersatz cowboys, Uncle Billy was the genuine article, driving as far north as the Dakotas on the legendary trails of Chisholm and Doan during their brief heyday in the 1870s and 1880s. As the open ranges of Texas disappeared and railroads displaced trails, Uncle Billy lit out once again, this time for ranch work in the Gila River country near the Arizona-New Mexico border. On his third day there, a large band of Chiricahua Apaches led by Geronimo himself swept down from the hills and stole away with horses and cattle from a nearby ranch. Uncle Billy had arrived in time to witness the final years of the vicious Apache wars, the most violent of all the Indian conflicts. He pursued Geronimo and other Chiricahua marauders both as a scout for the United States Army and as a vigilante stockman.

He might have stayed on to see the mighty Geronimo captured if not for the love of a mail-order bride. A year before the Apache warrior was caught in 1886, the foreman of the ranch where Uncle Billy worked paid for an immigrant bride from eastern Europe named Minnie Bublich. Instead of settling down with the foreman, Minnie married Uncle Billy, and the couple went off to the Sacramento Mountains to establish a ranch for themselves.

Although the famous Lincoln County War was over, the region was still rife with violence over land, money, and markets. Sheriff Pat Garrett, who had killed Billy the Kid in 1881, called upon Uncle Billy to serve on a grand jury that would indict one of the most powerful cattle barons in history, Oliver Lee, for the murder of a rival. Lee went to trial, was acquitted within minutes by an intimidated jury, and returned to the Sacramento Mountains to claim the water rights on Uncle Billy's homestead, still known today as Mauldin Springs. "If [Lee] wanted your woman or your place," explained his grandson Sid, "he'd take it or kill your ass. It was that simple." Uncle Billy yielded to Lee, moved to remote Mountain Park, and dedicated himself to the quiet business of apple farming.[11]

With diligence, savvy, and, most important, a strong global fruit market, Uncle Billy turned steady profits during the first two decades of the twentieth century. Then, in 1919, he handed the fifty-five acres of prime orchard over to his only child, Sidney Albert Mauldin, who had been adopted as an eleven-year-old frontier waif in 1902. An artillery corporal in the First World War, Sidney had just returned from the trenches of Europe traumatized by combat and partially disabled by a poison gas attack that had scalded his lungs. Uncle Billy probably hoped that farm life would help settle his son back into "normalcy." So he retired with his modest fortune to the desert floor only to watch with rising concern as Sidney drove the farm into the ground and the family into poverty.

At least, that's how it appeared to the family. Sidney, called "Pop" by Bill and his brother, possessed the energy and certainly the brains to run a medium-sized business, let alone a small family farm. Described by Bill as "a tall, wiry, swarthy man with a fierce beak and a black mustache," Pop was, by many accounts, brilliant. He had earned an electrical engineering degree by mail, could dismantle and rebuild virtually any engine blindfolded, and created farm machinery, such as an apple sprayer that still rests near the farmhouse, from the enormous junk pile he established in the pasture. "Pop was anything but lazy," Bill recalled, "he just needed a manager."

Bored and unfocused when he was without a grand scheme or an emergency repair, Pop thrived on crisis and whipped the household into periodic frenzies over his various "projects." One summer day, for example, Pop spied excursion cars heading up the mountain to Cloudcroft and decided to make Mountain Park a tourist attraction. He went broke before finishing the first of what he envisioned as several dozen cottages on a vast mountain estate. Declaring that Mountain Park held no future for him or his family, he then began planning his next move: growing citrus in the Arizona desert.

When in the midst of such preparations, Pop indulged in flights of oratory, never brooking the slightest interruption or contradiction. With his head tucked, dark eyes bulging, large nose whistling, and great ears wiggling ever so slightly, Pop harangued both his "sprouts" and his increasingly indifferent wife with the indisputable logic of his various schemes (see figures 2 and 3). As Bill recalled them, Pop's speeches all ran along the same theme:

> ". . . So I says the fact that nobody's done it before doesn't mean
> it can't be done and he says it takes a lot of money for something
> like that huh [the "huh" was for air, a quick gasp which was part

Pop didn't like
to be interrupted

**FIGURES 2 AND 3**
Two faces of Pop. Bill
drew the above portrait
for *A Sort of a Saga*, his
memoir of childhood
published in 1949. The
photograph is of Pop in
1975 at age eighty-four.

*Portrait copyright 1949 by*
*Bill Mauldin. Courtesy of*
*the Mauldin Estate.*

*Photograph courtesy of the*
*Mauldin Estate.*

of the sentence and left no breach for anybody to jump in] well I says it seems to me that a man who depends on money and not his own hard work can't make a go huh of anything anyhow I don't give damn he says you got to have money for something like that. . . . "

For smaller projects, such as trading a well-running vehicle for a jalopy or selling a Gila monster to an eastern zoo, Pop usually spared his family such oratory and simply acted on his own.[12]

Compared to his ambitious schemes or a truck in need of an engine overhaul, the humdrum routines of farming were deflating, even demoralizing, to Billy's father. To break the monotony, Pop would drink heavily from his crock of homemade beer. Then he would fight with his wife, play practical jokes, blast dynamite, chase women in Alamogordo, roar around the canyon roads on his motorcycle, or seek to settle old scores with Uncle Billy's single-action Colt .45. His was not a temperament congenial to farm life.

More devastating to the Mauldin family fortunes than Pop's volatility was the steady collapse of the agricultural economy in the 1920s. During and immediately after World War I, America's farmers enjoyed boom markets, selling their products to a devastated Europe. By the early 1920s, Europe had recovered, and American producers now found their crops competing with those grown a half world away. As farm surpluses grew, prices tumbled until it hardly paid farmers to even bring their products to market. In a business where producers had to worry about blight, drought, vermin, and summer hailstorms that knocked whole orchards of apples off their trees, the dismal market proved the last straw for many southwestern farmers. In the late 1920s, they began leaving the land to find work in cities. No one knew it yet, but the country was entering the earliest stages of the Great Depression.

Such hard luck turned out to be something of a happy coincidence for Pop, for it allowed him to unleash his wanderlust and drag his family along in pursuit of various will-o'-the-wisps. By the time Billy left Mountain Park permanently in July of 1936, Pop had worked the mines in Parral, Mexico; sold wrenches in El Paso; changed tires and picked cotton near Phoenix; prospected for gold in the Sonoran Desert; and built sanitary outhouses around the Tularosa Basin for the Federal Works Progress Administration (WPA). After each adventure, the family returned to Mountain Park, a little poorer and more frayed than when they had left. "Starchasing can be an interesting way of life," Bill explained, "but it's hard on a family."[13]

To Billy, Pop was the charismatic prime mover, the animating force of his world. Only later did he come to see his father as a victim of larger forces, a little man in constant battle against elements he could not control. And although Bill often imagined his tall, blustery father as his opposite, he also came to identify with Pop's pride, doggedness, and resourcefulness in the face of adversity.

He would never forget, for example, how Pop refused to allow his children to work alongside him in the cotton fields of Arizona during the Great Depression, even as the family was living out of its car. Bill also admired his father's many principled stands, especially against the American Legion, which Pop called "a chiselers' club trying to strip the taxpayers." Pop had been offered a one hundred percent disability rating for his lungs, but he accepted only ten percent, reasoning that his asthma still allowed him to work ninety percent of the time. Finally, Billy treasured the knowledge his father passed on to him, such as how to play stud poker. Pop introduced Billy to the game in part to teach his son a necessary life skill and in part to win back the seventy-five cents he owed the boy. "It was his way of being fatherly," explained Bill.[14]

This commanding, complex presence would appear time and again in Bill's writings and cartoons, informing the character of Willie in his wartime work and stealing the show in *A Sort of a Saga,* Bill's wry memoir of his childhood (see figures 4 and 5). To Bill, Pop represented the often whimsical, delusional, self-centered nature of authority. At the same time, Pop's character also embodied

FIGURES 4 AND 5 Long after the war, Bill finally admitted to a family resemblance between Pop and Willie. The drawing at left, which appears in *A Sort of a Saga* (1949), features a kneeling Pop and his young mining partner in Arizona, Pat, checking on their five-gallon crock of homemade beer. Below, the equally fierce-beaked Willie offers his mud bath to his younger partner Joe.

*Copyright 1949 by Bill Mauldin.*
*Courtesy of the Mauldin Estate.*

*"No, thanks, Willie. I'll go look fer some mud wot ain't been used."*

*Copyright 1944 by Bill Mauldin.*
*Courtesy of the Mauldin Estate.*

the humor, scrappiness, and bigheartedness of the disenfranchised. Pop was, in essence, both the blustery officer demanding obedience and the shivering buck private struggling to keep warm in the field (see figure 6). It was this double-sidedness of Pop's personality that strengthened Bill's reflexive sympathy for the underdog, his skeptical attitude toward power, and his intense desire to wield an authority of his own.

It is curious that given Bill's numerous depictions and reminiscences of Pop, he never divulged the great trauma underlying his father's turbulent personality. Four years before Uncle Billy adopted him, Pop had been orphaned in the desert without any family whatsoever. His birth father was a Louisiana Cajun of mixed Native American heritage named Bissell and his mother a Chiricahua Apache who had been forcibly resettled by the United States Army to Oklahoma. The couple had been working their way back to Chiricahua lands in eastern Arizona when their son was born in McKinney, Texas. Seven years later, by the time they had reached the Tularosa Basin, Pop's father and mother had both contracted tuberculosis and died. Young Sidney found himself alone in the brand-new frontier town of Alamogordo.

Frontier custom, or perhaps mere expedience, dictated that the boy be taken in by Alamogordo's brothel. The brothel was a sprawling enterprise connected to a saloon by an underground tunnel across First Street. Sidney lived and worked at the brothel for four years before meeting Uncle Billy and Minnie, who had recently miscarried and could not have children. In a gesture that embodies the hidden history of the multicultural West, Uncle Billy, the old Indian fighter, offered the mixed-blood boy a home, a horse, and the Mauldin name. Sidney accepted, although he resisted domestication and earned a reputation as a hell-raiser. "He loved whores and waitresses because he was raised in a whorehouse," Sid Jr. offers by way of explanation. "We're just sort of a weird bunch."[15]

There was weirdness in Billy's mother's family, too. Billy's maternal grandfather, George Bemis, was a dissolute member of

*"I don't want to have to warn you men again about building these confounded fires."*

FIGURE 6 Brigadier General Pop indulges in the hypocrisy of power in this maneuver cartoon from 1943. The Native American private "Joe Bearfoot," seated by the fire, also bears a resemblance to Pop and would eventually reemerge as "Willie" in Bill's overseas cartoons.

*Copyright 1943 by Bill Mauldin. Courtesy of the Mauldin Estate.*

the family that had founded the Bemis Bag Company of St. Louis. His uncles had invented the machine-sewn gunnysacks that carried virtually every grain of wheat transported on the Mississippi River. Oddly, George steered clear of the successful business and drifted West into New Mexico's empty quarter around the turn of the century.

George Bemis had the distinction of being able to convince people, including his grandsons, that in 1861 he had shared a stagecoach with Mark Twain on a trip from St. Joseph's, Missouri, to Carson City, Nevada. In his celebrated account of the journey, *Roughing It,* Twain describes a man named George Bemis as "dismally formidable," armed as he was with a gambler's "pepperbox" derringer that had a way of missing its target and hitting innocent bystanders. Although Billy's grandfather was only two years old in 1861, he lived up to the reputation of Twain's character and became known as one of the most violent, fiercely alcoholic ne'er-do-wells in the Sacramento Mountains.[16]

While her husband drank and terrorized the family, George's long-suffering wife Callie maintained a strict veneer of Victorian respectability. Nana forbade swearing, tobacco, and sex talk in her house and insisted on lace curtains and afternoon tea—that is, when George was not screaming and beating her and the children. As a member of the Alamogordo Order of the Eastern Star and the Daughters of the American Revolution, Nana took inordinate pride in her family's lineage and genteel background, regaling Billy with stories of his esteemed Chattanooga and Boston ancestors. Billy never warmed to his grandmother's pretense of gentility and good breeding.[17]

Nana's youngest daughter Katrina escaped the household at age sixteen by marrying Billy's father, a dashing ex-artillery corporal eleven years her senior. Compared to his affectionate and irreverent portraits of Pop, Bill's accounts of his mother are slight. This is probably because Bill found his mother's brand of instability far more disturbing than Pop's. When she was home, the pretty, diminutive Katrina indulged and doted on Billy, whom she called "her little ray of sunshine." But her protective, even possessive behavior made her sudden flights from the household puzzling and no doubt frightening to the young boy. She would simply disappear for days with no explanation, leaving Sid Jr. and Billy to fend for themselves as she drank, played cards, and otherwise cavorted in Alamogordo. Today, Katrina's behavior would probably invite the diagnosis of bipolar or borderline personality disorder. In the Sacramento Mountains of the 1920s and 1930s, she was merely eccentric.[18]

Despite her inconstancy, Katrina recognized early on her younger son's genius. It would have been difficult to overlook. Billy could render elaborately detailed drawings long before he could talk and started reading Robert Louis Stevenson, Mark Twain, Agatha Christie, and Tom Swift adventures at the age of four (see figure 7). Although he seemed unable to complete simple farm chores, he could master whatever academic assignment he was given, whether it be in math, science, literature, or art. He also possessed the odd gift of being able to read and write backward as well as he could forward, a talent that came in handy later when he lettered window signs from the inside.

In a region where intellectual prowess was rarely valued, both Katrina and her mother nurtured the boy's talents and somehow even scraped together enough money to buy a small library of leather-bound storybooks on installment. With Sid Jr. following in his father's footsteps as a mechanic, Nana Bemis invested in Billy her hopes for the family's redemption. Given Billy's manual dexterity, she assumed he would become a surgeon.

Such high expectations imprinted themselves on Billy's consciousness even as his parents' erratic behavior left him insecure, distrustful, and always braced for trouble. The family still has a photograph of a six-year-old Billy sitting outside in a Morris chair with a paper crown, an eggbeater scepter, and a fur collar draped around his shoulders. The family's only good carpet lies at his feet

FIGURE 7 Squatting next to his brother Sid, four-year-old Billy (right) holds the pencil and paper that would become his constant companions. Behind them is the brand-new Model T coupe Pop drove during his brief stint as a wrench salesman in El Paso. Pop would eventually trade the Model T, the finest car the family would ever own, for a broken-down truck.

*Courtesy of the Mauldin Estate.*

in the dirt. The boy wears a fierce look, as if displeased by the behavior of his subjects. It was his favorite make-believe role, one which in some ways he never outgrew. Even as an adult, he could still play the king on the throne, looking upon his kingdom and finding it wanting.[19]

IN 1929, Pop learned that half-section desert homesteads were being offered to veterans west of Phoenix. The prospect fired his imagination. The family would quit Mountain Park, he declared, and start anew by planting citrus in Arizona, where the climate allowed two growing seasons a year. Loading their old Maxwell touring car to the gunwales with suitcases, tools, and extra tires of various sizes, the Mauldins headed down the mountain for a two-year adventure in the desert.

Reaching the outskirts of Phoenix, Pop took a job changing tires on Greyhound buses in order to earn some start-up capital for the farm. Within weeks the stock market collapsed and the nation spiraled rapidly into the Great Depression. Pop lost his job and found himself scrounging for work just to keep his family living in a sheep pasture under a canvas tent stretched between a tree and their Maxwell. After several months he saved enough to file for a 320-acre parcel consisting of volcanic rock and greasewood brush with one ancient ironwood tree and a handful of paloverde trees scattered among the gravelly hills. The family set up house beneath the same canvas tent, supported by low walls and screens to keep out the rattlesnakes, tarantulas, and scorpions. Then Pop got busy trying to rehabilitate an abandoned gold mine he found near the property. The lack of water, he discovered, precluded citrus.

Nine-year-old Sid and eight-year-old Billy, meanwhile, roamed the homestead unfettered, wearing nothing but a pair of shorts and carrying a razor and potassium permanganate for snakebites. It was hardly the first time they'd kicked about on their own. Bill's earliest memory was of sitting on the banks of the Parral River in southern Chihuahua, Mexico, at age three, smoking a pack of Chesterfields with his brother. He also recalled trailing after some Mexican soldiers, who had taught him how to roll cigarettes, into a local bordello. The women there mothered him, feeding him fried tortillas and refusing to let him smoke. Billy became a regular at the brothel, until Pop finally discovered him there. Bill later joked that had he been allowed to remain, he might have kicked his smoking habit.[20]

Billy indulged that habit fully during the Arizona adventure, where he and Sid spent their days battling snakes and scorpions, playing with dynamite pilfered from Pop, and shooting at each other from foxholes with old .22 rifles they had gotten from a neighbor. The last game ended when Billy's bullet landed a little too close to Sid. Billy shot it into the two-inch iron pipe Sid had been using to peep through the loosely piled breastworks surrounding his foxhole. Luckily for Sid, his eye was elsewhere at the time, and the boys had enough sense to declare a cease-fire.

There was no live ammunition on the boys' desert schoolyard, but the pupils there did hurl rocks at each other at recess, turning over picnic tables and benches as barricades. The school itself consisted of one room for eight grades. Attendance was infrequent. "We were a rugged lot of little prairie wolves," Bill recalled, "toughened by desert life."[21]

Indeed, the experience hardened Bill so much he came to identify with the rattlesnakes, roadrunners, kangaroo mice, and Gila monsters that somehow managed to live in that parched landscape. He never gave up the pleasures of book learning and playacting, but his time in the desert taught him that the world outside Mountain Park was an inhospitable place, and that he had the stuff to survive it.

BILLY RETURNED to Mountain Park a testy, independent ten-year-old who rolled his own tobacco (or, if none was available, coffee grounds mixed with dried horse manure), drove cars up and down the mountain, drank whiskey on occasion, and fought constantly with those who called him "hillbilly," "desert rat," or some other name linked to his disreputable family, strange appearance, or penchant for books. Billy reserved his most belligerent behavior, however, for his easygoing, well-liked brother. Sid, too, probably resented the precocious, roosterish Billy, who was always at the head of their small class, while the dyslexic Sid was illiterate.

That the two survived boyhood without disabling each other is almost as astonishing as their making it through the Arizona adventure without succumbing to sunstroke. During one fight, Billy managed to throw his brother into a red-hot cast-iron stove with the word LIBERTY embossed on the front. Sid escaped the encounter with merely YTЯ and part of the Я branded on his buttock. Another time, after Sid had pushed his brother out of a closed bedroom window, Billy came back into the house, covered in blood and shards of glass, intending to pelt Sid with a handful of rocks. Only a rare intervention by Pop prevented what could have been an even bloodier retaliation.[22]

Despite their animosity, Billy and Sid each recognized that their fates were intertwined, if only because of their dysfunctional parents. As their parents grew apart, the boys saw that life in the Mauldin household would soon be untenable. "The atmosphere was changing," Bill recalled of the summer he was thirteen. "When people fight that much something vital begins to tear. Something else begins to calcify." The family ship, as Bill put it, was sinking beneath them. Both boys decided they'd be better served thrashing around on their own than clinging to either parent.

As Pop and Katrina planned their separate futures, Billy and Sid plotted theirs. By the following summer, they would be fourteen and fifteen respectively, old enough, in their estimation, to light out on their own. Perhaps they'd head back to the Arizona desert where Pop still owned the homestead and the boys had a few connections.[23]

Sid's future as a mechanic seemed certain—he had spent most of his childhood creating machines from Pop's junk pile—but Billy realized with alarm that his daydreaming had yielded surprisingly little in the way of marketable skills. Unwilling or unable to work on neighboring farms, he tried sales. He trudged up and down the mountain peddling magazines, salves, cast-off fruit, and soft drinks to tourists, and even bottles of bootleg whiskey he found buried in the woods. Once, he tried selling a bottle of skunk musk to Montgomery Ward and Sears, Roebuck for use in perfume manufacture. He never heard back. His biggest success came in a domino game in the back room of Shorty Miller's pool hall in Alamogordo, where he doubled what little money he earned selling fruit.[24]

His strongest talent—drawing—seemed to hold some commercial promise. He could hardly think without drawing, and protested as much when his teachers admonished him for doodling in class. Billy could sketch exact likenesses of Mickey Mouse and Donald Duck, a skill that won from his peers a measure of the admiration he craved.[25]

Billy's idea of art derived entirely from the cartoons he saw in popular magazines and newspapers. Although by the 1930s comics had branched out from slapstick and sex into more placid middle-class humor, they still had a whiff of the commercial sensationalism that had given rise to color cartoon supplements at the turn of the century. Tramps, orphans, hillbillies, hussies, and cuckolded husbands still dominated the comics, as they had during the great circulation wars between Joseph Pulitzer and William Randolph Hearst thirty years earlier. A handful of new pioneering adventure strips, led by Hal Foster's "Tarzan," Alex Raymond's "Flash Gordon," and Milton Caniff's "Terry and the Pirates," were just beginning to inspire a more illustrative and literate approach to the medium. Most comics, however, still employed the "big foot" style of cartooning, which relied on simple, bold contour lines and exaggerated human features, such as large feet, noses, and ears.[26]

In October 1935, in the midst of his vocational crisis, Billy was browsing through an old copy of *Popular Mechanics* near his father's junk pile when he ran across several ads for cartoonists' correspondence schools. One trumpeted the fortunes to be had, claiming that some cartoonists earned up to one hundred thousand dollars a year. Billy was sold immediately. "This was it," he recalled. "Not only was I going to save myself, but the family honor would also be salvaged. The answer to everything had been in my hands all along."

Cartooning also required little start-up capital or schooling. And the promise of big money kept the old daydreams alive. So Billy ventured over to Nana's house to offer to do some chores, bringing along the brochure he'd ordered from the Landon School's correspondence course. After he'd split some kindling, sipped some pale tea, and endured a few minutes of polite conversation, Billy raised the issue of his newfound vocation.

"I need twenty bucks," he blurted out, unfolding the brochure.

After worrying aloud about how Billy would preserve his artistic and moral virtue as he reached for the "bucket of dough" that lay in cartooning, Nana disappeared into her bedroom and returned with a handful of fives and ones.

Billy promised his grandmother he would do his best to uplift humanity in his artistic endeavors. Silently, he reasoned that it would probably be best to make the hundred thousand first before practicing benevolence. "If a poor cartoonist could bring joy to mankind," he thought, "think what a rich one could do."

The next day, his tuition left Mountain Park in a mailbag on a logging train bound for Alamogordo. Within weeks he submitted his first assignment.[27]

In choosing Charles N. Landon's School of Illustrating and Cartooning in Cleveland, Billy clearly knew what he was doing. For over two decades the Landon School had served as an important training ground for cartoonists, especially poor ones. Landon used his school to screen talent and funnel it to the National Enterprise Association newspaper syndicate, where he was art director. Roy Crane, creator of "Wash Tubbs," and Jack Cole, whose "Plastic Man" would become a comic book hit in the 1940s, were just two of the better-known cartoonists who had gotten their start with Landon. In return for his twenty dollars, Billy received back his completed assignments expertly corrected and resketched on transparency paper.[28]

The school's instructors taught some basic but important tricks upon which the trade of cartooning had relied since outgrowing the crudeness of the "Yellow Kid" and "Happy Hooligan" before World War I. The instructors showed that the palm of the hand is as long as the fingers, that the foot is shaped like a triangle, and that the torso is best sketched as a bean with a trapezoid attached as a pelvis (short side up for a female, short side down for a male). These tips, and several others concerning facial expression and caricature, gave Billy a foundation for his early cartooning and the commercial posters painted in his teenage years.

Billy supplemented his Landon School education with personal mentoring by "Hillbilly Larry" Smith, a cartoonist from nearby Ruidoso. Pop had built a WPA outhouse for Hillbilly Larry and had also caroused with him in the saloons. Smith's work appeared in various regional papers and magazines, and he is credited with inventing the still-ubiquitous southwestern "jack-a-lope" post-card. His bread and butter, however, was bartering his drawings for food, liquor, and much else in the cash-starved Depression economy.

Hillbilly Larry held the boy spellbound with his twitching, frenzied manner of composition. Nervous, rail-thin, and bursting with rapid-fire shots of advice, the artist emphasized product over process. He taught Billy never to waste a stroke, a drop of ink, a corner of paper, nor a second of time conceiving and executing a gag. Drawing from a reliable if limited stock of humor, Smith's rudimentary but expressive cartoons featured oversized women, bewildered tourists, bowlegged cowboys, wisecracking Indians, and automobiles that had minds of their own.

"Don't fool around," he told Billy. "The way to be a cartoonist is to draw. Keep busy and knock the stuff out. I'm hungry. Let's take these two drawings out and eat 'em."

"The muse was not on his shoulder," Bill recalled, "it was astride his ear, beating at his head."

Hillbilly Larry's hustling approach made sense to Billy. Whatever desire he had to develop his talent along more sophisticated lines fell to a need to feed himself. So Billy took Hillbilly Larry's hustle to heart, invested in supplies, and peddled his services throughout the countryside.

His first commission came from a local pottery company which ordered an advertising postcard in exchange for ten new one-dollar bills (Pop requisitioned half of them to pay a traffic fine). Soon Billy was painting window signs, posters, and banners at ten cents a square foot for businesses up and down the mountain. A gas station price war in Cloudcroft offered steady work, requiring new signs, with illustrations thrown in for free, every few days.

By July 1936, when his parents finally parted ways, Billy had acquired not only the cash but also the business acumen to launch his new life. "We were not tearful waifs adrift in a storm," Bill explained decades later. "We felt we knew how to survive on our own and had long ago plotted our course."[29]

As with so many teenage children during the Great Depression, that course involved moving West, to Phoenix in particular. It might seem shocking today for a pair of young teenagers to move out on their own, but such down-and-out migrations were common in the mid-1930s. The nation's highways and railroads were awash with well over a quarter million teenage drifters. Many had hit the road when their schools closed for lack of funds. When Billy and Sid left home, four out of ten American high school-age children were not in school.

With unemployment, divorce rates, and farm and business failures at record highs, many families simply disintegrated, with each member going his or her own way. Some parents pushed their older children out so as to ease the family's financial burden. Other youths ran away hoping to find work and be able to send money home. Nearly all traveled in search of a better life, exhilarated and confounded by their premature independence. Adults called it the "youth problem" and considered "road kids" a worrisome harbinger. "I have moments of real terror," confessed Eleanor Roosevelt in 1935, "when I think we may be losing this generation."[30]

The first lady's fears would not have been eased by the sight of Billy and Sid's departure. They descended from Mountain Park in an early Model T that burned almost as much oil as gas and consisted of hardly more than wheels, engine, and a frame strung together with baling wire.

*Phoenix, Arizona. 1936.* There could hardly have been a better place for an independent, talented poor white boy to land. A burgeoning city of over fifty thousand, Phoenix was as close to a boomtown as existed in Depression America, fed continually by rural castoffs like the Mauldin boys. The city also attracted tourists and wealthy invalids seeking a healthful climate. Rich and poor mingled, though the races did not. In perhaps the West's most segregated city, white students enjoyed a fine public school system and the largest high school west of the Mississippi. African American students, meanwhile, attended the tiny Phoenix Colored High School, and Native Americans were mostly enrolled in the federally funded "Indian School." As long as they spoke English, Mexican students were generally permitted to join their Anglo counterparts at the majestic Phoenix Union High School (PUHS).

With its six thousand students, acres of buildings, and broad quadrangles studded with mature palms, PUHS fooled most out-of-towners into thinking it was a university. The huge variety of classes and numerous extracurricular activities also mimicked college life. Its ROTC students were among the best trained in the country, and its yearbook and school paper regularly won national prizes. That Billy Mauldin distinguished himself in this large, rich pool of talent suggested to him that perhaps his childhood daydreams were not so misplaced after all.

Billy still had to rely on Hillbilly Larry's brand of hustle, however, for he and his brother were now paying rent. They lived at a boardinghouse in the commercial heart of the city on North Central Avenue, a block away from the stately childhood home of Barry Goldwater. This bustling thoroughfare fed Billy's dreams of riches. One of his favorite pastimes was to dress up in his only sport coat and his one good pair of trousers and loiter in the Westward Ho, a grand hotel located two blocks south. He would make his way to the sundeck, "strolling past bellhops and waiters with a cigarette hanging out of my mouth, hands in pockets, head down as if trying to remember where I had mislaid my last million." Then he would try out the various reducing and exercise machines until the staff chased him out. "This excursion always gave me strength for the coming week," he recalled. "It reminded me what lay ahead if I kept my nose to the grindstone and my eye on the ball."

Billy lived for the most part on twenty-five dollars a month, for which he received a cot on a sleeping porch and two meals a day. He met expenses by selling posters, painting white sidewall tires, and using the hard-nosed methods Pop taught him in Saturday night poker games. He also scandalized the city for a time by painting demure nudes on canvas tire covers, at four dollars apiece, for virtually all the hot-rodders in the area. The police eventually cracked down on that art, but not before Billy had won the esteem of Sid's friends, a regular "wolf pack" of petty criminals. Sid tried high school, but soon dropped out. He made his living by souping up and repairing Model A's and other cheap cars. Sid's fellow hot-rod enthusiasts treated Billy, as he recalled, with "the same wary gentleness that savage tribes traditionally show toward zanies and eccentrics." To demonstrate their respect, Sid's friends set Billy up with teenage prostitutes. They opened the artist's beer bottles for him so that he wouldn't damage his valuable hands.

Apart from this loose gang affiliation, Billy largely kept to himself, absorbed as he was in the education PUHS had to offer. His prior schooling had been spotty, taken between his family's road trips and his various childhood illnesses. The small mountain and desert schools he did attend had trouble keeping on top of him, since his easy mastery of schoolwork left him plenty of time to invent ever more disruptive ways of winning attention.

PUHS offered a far more sophisticated outlet for his clowning and youthful attacks on authority. The *Coyote Journal,* an eight-to-twelve-page student weekly of near-professional quality, attracted

Billy's notice immediately. The paper's sponsor, a teacher named Scott Nelson, recognized Billy's talents and eventually gave him the job of editorial cartoonist and commentator, a role Billy so relished that he almost lost sight of his larger goal of becoming rich (see figure 8). "God knows," Bill recalled, "if I wanted anything even more than money it was recognition."

It didn't take long for Billy to become a spokesperson for the student body. Once, he wrote a satirical essay with an accompanying cartoon to protest PUHS's ban on smoking within two blocks of school grounds. As a two-pack-a-day smoker (or its equivalent in Duke's Mixture and Bull Durham), Billy took special offense, though he also espoused the principle of student freedom. "I thought students had a lot to say about school policies," he explained. "When I decided a rule was chickenshit, I found a way to defy it in print."

In addition to winning notoriety, Billy also used his three years at PUHS to hone his skills as both a writer and an artist. While Scott Nelson tutored Billy in writing, art teacher Frances Kapanke developed Billy's drawing techniques. Kapanke knew that this immensely talented boy probably would never see another classroom after PUHS. So she placed him on a fast track to learn proper drafting techniques. Contradicting the Landon School and Hillbilly Larry, she emphasized such exercises as blind sketching and drawing from life. Billy tackled these lessons with determination. When not roaming Phoenix with pencil and sketchbook in hand, he often sat in the boardinghouse bathroom sketching his own arm from the double reverse image he created with two mirrors. When other boarders complained of Billy's bathroom penchant, the boardinghouse matron gave him a three-paneled mirror from her own dresser.[31]

Such loving, even obsessive devotion to craft would mark Bill's whole life. Scornful of dilettantism, he took on every new endeavor, from airplane piloting to machine tooling, with the intent of mastery. When he needed a special lock, he studied manuals and became a locksmith. When he learned to fly an airplane, he grasped

**FIGURE 8** Bill Mauldin's first political cartoon, published in the *Coyote Journal* in 1938, offers neutral comment on the radical Mexican president Lázaro Cárdenas's attempt to nationalize the country's mining industry. Cárdenas had seized the assets of seventeen foreign oil companies, much to the delight of Mexico's poor and the consternation of the United States.

aeronautical principles so well that he wrote articles overturning conventional wisdom about aviation. "I've never known anyone else like him," says friend Jon Gordon. "He could learn almost anything, any skill, simply by reading about it."[32]

Bill's quest for mastery was no doubt rooted in a desire for control over a world that always seemed unpredictable, even threatening. But his devotion to craft also represented a rather shrewd strategy on the part of a talented working-class boy who lacked other avenues of advance. Unlike middle-class kids who sought success through professional credentialing or start-up capital, Billy could imagine gaining economic independence only through mastery of a demonstrable skill. College was out of the question, and although he at first dreamed of opening a desert studio on his father's homestead, saving money for such a venture was nearly impossible in Depression-wracked Phoenix. So Billy fell back on virtually apprenticing himself to those who might teach him the art and mystery of cartooning, the one field that might deliver him from poverty. In addition to Frances Kapanke, the audacious boy also requested help from Reg Manning, an editorial cartoonist for the *Arizona Republic,* and every magazine and newspaper editor in town who would meet with him.

All along, Billy cared little for academic success. As an apprenticing cartoonist, he disregarded grades and credits, regressing into his role as a cut-up in math, science, and history. He simply ignored those activities that did not involve writing or art—with one significant exception: ROTC training.

Billy gloried in the well-ordered pomp and purpose of the ROTC. Much of his childhood had been spent listening to Pop's and Uncle Billy's stories of military adventure, and he had once sat spellbound at the sight of the old 1st Cavalry parading through Mountain Park on its way to summer maneuvers. The trucks and horses, sabers and scabbards, lanyards and guidons, and distinguished uniforms all fired his imagination. He even began dreaming of going on to

West Point, until Sid reminded him of his physical unfitness. "You couldn't pass the tests for a barracks rat," his brother sniffed.

The ROTC allowed Billy to indulge his romance for military drill and display. It also served more practical ends. Every ROTC student received free of charge a full dress uniform—including cap, trousers, khaki shirts, and serge jacket with brass buttons. Barely able to meet expenses, Billy wore his uniform four days a week, solving what he called his "clothing problem." Since it counted toward physical education credits, the ROTC also got Billy out of the humiliating ritual of gym class. Moreover, every cadet had free access to a firing range. "All in all," Bill explained, "the military offered a great many fringe benefits to kids who had no other way of obtaining them."

Best of all, the ROTC gave Billy a 1903 Springfield rifle for manual of arms training. With typically obsessive devotion, Billy practiced manual of arms to the point of exhaustion every day, flipping, twirling, throwing, and catching his nine-pound rifle with seemingly impossible dexterity. He made the exhibition drill team and perfected the Queen Anne salute. Perhaps the fanciest of all parade-ground exercises, the Queen Anne salute involves a cadet tossing his rifle in the air and landing its butt on the ground just behind a bent right knee. The rifle then somersaults overtop the shoulder as the cadet rises back into the "right shoulder arms" position.[33]

If the exhibition grounds held the trappings of glory, Billy's military uniform represented the finest thing he had ever owned. Every night, he borrowed the boardinghouse matron's electric iron and pressed his trousers under a damp towel. For a boy whose high school dress in Alamogordo had consisted of a union suit and overalls, the polished shoes and brass buttons signaled affluence, independence, and dignity of purpose. Billy's ROTC uniform was the source of his greatest pride as a young teenager (see figure 9). Perhaps because of that pride, the suit also later became for him an enduring symbol of disillusionment.

**FIGURE 9** A seventeen-year-old Billy Mauldin posing in his cherished ROTC uniform for the 1939 Phoenix Union High School yearbook. Although he would not graduate with his class, Billy designed the yearbook cover and spent several dollars to have his photograph included.

*Courtesy of the Mauldin Estate.*

After joining the ROTC, Billy visited his parents for the first time since leaving Mountain Park. He wanted to show them the visible progress he had made. His mother was now living near Phoenix, working as a live-in housekeeper for an elderly government mapmaker named George Curtis. When Billy showed up, Curtis made it clear that the boy was not welcome. So Billy headed for Mountain Park, where his father still lived. He arrived at the old homestead to find Pop drunk and naked, wallowing in a bathtub filled with homemade beer. "There he was," Bill recalled with laughter decades later, "pissing in the beer and then scooping some out for a drink." It would not be the last time he tried to return home.[34]

ONE DAY in biology class, Billy lit a cigarette and stuck it into the smiling jaws of "Gertrude," the class skeleton. When the cigarette burned out, Billy relit it, took a few drags, and placed it back into Gertrude's mouth.

"All right, Mauldin," said the teacher. "I tried to overlook the cigarette at first, but when you smoked it yourself I officially saw you."

Expelled from class, Billy lost and never recovered the lab credit he would have needed to graduate from PUHS in the spring of 1939. He would regret his lack of a diploma for years. School administrators would eventually award him the credit after the war, not in light of his Pulitzer Prize or service to his country, but because, they said, he deserved credit for having designed the 1939 yearbook cover.

"You've really burned your bridges, haven't you?" scolded Frances Kapanke when she learned the news of his failure to graduate. "From now on," she warned, "you can't afford not to improve your work."[35]

Even if college had been a possibility, Billy would probably have found its pace of learning too slow and its classrooms too stifling. In any case, the doting attention he received from Scott Nelson and Frances Kapanke convinced him that he did not need college after all. He saw himself on a fast track to success, one blazed by his innate talent and strength of will. Besides, at seventeen, he considered his life almost half over. Within the next twenty years or so, he expected either to burn out from success or commit suicide over failure.[36]

To complete his apprenticeship, Billy took Frances Kapanke's advice and sought admission to the Chicago Academy of Fine Arts (CAFA), which taught cartooning and did not require a high school diploma. More importantly, Chicago was home to some of the best cartoonists in the country, people Billy believed would be eager to help a gifted and ambitious kid like himself. The only problem was CAFA's $500 tuition. He would have to bank on Nana's continued faith in him as the redeemer of the family's fortunes.

Nana's husband, George Bemis, had died several years earlier, and she had since married the widowed Uncle Billy, who was over twenty years her senior. The match between in-laws only reinforced the Mauldins' reputation for eccentricity, even as it made Billy's request for a "grubstake" more formidable. Relying on his grandfather's frontier spirit, the mark of which, Bill claimed, was "tolerance and humor," Billy emphasized the cartooning, rather than the art, in framing his request. After laying down the rules of grubstaking and warning his grandson of the consequences if the boy failed to pay back the loan, Uncle Billy ordered Nana to give him the money. That he did so was remarkable, for the old frontiersman had lost almost his entire life's savings in an El Paso bank collapse early in the Depression.

In June 1939, the seventeen-year-old Billy took off in a Greyhound bus for Chicago. He was determined to cram as much learning as he could into one year at the CAFA and to emerge from his Chicago adventure as a professional cartoonist. "I had never forgot that I had bought exactly one year," Bill explained. "If I didn't make it by then I was sunk."[37]

Fortunately, in young Bill's view (he dropped "Billy" when he arrived in Chicago), there was not that much left to learn. Swaggering into the school director's office his first day in Chicago, Bill displayed samples of his work and explained that he intended to complete as much of the CAFA's two-year program as he could in twelve months. He already knew academic drawing and simply needed help cartooning. The director, Ruth van Sickle Ford, immediately led him to Wellington J. Reynolds, a formal portrait painter renowned for his classicism and contempt for cartoonists.

"Mr. Reynolds," Ford said, "here is a boy with some talent but absolutely no training. Please look after him. His ignorance is complicated by cockiness."

"All right," agreed Reynolds. Then the painter quizzed his new pupil on the basics of anatomy. "How far down the length of the average head is the center of the ear?"

"About a third," Bill replied.

"My God," Reynolds said to Ruth Ford, "what's he doing here—understudying to draw Popeye?"

50,000 YARS AGO

THEM WUZ THE DAYS

THE FIRST MAULDIN CHELLEA, FRANCE 250,000 YRS. AGO

**FIGURES 10 AND 11** Bill spent every weekend in Chicago on sketching expeditions around the city. One of his favorite haunts was the Brookfield Zoo, where he applied the lessons of Wellington J. Reynolds's life class. Ever the cartoonist, Bill made these sketches at the gorilla exhibit.

*Copyright 1939 by Bill Mauldin. Courtesy of the Mauldin Estate.*

Moments later, Bill took a seat in Reynolds' anatomy class and began his intensive yearlong study of formal drawing. Although he took cartooning classes with Vaughn Shoemaker, a political cartoonist with the *Chicago Daily News,* and Don Ulsh, a well-published gag artist, Bill's year at the CAFA concentrated heavily on life drawing and composition. He especially focused on portraiture. From Wellington J. Reynolds, Bill recalled, he learned "the structure of the human body from the bones outward," as well as movement. Ruth Ford, a watercolorist, also taught life drawing and reinforced Frances Kapanke's notion that even cartoonists needed classical academic training, a lesson Bill eventually took to heart. "In one year," he explained, "I learned enough to realize how little I knew, which was not bad going for me" (see figures 10 and 11).[38]

Cartooning, in fact, had changed dramatically since Bill's days in the Landon School. The "big foot" style still held sway, but the success of Hal Foster ("Tarzan" and "Prince Valiant"), a former book illustrator and reluctant cartoonist, had inspired numerous others to create sensual, realistic comic strips. In addition to adventure strip artists like Caniff and Raymond, humorists like Al Capp ("Li'l Abner") and the lesser-known J. R. Williams ("Out Our Way") also employed slick illustrative styles that betrayed formal training.

Although they never drafted a manifesto or founded a formal school of thought, these cartoonists were among the first to declare, if only through their painstakingly rendered illustrations, that cartoons were serious art. The finely illustrated details of Bill's wartime cartoons—the hunched shoulders, wrinkled fabric, blasted trees, and dented equipment—were born of both his classical training at the CAFA and his admiration of the new "little foot" style of comic art.[39]

Bill's realization that he had a lot left to learn did not totally puncture his arrogance, which perhaps more closely resembled ambition mixed with defensiveness. He continued to be something of a loner in Chicago, quiet, independent, and always alert. Vaughn Shoemaker told Bill years later that he remembered being scared of his intense young student.

"You sat there with those eyes burning out from under those sullen brows, and I was convinced that if I criticized your work too strongly you'd attack me right there in class," he said. "Who wants to get bitten by a chihuahua?"

Such intensity also characterized the informal apprenticeship the young cartoonist continued to pursue on his own. Bill regularly made the rounds of the city's newspapers, parking himself next to the drawing tables of Joe Parrish at the *Chicago Tribune,* Paul Battenfield at the *Chicago Times,* and George Lichty, who drafted his well-known "Grin and Bear It" comic in the same cramped studio as Battenfield. Bill's esteem for these men bordered on hero worship. He observed their styles, techniques, and very movements as they hustled to make deadlines. He picked up their rejected panels from the floor and took them back to his room at the Lawson YMCA to study. Once, he actually retrieved a used brush from Lichty's wastebasket—a Winsor & Newton No. 3, Albatta Series 7 for watercolor.

He immediately adopted the brand and kept Lichty's discarded brush for the rest of his life. Back at the CAFA, cartoonists Shoemaker and Ulsh supplemented Bill's growing stock of trade knowledge: always sign your name prominently to prevent plagiarism; do not lock into any one style, but remain versatile; and use the *Writer's Digest* to help with freelance magazine submissions.

As a young man in a hurry, Bill launched his freelancing campaign shortly after arriving in Chicago. It is not known whether he'd read Jack London's accounts of his own rise from poverty to celebrity through blind submissions to New York editors. If not, then his virtual mirroring of London's dogged, even masochistic submission regimen is all the more astonishing. Just as London had set himself an ironclad daily quota of words, so too did Bill force himself to produce ten well-developed cartoons sketched in pencil each night before going to bed, which was usually between two and four in the morning. All this came after a full day of classes and homework, and an evening of washing dishes at a local restaurant in exchange for his meals. Each night on his way to the YMCA on West Chicago Avenue, Bill bought cigarettes, or loose tobacco and papers, and a quart of milk to settle his stomach from all the smoking he did while producing his nightly sketches, or "roughs." Despite their name, the roughs had to approach finished quality, for anything less might jeopardize their acceptance.

In his tiny room cluttered with drawing paper, pencils, and fixative, the submission envelopes must have commanded a prominent place, for each night's work involved several dozen of them. Before collapsing into bed, Bill would bundle his ten new roughs and a return envelope into another envelope addressed to *The New Yorker*, which paid one hundred dollars and up for cartoons. *The New Yorker*'s rejects, which arrived daily in their return envelope to the YMCA mailroom, would then be placed in a new envelope addressed to the slightly lesser-paying *Collier's*. *Collier's* rejects, which also came daily, would go next to the *Saturday Evening Post; Saturday Evening Post*'s, in turn, went to *Esquire,* and so on

*"Don't worry, Zeb! It won't last!"*

FIGURE 12 One of two dozen or so cartoons that Bill sold to *Arizona Highways* during his year in Chicago. Most were cowboy, Indian, and car gags. This one, published in February 1940, was reprinted in the *New York Times* travel section. Fellow students hoisted Bill on their shoulders and paraded him around the CAFA in celebration.

down the line until Bill had exhausted his list of some twenty-five magazines.

Sometimes the roughs would come back smeared or manhandled, and Bill would have to redraw them. Other times, Bill tailored the roughs to meet a particular specialty: military humor for the *American Legion Magazine,* hunting jokes for outdoors magazines, and western and travel gags for *Arizona Highways,* one of Hillbilly Larry's favorite outlets.

Bill credited *Arizona Highways* with keeping his submission system going, for, at two dollars a cartoon, the glossy travel magazine bought just enough of them, about two dozen, to cover a year's worth of postage and envelopes (see figure 12). None of the other 2,500 or more cartoons Bill created and sent out that year ever saw print. Unlike Jack London, who stacked his rejection slips on a five-foot skewer next to his desk, Bill simply tossed his daily quotient into the wastebasket.

Years later, during his last days in Europe in the spring of 1945, Bill received a return envelope from Harold Ross, the legendary founding editor of *The New Yorker.* Ross had okayed a rough Bill had submitted during the war. When the two met back home several months later, Ross asked Bill why he had never sent the finished drawing. Bill explained how as a struggling art student in Chicago he had submitted thousands of rejected roughs to *The New Yorker.* After he achieved success, he just wanted to see if he could get a submission accepted by the magazine in order to confirm that he had indeed "*really* made it." Bill then offered Ross the finished drawing; that is, if the editor still wanted it.

"Nah," Ross replied, "it was a soldier cartoon and the war's over."[40]

IN CHICAGO, Bill wrote regularly to his mother and grandmother, mostly detailing the wonders of big-city life. He told his mom that the YMCA was a "magnificent hotel," and that Chicago had a mind-boggling 1,156,000 telephones, 5,100 lawyers, 3,400 dentists, and 9,200 physicians. His first letter described sketching a nude model in Wellington J. Reynolds' anatomy class. "Man, does she have a shape!" he exclaimed. Bill also passed along the good news about *Arizona Highways* buying his first cartoons and all but assured his mother and Nana that success was just around the corner. "By return mail will come a BEE-OO-TIFUL check for $16!" he wrote, admitting, "Of course, $2 isn't a heck of a lot to get for a gag, but—"[41]

Bill's failure to sell his roughs to even one national magazine or land a job as a commercial artist when his tuition money ran out left him with few options. Some of his classmates prepared to move to New York City; others sought jobs with Walt Disney, a CAFA alumnus, who was expanding his studios in Burbank after the stunning success of *Snow White and the Seven Dwarfs* a few years earlier. Disney's animators were notoriously underpaid and overworked, but, recalled Bill, "if his talent scouts had tapped me at that point I'd have jumped into their pockets." Unemployment was still high in the spring of 1940, even for young talented cartoonists who required just one meal and a few hours' sleep a day.

Having failed to earn back Uncle Billy's grubstake, Bill returned to Phoenix in June. His mother continued to live there with the mapmaker George Curtis, who was now her husband. Curtis begrudgingly agreed to allow Bill to sleep on their porch for a few weeks until he found a job. Not long afterward, Curtis began offering to buy his stepson a one-way ticket back to Chicago.

Despite days of toting his samples around Phoenix, Bill landed only a few commissions to draw campaign posters for local political candidates. The work, which Reg Manning at the *Arizona Republic* directed his way, was purely mercenary. At eighteen, Bill possessed few political convictions. His parents had been Hoover Republicans, at least before the Depression. The posters he drew in 1940 were for Democrats, Arizona being a virtual one-party state rooted in southern tradition. The most exciting primary race that summer was between the Democratic governor Robert Taylor Jones and a rival candidate, Sidney Preston Osborn. As if to demonstrate his sheer moxie, Bill determined to work both sides of the race. The stunt served as the coup de grâce of his civilian career.

Bill managed to get an appointment with Osborn by claiming to be an out-of-town observer. After recovering from his shock upon meeting the prepubescent-looking cartoonist, Osborn ordered two posters attacking the governor at twenty-five dollars each. Bill delivered the drawings, which depicted Robert Taylor Jones as both a rodeo clown and a vulture, and then made his way to the governor's office, where he informed Jones' advisers of their opponent's hatchet work. Bill offered his services to counter the unnamed cartoonist working for Osborn. The governor's advisers reluctantly agreed to buy one drawing extolling Jones' statesmanship. Like Jack London's autobiographical hero Martin Eden, who penned prize-winning essays for both the Democratic and Republican parties, Bill had brought his street hustle to the statehouse, fusing the grit of a Horatio Alger hero with the guile of a con artist. His only mistake was in signing all the posters. Reg Manning joined George Curtis in urging Bill to leave town.

Bill did leave Phoenix that fall, but only because he'd given up on achieving immediate success as a commercial artist and cartoonist. Unwilling to go back to painting white sidewalls on tires, Bill allowed his old enchantment with the military to solve his unemployment problem. An old ROTC friend, Jack Heinz, persuaded Bill to join the Arizona National Guard, where Heinz was a corporal in the 120th Quartermaster Regiment. Bill did not need much convincing.

His poverty aside, he believed strongly that the United States should come to the aid of Great Britain and Western Europe generally in their struggle against Hitler's Germany. Having sparked World War II with its invasion of Poland a year earlier, Hitler's army had just conquered France and appeared poised to invade Britain, which was also being pounded by the Luftwaffe's terror bombings. Bill agreed with Heinz that the United States would eventually be drawn into the conflict, and that joining a quartermaster unit would preclude being drafted into the infantry. "I'd decided I'd rather drive than walk my way through any war we might find ourselves in," Bill explained.[42]

As with his youthful ROTC experiences and West Point ambitions, practical concerns mixed with dreams of glory as he envisioned somehow rising through the ranks on the basis of his talent. "I wouldn't be the first hayseed to begin a distinguished military career from hunger," Bill had reasoned at age thirteen. Similar hopes were guiding him still.[43]

If Bill had waited any later than mid-September of 1940, his military career might never have happened. Standing five feet ten inches tall, Bill weighed perhaps 110 pounds, more than the "ninety-seven-pound weakling" he imagined himself to be, but much less than the minimum weight required for army induction. Fortunately for him, the Arizona Guard, which was part of the 45th Division, had yet to be "federalized," or taken on as a full-fledged component of the United States Army. Bill's enlistment on September 12 beat the Guard's mobilization by four days, so he never had to submit to an army physical. "They didn't really test our eyes," Bill recalled of the perfunctory exam he received upon induction, "they sort of counted them. I didn't see so much as a stethoscope that day." The examining doctor's sole interest was in hemorrhoids, which might have prevented a new enlistee from making the thousand-mile ride to Fort Sill, Oklahoma, where the newly mobilized 45th Division was headquartered.[44]

The roughly 13,000 soldiers who converged on Fort Sill that fall were all volunteer Guardsmen from Arizona, Colorado, New Mexico, and Oklahoma. The division was a child of the American Southwest with roots reaching back to the Indian Wars of the nineteenth century. Its insignia had been a gold swastika on a red background, a mystical thousand-year-old Native American symbol of eternal migration and return. The division did not see fit to change the emblem until shortly before the outbreak of war in Europe. In 1939, the men removed their shoulder patches and replaced them with a gold Thunderbird, another Native American symbol signifying the promise of rain and bounty.[45]

Most of the 45th's men came from hardscrabble backgrounds. Many grew up in the heart of the Dust Bowl, where drought, mechanization, farm foreclosure, and depressed agricultural prices had devastated local communities and prompted a mass exodus of poverty-stricken "Okies" from the region. The typical soldier in the 45th Division had originally enlisted for the twelve-dollar quarterly check the Guard offered in return for weekly drill sessions and an annual summer camp. Woefully underequipped and undertrained, the 45th Division, in the words of one military historian, represented "a very secondary second line of defense."

During the previous decade, these Guard units had quelled miners' strikes, hunted down jailbreakers, and battled locusts in the wheat fields of eastern Colorado. Now, fifteen months before the attack on Pearl Harbor, they were being prepared for a possible ground war in Europe. Their standard issue was used World War I surplus: 1903 Springfield rifles, cracked hobnailed boots, peaked campaign hats, heavy wool tunics and jodhpurs, and long puttees, leg wrappings that practically cut off circulation when properly cinched. Bill signed on to drive trucks for Company D of the 120th Quartermaster Regiment. It was hardly the stuff of glory.

Bill awoke to his mistake a couple of weeks after induction on a baseball field in Midland, Texas. He'd pulled sentry duty after a jarring all-day ride in the back of a truck he'd hoped to be driving. Just after midnight, his company's first sergeant, or "topkick," approached him, along with a lieutenant. They reeked of whiskey.

"Who goes there?" Bill shouted, blocking their path with his unloaded Springfield rifle. He suspected the pair were trying to trick him into departing from the general orders for sentries, which, of course, Bill had mastered.

"If you don't know by now, you never will," the sergeant replied. "Who are *you,* anyway?" Shining his flashlight into Bill's face, the sergeant moaned, "Aw, it's *him.*"

Bill stood his ground.

"What the hell do you want from us?" the topkick shouted. "Get your silly ass out of the way and get back to your job." The sergeant brushed by Bill and disappeared into the guard tent. Bill had made the topkick's "shit list," and basic training had yet to begin.

The next day, bouncing over several hundred miles of rutted Texas road, Bill decided that, at age eighteen, he was probably a failure. After deductions for insurance and repayment of his grandparents' grubstake, Bill's twenty-one-dollar-a-month job in the truck company barely left enough for cigarettes and candy. He had run out of outlets for his ambition. "I had a crazy notion in the back of my head," Bill recalled of his decision to join the army, "that maybe there would be some way in which I could combine my artistic and soldierly talents." Nothing he'd seen in the army so far suggested any demand or respect for his kind of talent. "Hell, at the rate I was going," he remembered thinking on his way to Fort Sill, "I would be lucky to get a job painting latrine signs."[46]

Given his lonely teenage desire for recognition and mastery, as well as his all-or-nothing approach to life, Private Mauldin was probably destined either for special punishment or special promotion. As was so often the case in his career, he got both.

# Chapter Two

# Maneuvering

*(September 1940–June 1943)*

"YOU ARE BAD NEWS, KID," groaned Bill's tentmate as the foam from a twenty-gallon can of urine splashed in his face. The two men staggered in the predawn darkness of Fort Sill carrying the 155-pound can between them. Bill consoled himself that at least he'd drawn the upwind handle this time. His tentmate, a good-natured Mexican-American boxer, meanwhile, cursed his luck for being thrown in with such a screwup.

The urine can was the brainchild of Company D's first sergeant. He'd installed it outside the company's tents in order to prevent his men from relieving themselves on the dirt street and footpaths at night. Before the barrel, so few had bothered to make the long walk to the latrine that Bill's quartermaster company had turned their patch of the Oklahoma Dust Bowl into a field of reddish molasses. The honey bucket solved the problem. It also provided an ideal opportunity for chickenshit.

The job of hauling the can to the latrine normally went to the last two men out of their tents at reveille. Bill managed to catch the detail twice in the first week. After that, he practically slept in his uniform and bolted awake at even the suggestion of a whistle or bugle call. One morning, inevitably, Bill beat the entire company out of their tents, and found himself alone standing at attention before his incredulous topkick. Poking the honey bucket's foamy head with his swagger stick, the first sergeant mischievously ordered Bill to remove the can, designating his tentmate as an assistant. As they trudged toward the latrine, the boxer muttered about transferring out of Bill's tent, while Bill pondered the illogic of military chickenshit. "In the army," he realized, "it does not pay any more to be eager than to be tardy."[1]

More profound was his dawning awareness that successful soldiering had little to do with skill, cunning, innovation, or even efficient execution of orders. Rather, it was conformity, anonymity, and the lackluster adherence to protocol that the army seemed to value. Proficiency, exceptional performance, intellectual curiosity—these were the targets of chickenshit, that common blend of sadism, corruption, and petty harassment.[2]

With the indignity of the urine can fresh in his mind, Bill resolved to achieve anonymity in Company D, "to do no less than my share of goldbricking and no more than my share of working." His commander provided ample opportunity for such inconspicuous mediocrity. Rather than putting the men through basic training, he had them hauling supplies, shoveling coal, washing trucks, and chopping and stacking the wood that heated their tents. Even Bill could resist the urge to shine under these conditions.

But then, one day at reveille, the topkick announced a new policy straight from headquarters that all units of the 45th, including the quartermasters, had to demonstrate proficiency in close-order drill. The first sergeant admitted he knew nothing about parade-ground exercises and asked if anyone there did. Bill's hand shot up, and the topkick assigned him a squad. By midmorning, the baby-faced private had his men marching in step for the first time since they joined the army. By the end of the day, they were performing the fanciest footwork in the regiment. The culmination of Bill's efforts was an exercise choreographed around a series of "to the rear HARCH!" commands where the rear ranks reversed direction, marched awhile, and then reversed again, along with the front ranks, so that the two were brought marching directly toward each other. At the moment before impact, Bill commanded the front ranks to reverse a final time so that the entire squad was once more marching together in the same direction.

"Well, well, well," observed the first sergeant. "How are you at manual of arms? I'll bet you're great at that, too."

Rising to the bait, Bill told the topkick to wait while he fetched a rifle. Then he conspicuously prepared the rifle strap before launching into a Queen Anne salute. "Never was it done so well," he recalled. He then proceeded through the manual of arms, running through it forward and then backward, spinning the rifle into position with each move. He finished with an "inspection arms" flourish that automatically snapped the bolt open and brought the rifle up to the first sergeant for inspection. "It was gratifying to observe," gloated Bill many years later, "that he didn't even know how to receive it."

Despite, or rather because of, this triumph, Bill spent the next six weeks on KP, guard, and latrine duty. He gave up trying to achieve anonymity and searched for any angle that might bring him closer to those things he craved most: money, recognition, and the opportunity to develop and demonstrate his skills. When not scrubbing out pots and toilets, he worked furiously on his sketchbook and began developing cartoon ideas again. But his hustle yielded only one paying job: drawing caricatures on the name patches of soldiers' denim fatigues for a quarter apiece. All other enterprises in Company D, Bill learned, were controlled by two surly noncoms, a mess sergeant and a supply sergeant, who were known as "the Gold Dust Twins." Abetted by the company commander and regimental brass, the Gold Dust Twins controlled gambling, prostitution, bootlegging, loan-sharking, and every other profitable racket around Fort Sill.[3] Truly, the 120th Quartermasters was a corrupt corner of the United States Army, a fetid backwater of a second-class National Guard division. Unredeemable. The only solution was somehow to escape it.

A way out landed in his six-man tent on October 4, 1940, in the form of a new four-page tabloid titled the *45th Division News*. This weekly newspaper originated in the division's intelligence section, far removed from Company D. Noticing that it lacked cartoons, Bill wrote a glowing letter to the paper's editor about a gifted cartoonist stuck in the quartermasters who would be a terrific addition to the newspaper's staff. Then he persuaded his tentmate to sign the letter. Days later, Bill was summoned to division headquarters to meet with Lieutenant Colonel Walter M. Harrison, the assistant chief of staff for intelligence.

Like the other Guardsmen in the division, Harrison had recently been called to active duty, taken away from his civilian job as editor of the *Daily Oklahoman* and the *Oklahoma City Times*. A trim, wiry fifty-two-year-old reminiscent of Uncle Billy, Harrison had launched the *45th Division News* shortly after his arrival at Fort Sill. He believed that a free press was as necessary to soldiers as it was to civilians. The *45th Division News* was, at that point, the only divisional newspaper in the army. Harrison had had to duck the printer for three and a half months before scraping up enough money to pay the first printing bill. He kept the project afloat through the division's morale and entertainment funds and probably his own deep pockets. He also had been forced to dodge certain officers at headquarters who considered the paper's seven-person part-time staff as "a bunch of wild men" who did not properly belong on a table of organization. Some even murmured about Communists running loose in the intelligence section. In response, Harrison shrewdly exploited the latitude customarily afforded intelligence units to escape oversight. It didn't hurt that he wielded considerable clout as an Oklahoma power broker, plenty to protect his small experiment in military journalism. "Most of the division's highest-ranking officers were in business or politics in Oklahoma and knew they would have to reckon with the waspish Harrison when he went back to being a journalist himself," explained Bill.[4]

Harrison also drew critical support from the division's commander, Major General William S. Key, who, like Harrison, was at heart a part-time soldier. As a Democratic businessman, New Deal bureaucrat, and statewide politician, Key understood the public relations value of the *45th Division News*. Both men believed that the division's morale, and hence performance, would improve if enlisted men had an institution of their own, a medium that spoke *for* them and not just *to* them.

In Harrison's office, Bill stood at attention while the colonel riffled through Bill's samples and then hired him on the spot. My luck has turned, Bill thought. "Farewell to Company D, to KP, to latrine duty, guard duty; goodbye Gold Dust Twins. Watch my smoke, you bastards."

Then Harrison informed Bill that he would be released from Company D only on Friday afternoons to draw his weekly cartoon, a task the colonel guessed would take only three or four hours. "His time estimate," Bill later admitted, "was distressingly accurate." Bill tried to protest but Harrison cut him off, explaining that personnel would hit the roof over a transfer for a gag artist. The paper was on thin ice already. Harrison had so far rebuffed every attempt to turn his experiment into a mere organ for official news releases and puff pieces on commanders and staff officers. Taking on a jug-eared kid cartoonist full-time would surely be just the weapon division brass needed to kill the paper. Bill would have to remain in the quartermasters.[5]

Even so, Colonel Harrison had opened the door a crack, and Bill pushed with all his might to widen it. He worked at a drawing board in the corner of the small newsroom every Friday afternoon and every evening while off duty, spending four or five hours a night sketching roughs for magazines again, as he had in Chicago. Military life, for all its frustrations and disappointments, gave him

FIGURE **13** Bill Mauldin's first *45th Division News* cartoon, published on October 25, 1940. The characters' hobnailed boots, irregular clothes, and lazy, uninspired behavior reflect Bill's disenchantment with the 120th Quartermaster Regiment. Joe the Indian, far left, would grow in physical, mental, and moral stature after Bill's transfer to the 180th Infantry in January 1941.

*Copyright 1940 by Bill Mauldin. Courtesy of the Mauldin Estate.*

ample material for his new cartoons. Indeed, it was his only material. Even the generic gags he scratched out again for *Arizona Highways* involved army subjects. One depicted a soldier with a teddy bear and newspaper hat complaining of the general's "overdoing this camouflage stuff." Another showed a convoy stalled behind a general's staff car which had stopped for directions from a buckboard-riding hillbilly.[6]

In contrast to these simple gags, Bill's earliest work for the *45th Division News* shows enormous effort: busy, detailed panels, a more

FIGURE 14 Bill's second army cartoon, from November 1, 1940, takes aim at the Gold Dust Twins' loan-sharking operation. Shortly after this cartoon, the Twins somehow ran afoul of brass, were temporarily demoted, and then were sentenced to thirty days' hard labor. Inevitably Bill drew guard duty. Not long after Bill arrived with his empty rifle, the Twins threw down their shovels and announced a coffee break. Bill ordered them not to leave. The Corporal of the Guard broke the standoff by chewing Bill out for not giving the men a break. "No hard feelings, kid," grinned the ex–mess sergeant over the brim of his coffee cup.

illustrative style, and a focus on character development. From the beginning, Bill's feature, titled "Star Spangled Banter" (Bill never explained where he got the title), adhered to the newspaper's mandate of speaking to and for the enlisted men of the division. Predictably, his first army cartoon, published on October 25, 1940, shows four unsoldierly privates peeling potatoes (see figure 13). Other early panels similarly poked fun at the follies and inconveniences of military life: mud, marching, and clogged stovepipes that smoked men out of their tents (see figure 14). Some were edgier than others. One showed a sergeant pulling men out of sick bay, charging them with malingering. Another depicted an officer's jeep splattering mud on soldiers. "Dad blasted ossifers!" yells one enlisted man. "They come tearin' by on them puddle jumpers, an' then raise whoopee on accounta tha mud on our uniforms!"[7]

By his later wartime standards, these first cartoons were tame, but they troubled some at headquarters who were not accustomed to any kind of public criticism, playful as it was, from enlisted men.

"Your cartoons have an irreverent quality about them which has not escaped notice," Colonel Harrison informed Bill.

The comment was meant as both encouragement and warning. On the one hand, Harrison promoted and defended the paper as an experiment in morale boosting. "Soldiers need outlets for their gripes," he explained to Bill, "and if they can pick up a paper and see somebody griping for them they can go back to work feeling better." On the other hand, Harrison had to be careful not to ruffle too many feathers. And he certainly did not intend the *45th Division News* to become a vehicle for vendettas or insubordination. The paper's very existence depended on the staff's ability to strike this delicate balance, to serve as an authentic voice of the enlisted man without challenging the authority of division brass.

Harrison's experiment certainly boosted Bill's morale. "Life in Company D became almost bearable," Bill recalled. "It didn't matter now that I wasn't making it in the army. I was back in my professional bag."

Just as he was accommodating himself to the quartermasters, Bill fell victim to an act of chickenshit exemplifying everything that rude term implies. The occasion was an IQ test, the general aptitude test battery administered to all United States Army personnel, from generals on down, in the fall of 1940. Intended to match soldiers with their most appropriate roles in the vast military bureaucracy, the exam played to Bill's prowess in arithmetic, word association, and problem solving. He scored above 140, the highest in the 120th Quartermaster Regiment and the second highest in the entire 45th Division. The first sergeant rewarded Bill by putting him on permanent KP.

Bill pleaded with Harrison the following Friday afternoon for a transfer to the intelligence section, but the colonel again refused. Now desperate, Bill threatened to move to the infantry.

"The infantry?" asked a startled Harrison. "Nobody—absolutely nobody in the entire military history of the world—ever voluntarily transferred out of the quartermasters into the infantry."

But Bill had made up his mind, and after some discussion, Harrison approved the cartoonist's transfer to Company K of the 180th Infantry Regiment.

When Bill returned to Company D to gather his things and receive his transfer papers, he found a crowd of men staring at him.

"Holy cow, Mauldin," said the orderly-room clerk, "we knew you were a fuckup, but what have you done to somebody up at division?"

Even Company D's commander took mercy on Bill. "I feel bad for you, kid," he confided. "I'm going to have somebody drive you over there with all of your gear. Save your feet. You'll need them."[8]


THE 180TH INFANTRY was a world apart from the quartermasters. The men of the 180th were far rougher than those in Company D, and certainly less savvy in the scrimmage for supplies, favors, and cushy assignments. Their tents had no floors or electricity for the first several weeks of basic training. The quartermasters had not seen fit to issue the regiment overcoats until November, after temperatures had dipped to well below freezing.

But Company K shared a bond and a pride in soldiering that the quartermasters lacked. Bill noticed the difference his first morning in the new regiment. "When K Company fell out for reveille," he recalled, "we found our officers dressed, shaven, and waiting for us, instead of a red-eyed first sergeant wearing bedroom slippers and tucking in his shirttail beside a can of foaming quartermaster piss."[9]

The infantrymen actually stood at attention in straight lines, with their weapons properly presented, while the regimental band played and the clear, almost songful, reports of the corporals, sergeants, and lieutenants rang out in the frosty morning air. Bill's old enchantment with the army began to creep back.

The very pride and camaraderie of K Company, however, made breaking into the outfit difficult. These men had gone through basic training together, and many had known one another as civilians near McAlester, Oklahoma, where most of them had been part-time Guardsmen. Bill arrived, therefore, as a double outsider, preceded by his reputation as a quartermasters dropout who took off every Friday afternoon to scribble cartoons. He didn't know how to roll a pack, let alone handle a bayonet, prepare for a thirty-mile march, or drill in hand-to-hand combat.

Fortunately, one tentmate in Company K took a liking to the scrawny newcomer and mentored him through his initiation. He was Private First Class Rayson J. Billey, a Choctaw Indian from Keota, Oklahoma. Some referred to Billey as "the Medicine Man," an honorific that supposedly derived from his father's tribal status. Bill described him as having "the eyes of a turkey buzzard, a broken beak, a slit mouth, a lantern jaw, a deadpan sense of humor, a degree from the University of Oklahoma, a talent for memorizing and reciting epic poems, and a conviction that there would never be peace with the white man until it was legal for Indians to buy whiskey." By all accounts, Billey was a remarkable soldier who could hit a bull's-eye from two hundred yards standing upright, defeat any man in hand-to-hand combat, and discourse on the art of William Hogarth and Honoré Daumier, two satirists Billey considered the forefathers of Bill's esteemed craft.[10]

Such talents were not unusual in Company K. Despite its hard-scrabble character, the outfit contained a number of well-educated soldiers, especially among its Choctaws. Many had graduated from the best academies in Oklahoma. Bill, in fact, was the only man in his company, apart from the first sergeant, also white, to lack a high school diploma. The company's talent came largely from its ethnic and racial minorities. Representing Anglos, Mexicans, and dozens of American Indian nations at a time when segregation in the army was the rule and African Americans were relegated to their own noncombat units, the 180th Infantry was the most integrated regiment in the country, claiming more Native Americans than any other.

These Indian soldiers left a profound imprint on the regiment, one visible not only on the 180th's insignia, an Indian head with the motto "Ready in Peace and War" written in Choctaw, but also in the unit's esprit. For Native Americans, volunteer soldiering was part of a larger struggle to claim the full benefits of citizenship. Forcibly resettled to "the Indian Territory" of Oklahoma in the nineteenth century, the state's various Indian tribes had long pledged their armed service to white authorities in return for civil rights and recognition. In the Civil War, some tribes had fought with the Union, others with the Confederacy, all depending on the guarantees each side offered. In 1898, Oklahoma's Indians charged up Kettle Hill and San Juan Heights with Teddy Roosevelt's Rough Riders. In World War I, they served in the 142nd Infantry and saw some of the fiercest fighting in France. The reward for such service was citizenship, from which most Native Americans were otherwise barred. So when Oklahoma christened the 180th Infantry as its National Guard after World War I, Indians joined as a matter of course. By 1941, the regiment had become more than a mere Guard unit; it was an institution of racial uplift, advancement, and empowerment.[11]

Having come from the margins of American society himself, Bill Mauldin identified with the regiment's unofficial mission and also with its rough and literate men who seemed to delight in

defying stereotypes. He wanted desperately for these men to recip-
rocate the respect he had for them. So he hunkered down to mastering the survival skills of combat. Like his mentor Rayson Billey,
Bill thrived on bayonet drills, marksmanship, and various field
exercises that required tactical training and finesse. He preferred
the accuracy and "lusty recoil" of the old 1903 Springfield rifle,
for example, over the new semiautomatic M-1. His enthusiasm
for such expertise and training would survive well into the war
until he learned the lesson of every combat soldier: on the line, no
amount of knowledge, preparation, or skill can save you.

Bill completed his initiation into Company K on a cold damp
Thursday in early 1941. He woke up that day feeling awful, as with
the flu, but nonetheless joined his outfit on its weekly thirty-mile
march. His company marched every weekday, beginning with a
fifteen-mile hike on Monday and ending with a thirty-five miler
on Friday. Bill's Friday afternoon cartooning assignment excused
him from the longest marches, an absence the company recognized by assigning him to carry the unit's twenty-pound BAR, or
Browning automatic rifle. The BAR remained in his hands on that
Thursday when, after completing the thirty-mile hike in the freezing rain, Bill's new buddies led a feverish, delirious Private Mauldin
across the parade ground and into the division hospital. When he
returned to his outfit several days later, recovered from the measles,
the men traded his BAR for a ten-pound M-1. He was now part of
K Company.[12]

AND YET, he was not part of it. Bill continued to lead a double life,
"struggling with the sword by day and the pen by night," as he put
it. Still aspiring to full-time status on the *45th Division News,* Bill
diligently pursued his craft. After the division moved from Fort
Sill to Camp Barkeley near Abilene, Texas, in early March 1941, Bill
spent every Saturday afternoon and Sunday among the presses at
the *Abilene Reporter-News,* which printed the division's newspaper.

There he discovered how the photoengraving process worked. After Bill completed a cartoon, it was passed to the engravers, who photographed the original drawing and then exposed the negative onto a zinc or copper plate that was then washed in a solvent and etched with acid. The photoengravers, Bill realized, could "make a bad [cartoon] seem passable or a good one seem terrible, depending upon their ability or their mood." He therefore made sure to ingratiate himself with the engraving crew and, for good measure, to learn the process himself. Within a few weekends he had mastered it well enough to oversee and sometimes even execute the engraving of his original drawings.[13]

The drawings themselves evolved rapidly after Bill's transfer to Company K. The first installments of "Star Spangled Banter," drawn while he was still in the quartermasters, had attempted to establish distinct characters and even narrative continuity from week to week. The earliest cartoons had centered especially on the antics of "Joe," an arched-nosed Indian who spoke broken English and expressed bafflement at the ways of the white man's army. His companions were a nameless square-jawed Oklahoma farm boy who, except for his blond hair, resembled Li'l Abner, and a rather nondescript pug-nosed character occasionally referred to as "Willie." The humor was rudimentary, relying heavily on dialect and slapstick. In one early panel, Joe buys a stray dog from an African American street urchin whose speech and facial features were the stuff of racial caricature. In the following week's cartoon, Joe's dog runs roughshod through the camp, stealing a major's cap and dragging it through the mud.[14]

As his army experiences broadened in Company K, Bill shifted away from these kinds of stock characters, storylines, and stereotypes. He depicted Joe and Willie much less frequently and dropped the blond farm boy altogether. By mid-1941, Willie had become a stocky mustachioed straight man resembling Bill's friend Johnny Waddell, a reporter on the *45th Division News*. Joe's transformation was more striking. He now spoke Standard English, instead of cartoon-Indian dialect, and delivered lines expressing comic insight, rather than a dim understanding of army life (see figure 15). No longer a caricature, Joe nonetheless retained his Native American identity, even adopting the surname "Bearfoot" in October 1941. By then, however, he had become barely distinguishable from the cartoon's other burly, broken-nosed enlisted men. Along with Willie, Joe would eventually disappear from "Star Spangled Banter," though his rough, independent, wisecracking traits would live on in Bill's other characters.[15]

So enchanted was he with field exercises, maneuvers, and other combat-related training that Bill willingly sacrificed Joe, Willie, and the farm boy in order to exploit other rich illustrative and comic material. Drawing its humor increasingly from the customs and conventions of army life rather than idiosyncratic characters, "Star Spangled Banter" employed a growing pool of indistinct cartoon soldiers. The characterization grew so weak that by 1942 it was difficult to tell the soldiers apart, even when they shared the same panel. Bill's characters would remain in this stunted state for another three years until, after about seven months of combat, Willie and Joe were reborn.

The shift to occupational situations and humor coincided with a renewed attention to draftsmanship and composition. Bill stopped using speech balloons, which had previously cluttered his panels, and switched instead to one- or two-line captions. He also worked tirelessly to refine the illustrative techniques he'd learned at the Chicago Academy of Fine Arts. Bill's ability to draw from life met the peculiar challenges of cartooning for the *45th Division News*. His audience, as he put it, "lived intimately with a few pieces of equipment and resented seeing it pictured inaccurately." In *Arizona Highways* and other general-market publications, Bill could get away with the "big foot" style, relying on his pen and simple contour lines to get his gags across. Bill's charge in "Star Spangled Banter," however, was not only to make his readers laugh, but also, in a sense, to document them and their world.[16]

**FIGURE 15** This cartoon from May 9, 1941, debuts a new Joe: no comic dialect, a beefed-up physique, and a common infantry gripe: mud.

*Prints and Photographs Division, Library of Congress, LC-DIG-ppmsca-13569.*

*Copyright 1941 by Bill Mauldin. Courtesy of the Mauldin Estate.*

Bill's panels for the *45th Division News,* therefore, betray painstaking attention to the accoutrements of soldiering. Rifles, packs, tents, kitchens, jeeps, tanks, artillery, fence posts, even boots, uniforms, and insignia appear in fidelity. Bill relished the challenge of achieving such realistic effects. Next to his drawing table he kept books on anatomy and files of magazine clippings—"everything from azaleas to zebras," he said.[17]

**Figure 16** This panel, sketched aboard a troop train to Fort Devens, Massachusetts, in April 1942, betrays the influence of Milton Caniff and other comic strip artists who used the chiaroscuro technique to indicate shape and texture through light and shadow. In this case, there are two light sources: the train window and the foreground. Bill relished the opportunity to do the kind of detailed sketch work he could not always include in "Star Spangled Banter."

*Copyright 1942 by Bill Mauldin. Courtesy of the Mauldin Estate.*

To achieve visual authenticity under the pressure of deadlines, Bill relied on chiaroscuro, a brush technique used by adventure strip artists that created impressions of light and shadow. Chiaroscuro allowed Bill to invoke a sense of reality without having to draw every plank in a tent floor or wrinkle in a pant leg. The effect was to render in distilled, enhanced form a unique environment that readers of the *45th Division News* recognized immediately as their own (see figure 16).[18]

Unlike other army-oriented comics that would flood the market after Pearl Harbor, Bill's humor did not generally play upon naive draftee encounters with military regimentation. Rather, Bill represented the army as a fully realized social world, familiar and taken for granted, with the humor arising from the tensions and conflicts within that world itself. While a few of his characters could sometimes be seen trying to clean their M-1s in a utility sink or sight an artillery piece like a rifle, most were competent soldiers who could hardly be imagined in any other setting. Bill's realism, then, suggested a fundamental respect for army life, a belief in soldiers' abilities, and a sense that, in the end, he was at home in the 45th Division.[19]

"STAR SPANGLED BANTER," Bill's cartooning career, and the 45th Division reached a turning point in August 1941 when the division joined almost a half million other troops in Louisiana for the largest field maneuvers ever held in the United States. The war games, referred to simply as "the Big One," were an attempt by Army Chief of Staff General George C. Marshall to prepare his ill-trained soldiers for the real combat zones that, month by month, were claiming a greater share of the globe. Many of those destined to lead on the battlefields of Europe were tested in Louisiana. Major General George S. Patton Jr., Colonel Dwight D. Eisenhower, Lieutenant General Mark W. Clark, and Brigadier General

Omar Bradley all played major roles in the exercises. It was their final dress rehearsal before a growing global crisis finally engulfed the world's only remaining nonbelligerent power.[20]

Two years earlier, Germany had triggered World War II by invading Poland. Since then, the Third Reich and its allies, Italy and Vichy France, had taken over most of western Europe and much of northern Africa. Six weeks before the Louisiana maneuvers, Hitler's Wehrmacht launched a surprise attack against the Soviet Union, deploying 3 million of its soldiers and thousands of Panzer tanks along a 2,000-mile front. By the time the 45th arrived in Louisiana, the German army had overrun Minsk and appeared poised to take Leningrad, Kiev, and Moscow. Soviet Russia and the Red Army, the world's largest, were on the brink of collapse.

In response to the crisis, President Franklin Roosevelt had pledged to Britain and Russia all the munitions, foodstuffs, and other materials necessary to keep their war efforts going. Shipping such cargo, however, meant crossing a cordon of German U-boats in the North Atlantic. To fend off these submarines, which were sinking a half million tons of supplies a month, the president ordered U.S. destroyers to escort the merchant ships. At first these escorts merely radioed information on submarine movements to British vessels. But when the U-boats began attacking American ships directly, FDR approved an undeclared naval war against Germany. It was merely a matter of time before the conflict spread.

Meanwhile, on the other side of the globe, the Pacific war was already in its fifth year. Japan's imperial war machine, now allied with Germany and Italy, had conquered much of China and was looking to fill the vacuum left in Asia by Europe's preoccupied colonial powers. In July 1941, Japan seized the French colony of Vietnam in preparation for a campaign against British and Dutch possessions to the south. President Roosevelt responded by freezing Japanese assets in the United States and declaring a total trade embargo that choked off Japan's oil supply. The Japanese now

faced a stark choice: they could either avoid war by granting con-
cessions to the United States or ensure it by seizing more territory,
including oil fields in the Dutch East Indies.

Facing the possibility of a two-front global war, the United States
Army put its half million troops to the test across 3,400 square
miles of public and private land in Louisiana. The army had come
a long way since 1939, when it had ranked, at best, as the world's
seventeenth largest. The nation's defense budget was so meager
then that the army could equip only about a third of its soldiers.
An unpopular peacetime draft the following year had doubled the
army's size, but the War Department still struggled to keep it fur-
nished with rifles, tanks, planes, vehicles, and artillery. In Louisiana, two-by-fours substituted for machine guns, sacks of flour for
grenades, stovepipes on wagon wheels for artillery, painted white
color guard rifles for shoulder arms, and World War I vintage
biplanes for observer aircraft. The War Department banned the
use of live ammunition, concerned about both its scarcity and the
danger it posed to untrained troops.[21]

Much of the modern equipment the army did turn out in Louisiana later proved useless in combat. The new 37-millimeter antitank
gun, for example, fired shells that bounced off German armor.
The Stuart tank featured the same ineffectual gun, side armor only
an inch thick, fuel tanks that exploded on impact, and tracks so
narrow they sank in mud. Perhaps the most striking expression
of American naïveté about the war to come was the army's boast
that it had acquired 20,000 new horses for its cavalry, the largest
number since the Civil War. When surrounded by horse-mounted
soldiers in Louisiana, Bill and his fellow correspondents with the
45th Division News simply hauled off in their truck. "If the Germans
or the Japanese had any spies watching us," Bill recalled of the
maneuvers, "they must have laughed their heads off."[22]

To publicize the 45th's role in the Louisiana maneuvers, the division assigned the newspaper staff to work as press agents who would
gather material from the field and send stories back to hometown

papers. For the first time in his short army career, Bill was a full-time cartoonist and intended to take every advantage of the opportunity. Working part-time, he'd already increased production to three or four cartoons a week, with Walter Harrison's *Oklahoma City Times* buying up his surplus. In Louisiana he produced even more and persuaded the *Shreveport Times* to publish his cartoons for the duration of the maneuvers.

The war games introduced Bill to a method he would use in Europe of visiting combat units in the field, observing their conditions for a day or two, and then returning to his tent or room with sketches and cartoon ideas. With a breadboard on his knees as an easel, Bill sketched constantly as he and other staffers crisscrossed swamps, farms, small towns, and pinewoods in a pickup truck fitted with a canvas cover. At night they slept in tents and, on occasion, in an office they'd set up in Shreveport's Washington-Youree Hotel. By the end of the two-month exercises, they'd traveled over ten thousand miles.[23]

The scale, sweep, and realism of the maneuvers, diminished, to be sure, by the makeshift weaponry, clearly fired Bill's imagination. Indeed, the constant movement and extreme field conditions—which included 107 degree heat, marches through bogs, and torrential downpours that flooded pup tents—seemed to sharpen his humor and visual sense. A few of his maneuver cartoons even foreshadowed his later wartime work for the *Stars and Stripes*. One, inspired by a visit to K Company, depicts a grim unshaven soldier crawling in mud during a rainstorm. His companion gestures to a reporter standing behind them with an umbrella. "It's the press," the kneeling soldier says, "he wants to know how's our morale."[24]

As if in response to Bill's newfound inspiration, two men from San Antonio, Texas, drove their big Oldsmobile up to the press section's tent one day and asked for the "renowned" soldier-cartoonist. Wearing "straw hats, seersucker suits, and two-toned shoes," the men said they represented Universal Press and asked if Bill was interested in publishing a special souvenir book of original cartoons for the maneuvers. It didn't take long for Bill to sign the contract drawn up for him by the division's judge advocate general.

Securing a three-day pass, Bill spent all his pocket money on a motel room at the edge of Shreveport where, in forty-eight hours, he turned out fifteen cartoons and twenty-five sketches. After finishing the job at the offices of the *Shreveport Times,* he fell asleep atop a large conference room table. Just before the end of maneuvers, his drawings came back from San Antonio in the form of a twenty-five-cent paperback titled *Star Spangled Banter* (see figure 17). The book was a hit in the 45th Division. "I was nineteen years old and suddenly I was watching people with their noses buried in a book I had published," Bill recalled. "The fact that I didn't hear another word from Universal Press and never learned where they mailed my royalties hardly hurt at all."[25]

As for the division, it passed George Marshall's test, but not by much. The men weren't so inept as the year before, but General Marshall still had strong reservations about the 45th's National Guard officers, who had a well-deserved reputation for corruption and incompetence. After the 1941 maneuvers, Marshall massively restructured the army's Guard divisions, replacing corps commanders and other senior officers with professionally trained regular army personnel. Marshall also targeted inefficient and unreliable units. Bill must have been pleased when, a few weeks into the war, the 120th Quartermaster Regiment was dissolved, replaced by a single company less than one-tenth its size.[26]

THE JAPANESE ATTACK on Pearl Harbor on December 7, 1941, hardly caused a stir in the 45th Division. Long convinced they were headed for combat somewhere sometime soon, the men of the 45th responded to the declaration of war almost with relief. The uncertainty, at least, was over. "We didn't even have sense enough to get scared," Bill recalled.

Apart from a mad scramble for cardboard boxes for mailing

*"O.K.—it's a swap, if ya throw in yer tin hat."*

FIGURE 17 Bill comments on the army's unpreparedness in this cartoon, drawn during Bill's marathon drafting session for his first book, *Star Spangled Banter*. The mustachioed soldier is Willie.

*Copyright 1941 by Bill Mauldin. Courtesy of the Mauldin Estate.*

home their civilian clothes—uniforms being required for the war's duration—the only immediate change at Camp Barkeley was an epidemic of marriage proposals. Within weeks, it seemed, every young woman in Abilene was spoken for. "Nature always seems to step up the mating instinct when killing is afoot," Bill observed. "In Abilene apparently our libidos grasped the situation ahead of our brains."[27]

This is how Bill explained his truncated courtship of an eighteen-year-old college sophomore named Norma Jean Humphries and his marriage to her less than three months after Pearl Harbor. Bill had dated other girls around Abilene before Jean, but none did he pursue as single-mindedly. Bill had blushed when George Tapscott, the *45th Division News'* photographer, had introduced him to Jean on the street and had called her a half dozen times a day for five days until she agreed to go on a date with him. He knew he had won her over when she broke a date with a glamorous air force pilot—a lieutenant, no less—in order to see him exclusively. Using the five dollars he'd earned from selling a half-page cartoon to the *Daily Oklahoman*, Bill made a down payment on a diamond ring costing $27.50 and presented it to Jean. "If you held it up to the light," Bill later told a reporter in Italy, "you could see the diamond real good—at least, I think it's a diamond."

On February 28, 1942, Bill and Jean stood before the division chaplain, who, in the spirit of the army, performed a perfunctory marriage ceremony and then moved to the next couple in line. Hearing the news in California, where he was now working in a shipyard as a steamfitter, Pop expressed his delight that Bill, still a minor, had chosen to forge Pop's signature on the marriage certificate rather than his mother's.[28]

Though they hardly knew each other, Bill and Jean were a pretty good match. An attractive petite brunette, Jean shared Bill's intelligence, ambition, independence, and hardscrabble background. She had grown up in Toyah, Texas, a railroad stop well on its way to becoming a ghost town when she left it in 1940 for Hardin-Simmons University in Abilene. Jean had initially resisted marrying

Bill because she didn't want to interrupt her studies. She stood at the top of her class and expected to move on to medical school after graduation. But Bill convinced Jean she could be both a student and a wife, and the two of them settled into a small rented room in town, the division allowing married men to live off base.

If his subsequent marriages are any indication, Bill was probably ambivalent about Jean's brains and ambition. On the one hand, these qualities pleased Bill, who enjoyed seeing his own best traits mirrored in others. On the other hand, Jean's careerism and academic success threatened Bill's fragile sense of self. Always maneuvering for the upper hand in any relationship, Bill faced the real possibility of slipping behind Jean in importance. He was still, after all, little more than a twenty-one-dollar-a-month rifleman, desperately clinging to his part-time job with the *45th Division News* and hustling to sell his product. Already surpassing him in terms of credentials, Jean was halfway to valedictorian status at Hardin-Simmons. In a few years, she might have not only overshadowed Bill, but supported him.

As if responding to the threat, Bill poured increased energy into his weekly cartoon. Waking every morning at three o'clock in order to make reveille, Bill commuted to Camp Barkeley, where he spent more hours at the drawing table than ever. The division newspaper had expanded after Pearl Harbor and had given Bill a half page a week for his feature. He also drew original "Star Spangled Banter" cartoons (not reprints from the feature) for the *Daily Oklahoman*. The *45th Division News* had grown into a more visually sophisticated montage of gags and illustrations that practically exhausted Bill's attention. Finally, he debuted a humor column about infantry life titled "Quoth the Dogface," a slang term for foot soldier. Even Captain Fred Stoft, the new officer in charge of the newspaper—Walter Harrison having left for staff officer school at Fort Leavenworth—expressed concern over Bill's frantic schedule.

"If you aren't careful," he said, "you'll be a burned-out has-been before you're old enough to vote."

Hardly a martyr, Bill needled Stoft constantly for more time, better supplies, higher pay, and special privileges. He demanded, for example, a private office, which the newspaper granted in the form of a cubby smaller than a closet. "Bill would retire into this when he wanted privacy," recalled reporter Don Robinson, "but, by tilting back about six inches, he could come out and join the conversation."[29]

Stoft temporarily appeased his prima donna cartoonist by wresting from the infantry more special-duty time for Bill along with a promotion to private first class. The stripe and the time came out of Company K's allotment. The company's commander made it clear that Bill was now more a liability than an asset.

"You goddamn quartermaster fugitive," he groused, learning of the promotion, "you've cost me a third-cook's rating."

The commander took to calling Bill "the Unknown Soldier" for all his absences from the company and even tried to goad him into handing back the stripe. Rayson Billey, however, encouraged Bill, reassuring him that the chevron was not the commander's property and that the men of Company K enjoyed having the popular cartoonist among them.

Also, Jean welcomed the pay increase, which let her quit a part-time job at an ice cream parlor, but equally she resented Bill's increasing absorption in his work. A night owl who required little sleep, Bill always worked into the wee hours, either in his cubby or at home with Jean. He also disappeared for days on maneuvers, both to train with Company K and to gather fresh material for his feature. Feeling abandoned and isolated, Jean increasingly lashed out at Bill, who, in turn, only grew more defensive.

"At these moments I became the one who felt threatened," Bill explained. "My drawing hand had become my Rock of Gibraltar. With it, I was convinced the world might be mine. Without it, I felt like an insignificant jerk."

It was probably with some relief that Bill learned in early spring of the division's imminent transfer to Fort Devens, Massachusetts.

What prompted the move remained secret, though most soldiers understood they were headed for final combat training before being shipped overseas to strike the first American blow against the Wehrmacht.

So, after less than two months of marriage, Bill left Jean behind in Abilene and took his turn standing guard on the freezing, soot-covered railcars that sped the 45th Division across the continent.

One cold afternoon in Pennsylvania, with the train stopped on a siding, a farm mother emerged from her house bearing coffee and a basket filled with cookies, doughnuts, and sandwiches. She handed them up to Bill to share with his comrades. The train began to move, and Bill asked how he could get the basket and coffee pot back to her. She told him not to worry about it. "God bless you," she said, as the train pulled out.

It was a simple act of generosity Bill would never forget. He felt like a white knight. "She was my country," he said, "and she was worth all the soot and chilblains."[30]

THE PROSPECT of combat frightened Bill less than the indefinite suspension of the *45th Division News*. Because of the need for secrecy, the army eliminated all public signs of the division, from its newspaper to its Thunderbird patches. Apparently the paper was dead, and the staff would soon be landing on a beach somewhere in full gear.

When not practicing amphibious assaults on Cape Cod or Martha's Vineyard with Company K, Bill stormed up and down the East Coast trying to keep his cartooning career alive. In nearby Boston, he called at every newspaper, magazine, and book publisher he could locate. The war had created a demand for army cartoons, and both the *Boston Herald* and the *Boston Globe* bought some of Bill's work. The *Herald* even paid twenty-five dollars for a full-page color layout. He also won two hundred dollars in an Elks cartoon contest intended to encourage letter writing to soldiers.

Bill placed second for a cartoon of a private in the field with an opened envelope surrounded by his mates: "No news, fellas," the caption reads, "just *Garden Beautiful* asking if I wanna renew my subscription."

The contest represented Bill's high-water mark that summer. Most of the editors he met were wary of the sullen-looking, chain-smoking, downy-faced kid cartoonist. To them, Bill's plebeian, wisecracking cartoon soldiers were something of a puzzle. The characters belonged neither to the military adventure strip, which recounted the exploits of daring pilots and intelligence officers, nor to the standard army gag strip, which featured bespectacled draftees, bullying drill sergeants, and exasperated officers. Russell Hall, an editor at Charles Scribner's Sons, agreed with Bill that a book of army cartoons would be popular, but could not imagine this all-but-prepubescent soldier as its author. Indeed, Hall suspected that Bill was an impostor. "I thought maybe you had stolen that uniform," the regretful editor told Bill years later.[31]

Given so much rejection and the death of the *45th Division News,* Bill felt resurrected when a new army weekly, titled *Yank,* began actively recruiting enlisted men for its staff. The magazine had been inspired in part by Walter Harrison's modest experiment. Sometime before, the *News* had attracted social scientists in the War Department who fretted about the stability and cohesiveness of an army that had ballooned to fantastic proportions. Personnel experts especially focused on the influx of draftees chafing against the restrictions, low pay, and drudgery of army life, as well as the extreme deference expected by officers. In early 1942, the army replaced the "Morale Branch" with a larger, more powerful agency known as the Information and Education Division. Here *Yank* was born.

The idea, championed by George Marshall, was to publish a nominally independent news and entertainment magazine staffed exclusively by men from the ranks. Official oversight would be from a distance. The magazine would adopt a credo that the *45th Division News* had left publicly unstated: "By and for the enlisted men."

The first mock-up, created by seven civilian advertising and publishing professionals, was approved by Secretary of War Henry Stimson in March 1942 and contained one Mauldin cartoon. Two months later, just after the 45th Division's arrival in the East, a staff of sixteen hastily inducted editors, writers, and illustrators opened an office on East Forty-second Street in New York. The office was immediately besieged by hundreds of applicants seeking a transfer to the magazine's staff. Bill, who had made initial contact with the staff months earlier, pressed as hard as any of them. He sent a steady stream of drawings and visited the office in person with a letter from Walter Harrison in hand. He also traveled to Washington, D.C., where he entreated Mike Monroney, a United States congressman from Oklahoma City and advocate for the 45th Division, to promote "Star Spangled Banter" in the War Department.

*Yank* not only refused to hire Bill but also largely snubbed him as a contributor, publishing only a half dozen of his numerous submissions. To feature editor Douglas Borgstedt, Bill's characters were "too unsoldierly." A more accurate critique would have pointed out the differences between "Star Spangled Banter" and *Yank*'s regular cartoon features, such as George Baker's "The Sad Sack" and Dave Breger's "G.I. Joe." While Bill's cartoon bore the marks of a seasoned army insider, Baker's and Breger's work represented the perspective of lowly draftees. "The Sad Sack" and "G.I. Joe" pit inept, intractable, diminutive privates against a stubbornly rigid army environment. Like the magazine's staff itself, these cartoon characters were *in* the army, but not *of* it. Bill's best work drew on the intricacies of infantry maneuvers, training, and equipment, but such fare had no place in the pages of *Yank* (see figures 18 and 19).

After several months of rejection, Bill would eventually lash out with a scathing letter to Borgstedt itemizing the editor's, the magazine's, and the other cartoonists' shortcomings. Borgstedt thought Bill such a crackpot that he pinned Bill's letter on the office bulletin board for all to read. It would be Bill's final submission to the magazine.[32]

FIGURE 18 If Bill's maneuver cartoons represented "light duty," then *Yank*'s early comics were hardly even military. This panel, from Corporal Dave Breger's inaugural "G.I. Joe" cartoon, appeared in the original *Yank* mock-up in March 1942. Breger, who was taken on staff by *Yank* and eventually promoted to lieutenant, would go on to enjoy enormous success with the feature. Given the cartoon's title, some readers on the home front later confused Breger's "G.I. Joe" with Mauldin's "Willie and Joe," to Bill's profound annoyance.

While Bill wrestled with *Yank*, the 45th's fate was unveiled in a staff officers' meeting called in late summer 1942 by Major General George S. Patton Jr. Patton's daring nighttime tank maneuvers had propelled him to stardom during the Louisiana war games. He and other planners had selected the 45th to participate in Operation Torch, the Anglo-American invasion of Vichy-controlled Morocco and Algeria.[33]

"WE DO IT WITH DOGS BACK IN THE STATES—ON A SOMEWHAT SMALLER SCALE, OF COURSE—"

**FIGURE 19** *"Yank,"* groused Bill, "encouraged my penchant for dumb gags." The above, published on July 15, 1942, was one of only six Mauldin cartoons accepted by the magazine. Bill's grudge against *Yank* lasted a lifetime.

A decision to launch the North African campaign had come after months of fractious negotiations with British Prime Minister Winston Churchill. President Roosevelt, strongly influenced by George Marshall, had initially preferred to strike at Hitler's *Festung Europa* directly in northwestern France. Such a campaign would put the American army on a short route to Germany and also aid the Soviet Union by drawing Hitler's troops from the Eastern Front. But Churchill, whose soldiers had already suffered defeat in France, Norway, and the Balkans, shuddered at the thought of a green American army blundering into catastrophe on the beaches of Normandy or Calais.

Centuries of imperial rule, as well as personal memories of slaughter on the Western Front in World War I, had taught Churchill and other British planners to minimize the risks of large-scale land wars by fighting from the periphery and controlling vital seaports. For their part, American strategists suspected that the conservative prime minister's "soft underbelly" Mediterranean strategy was motivated by his desire to gain access to old British colonies in the Middle East and the Balkans and to see the Red Army worn down. But by the end of July, Churchill's repeated cautions had tempered Roosevelt's impulse for a swift decisive campaign. Preparations began for the invasion of North Africa.[34]

Shortly after Patton's announcement, Army General Headquarters replaced the 45th's General William Key, the easy-going National Guard commander called "General Bill" by his men, with a veteran from the Regular army, Major General Troy Middleton. At the same time, the War Department pulled the 45th off of Operation Torch. As American troops landed in Casablanca, Oran, and Algiers on November 8, the 45th pulled out of Fort Devens for winter training at Pine Camp, near Watertown, New York. Most of the men guessed they were being prepared to invade Norway.

Bill's disappointment in missing out on the North African invasion surprised him, especially since the change of plans meant a reprieve for his career and the *45th Division News*. "Esprit has a way of sneaking up on the worst of us," he realized after months of training with Company K. The stand-down also meant reuniting with Jean, who quit college and joined Bill in Watertown.

While Bill and the rest of the *News* staff sized up Middleton, winter descended on Pine Camp with such ferocity that training practically ground to a halt. Ten-foot snowdrifts, subzero temperatures, and strong winds sweeping off Lake Ontario made venturing outside hazardous and maneuvers impossible. The *Watertown Times,* which printed the resurrected *45th Division News,* bought most of Bill's Pine Camp panels but balked at his offer to supply the paper with a weekly cartoon for the duration of the war. After two months in Watertown, when Bill had just about run out of snow-and-ice gags, orders came down once again for the division to relocate. Like an armchair strategist moving a pin on a map, general headquarters shifted the 45th to Camp Pickett, Virginia.[35]

A lot of overseas soldiers called upon the War Department to "draft the 45th" and derided Bill's outfit as the "trainingest division" in the army, but Washington was actually positioning the 45th Division for the next phase of the Mediterranean war. Roosevelt, Churchill, and the Allied Chiefs of Staff had met in newly liberated Casablanca and agreed to launch Operation Husky, the Allied invasion of Sicily, after concluding the North African campaign. While General Middleton and his staff flew to Morocco to plan the invasion with General Patton, the 45th Division stepped up their amphibious training on the beaches of Little Creek, Virginia, and Solomons Island, Maryland. A visit by General Marshall to Camp Pickett only confirmed a wide suspicion: the 45th would make an amphibious assault against Axis forces in Europe within a matter of weeks.

When the remnants of the German Afrika Korps finally surrendered in Tunisia on May 12, 1943, the men of the 45th brawled, whored, drew up wills, bought life insurance, wrote letters home, and otherwise behaved as generations of departing soldiers had before them.[36]

As the planning, training, and hell-raising reached fever pitch,

Bill became frenetic. Jean had recently informed him that she was pregnant, and he was determined to build up their savings account before heading overseas. Between his five dollars a week from the *Daily Oklahoman,* the cash won in the Elks contest, and the money earned freelancing, Bill had put aside two hundred dollars. A private Washington-based publishing company that put out the *Army Times* newspaper had recently offered to publish a collection of his old cartoons. Bill struck a hasty deal with the company's president, Mel Ryder, two days before heading for the loading docks at Newport News. Bill's contract for *Star Spangled Banter,* as his second book was titled, called for a one-hundred dollar advance against a royalty of two cents a copy. Ryder also pledged an effort to try to syndicate whatever cartoons Bill sent from overseas.[37]

On May 25, the invasion task force began combat-loading its men, equipment, and vehicles aboard twenty-five large ships. Everything entered in reverse order, so that when the doors flew open on a hostile shore, the first wave would be at the ready. On June 4, the ships and a dozen destroyer escorts shoved off for a two-week journey through U-boat-infested waters. It was the largest convoy ever to cross the Atlantic.[38]

Crammed three feet below the waterline in Hold 4-D of the troopship *James O'Hara,* Bill Mauldin felt blessed by fate to be traveling as a member of the *45th Division News* staff, rather than with Company K of the 180th Infantry. Before leaving Camp Pickett, Bill had darted about like a magpie, stealing pencils, pens, erasers, glue—anything that might "come in handy overseas," as he put it. "He bought ink by the quart and fixative by the gallon," *News* editor Don Robinson recalled. "He purchased paper, hoarded envelopes, and soon had more stuff than the rest of us together."

Lying in his billet contemplating the fifteen-inch opening between his canvas bunk and the one above him, Bill surveyed the gang of combat engineers who shared the stifling hold. He pulled a bottle of ink from his barracks bag and offered to draw caricatures on the soldiers' name patches for fifty cents apiece.[39]

# Chapter Three

# Going In

> *The front cannot but attract us, because it is, in one way, the*
> *extreme boundary between what you are already aware of and*
> *what is still in the process of formation. Not only do you see*
> *there things that you experience nowhere else, but you also see*
> *emerge from within yourself an underlying stream of clarity,*
> *energy, and freedom that is to be found hardly anywhere else*
> *in ordinary life.*
>
> —PIERRE TEILHARD DE CHARDIN,
> STRETCHER-BEARER, 4TH MIXED REGIMENT
> OF ZOUAVES AND MOROCCAN TIRAILLEURS,
> FRANCE, SEPTEMBER 25, 1917[1]

IN BOARDING the *James O'Hara*, Bill Mauldin and his fellow
passengers had passed from garrison life into the world of war.
Few, at first, understood the difference. U-boats prowled Atlantic
sea-lanes. That much, everyone knew. But the danger remained
abstract. "None of us," as Bill recalled, "had yet adjusted below our

necklines to the idea that a real war was going on somewhere. . . . We just hadn't *felt* our knowledge yet."

Then, one morning after several days at sea, Bill felt it. He was standing in a chow line so long that any soldier wanting a meal had to shuffle for several hours along a twisting route that took him into virtually every hold, through every passageway, and up or down every ladder on the ship. Once in a while he even popped up on deck, the only time he saw the sky and breathed fresh air. It was at just such a moment, as Bill gazed at the vast empty ocean to his left, that fear seized him. He and the other men of Hold 4-D were stowed low on the port side of the extreme port flank of the convoy. Nothing stood between them and the guided torpedoes that ripped so easily into steel-plated hulls. Imagining a horror that might await in the hold, Bill volunteered for antiaircraft duty on deck. There, he reasoned, he might survive a direct hit with mere flash burns. Bluffing his way into the job, he relied on his memory of photographs of the 20-millimeter cannon. Thus occupied with his weapon, he spent most of his journey studying it, making sketches, soaking in the sunshine, and enjoying cool evening breezes as the ship approached the Azores.[2]

If the trip aboard the *James O'Hara* alerted Bill to the dangers of war, it also drove home as nothing else had the stakes of military rank. Nowhere was the gulf between officers and enlisted men more apparent than on a troopship. Except when snaking their way to the galley, common soldiers languished below deck in cavernous billets scaffolded with bunks sometimes twelve levels high. Stowed on canvas shelves in dark, narrow holds, soldiers found even reading difficult. Air, fetid on good days, grew fouler in hot, sunny weather. Seasickness compounded the problem as soldiers in the upper bunks vomited on those below. Lack of space made cleaning up almost impossible; herding the men to one side of the vessel to hose off the floors could cause the ship to roll and capsize.

Few officers ventured below deck. Most remained in the comforts of "Officers' Country"—the lounges, staterooms, dining halls, and deckside promenades designated as off limits to enlisted men. Officers' Country comprised half of the ship or more, even though commissioned passengers made up only a tiny fraction of the men on board. With little else to occupy them, army brass policed its domain as if on sentry duty. "Where we can go, where we can't go," complained one Europe-bound soldier in a letter back home, "seem to be of primary concern to the officers."[3]

Bill managed to infiltrate Officers' Country at two o'clock in the morning via a dumbwaiter that took him to an unguarded corner of the officers' galley. A cook assigned to the galley had invited him up, hoping to get a full-size Mauldin caricature out of the deal. Every night thereafter, Bill worked on the watercolor portrait in exchange for all the steak, baked potatoes, and ice cream he could eat.

He also, of course, sketched cartoons. While Bill was maneuvering his way out of Hold 4-D, Don Robinson, editor of the *45th Division News,* had somehow managed to gain nighttime access to a mimeograph machine in the officers' wardroom. He got permission from the ship's captain to crank out a daily shipboard paper complete with Mauldin cartoons cut from stencils. The liberal-minded captain apparently enjoyed Bill's drawings, which targeted Officers' Country, the chow line, the restricted access to showers, and other irritations of life aboard the *James O'Hara.*[4]

The two-week journey ended at 1500 hours on June 22, 1943, when the convoy carrying the 45th Division dropped anchor off the coast of Oran, Algeria. Oran had been in Allied hands since the second day of Operation Torch, the Anglo-American invasion of North Africa launched the previous November. The 45th disembarked in darkness the following morning, using the occasion to practice the amphibious landings to become so familiar in coming months. Men clambered down cargo nets in full gear, carrying at least fifty pounds of equipment, clothing, ammunition, and weaponry. Landing craft piloted by navy coxswains churned toward the shoreline. Dawn broke with only one regiment having reached its objective. Some boats landed ten or twelve miles away from the correct beach. "Good Lord!" exclaimed General Omar Bradley, who would soon take the division under his command as part of II Corps. "Suppose they miss it by that much in Sicily?"[5]

As the division drilled and practiced amphibious assaults near Oran, Bill, Don Robinson, and the three other members of the newspaper staff, desperate, as always, to justify their absence from the infantry, tried to put out a paper. Failing to find a printer, they fell back into the village of Port-au-Poule and waited out their twelve-day layover, taking in the town's cafés and wine bars.

What they saw of local color was gruesome. "The Arabs were easily the sorriest human beings I had ever seen or imagined," Bill recalled. So brutal was French colonial rule that the population of Algeria had shrunk by almost half during fifty years of colonization. Shoeless, emaciated, and wearing used army mattress covers as robes, the Arabs appeared to Bill almost as apparitions skulking in the desert. The French treated them as subhuman. Any Frenchman found guilty of accidentally running over an Arab child with a truck paid a five-dollar fine. A dead goat or donkey brought double the penalty.[6]

American soldiers, for the most part, adopted the French contempt for the Arabs. Racial hatred of native Moroccans, Algerians, and Tunisians among the GIs was intense. Soldiers called them "wogs," and some shot them for sport, "like rabbits in the States during hunting season," as one American explained it in a letter home. During the North African campaign, rape and murder by American troops occurred with such frequency that some at Allied forces headquarters worried about a general breakdown in discipline. Soldiers usually justified their behavior by pointing out that the Arabs were sometimes German collaborators, or that they sliced Americans' throats to steal their boots.[7] More liberal and civilized observers sublimated their fear and disgust into condescension.

Bill's firsthand encounter with the Algerian underclass came when a lieutenant happening through Port-au-Poule spotted the cartoonist and ordered him to stand guard over some headquarters tents. Within minutes of taking his post, Bill spied an Arab youth dragging away a barracks bag filled with shoes. Bill raised his unloaded rifle and ordered the boy to drop the bag. The kid looked up, grinned, shrugged, and continued on his way. Bill conspicuously pulled the bolt on his rifle and loudly repeated the order. Not wanting to be shot in the back, the boy turned around, put down the bag, spread his arms, and invited Bill to shoot him in the chest, as was Bill's legal right. "It was my first experience with someone who really had nothing to lose," Bill recalled almost thirty years later. "It was disturbing."

When Bill failed to shoot him, the boy picked up the bag of shoes and hustled out of sight.

Angry voices soon emerged from the tents.

"Goddamn that lousy Mauldin," they cried, "some son of a bitch got my shoes."

Bill pleaded that an unloaded Springfield was no match for the band of knife-wielding "A-rabs" who had escaped with the barracks bag. The men then directed their verbal wrath at the lieutenant who had issued the empty weapon.

"I couldn't have taken a shot at that boy if I had been holding a loaded and well-oiled Tommy gun and my life had depended on it," Bill said, "but I kept that fact to myself."[8]

THE DAY of the Sicily invasion found Bill rolling on the floor of Hold 4-D covered in vomit. Sailing had been smooth during four days of the thousand-mile trip from Oran to Sicily. But on the fifth day, a northerly wind picked up, the Mediterranean Sea grew choppy, and soon the ship wallowed in a gale storm.

Every man on board, by most estimates, succumbed to seasickness. Bill held out fine until he went below deck to the head, where vomit an inch deep covered the tiled floor and masses of men convulsed around toilets lining the walls. The ship tipped bow-first into a thirty-foot trough, sending the men down the floor's slithery incline, and as the bow rose to climb the next wave, the soldiers tumbled backward in heaps. After scratching and clawing his way to the hatch, Bill managed to regain his position topside, where, perched by the cannon, he watched hundreds of sick men preparing to descend the cargo nets into the heaving landing crafts below. Around midnight, back in Hold 4-D, a captain from the 120th Engineer Combat Battalion came looking for Sergeant Mauldin and the *45th Division News* staff. The engineers needed extra hands for shore party duties, such as clearing mines and barbed wire. Engineers would be landing first, ahead of the infantry.

Don Robinson relinquished two reporters, Fred Sheehan and Bill Barrett, holding back his photographer, George Tapscott, on the grounds that he was a medic. Robinson himself, as head of the news section, also escaped being dragooned, as did Bill, for whom Robinson covered simply by reporting him missing. When Bill returned to the hold after dawn to gather his gear for the landing, Robinson told him the news.

"It was bound to end, anyway," he screamed over the sound of navy escort guns, which were now bombarding the island to support the invasion. "Goddammit, Mauldin, we're soldiers now," he scolded unprovoked, "and we'd better face up to it."

The three remaining members of the newspaper staff climbed into the shaft of light streaming through the open hatch. The storm had ended, but the ship still bucked. The invasion's first wave had landed hours earlier on Sicily's southeastern shore near the village of Scoglitti. As the ship's 20-millimeter guns opened up on enemy aircraft, Bill, Tapscott, and Robinson stood ready to debark.

Compared to combat soldiers, who were weighed down with rifles, mortars, bazookas, radios, grenades, machine guns, and ammunition, the three newsmen traveled light. They wore steel pot-like helmets, olive drab woolen shirts and pants, cotton waist-length jackets, and leather ankle-high shoes topped by canvas leggings. Around their waists they carried life belts with $CO_2$ canisters just in case their landing craft sank. On their backs were canvas musette bags or haversacks stuffed with rations, utensils, toothbrush, comb, blanket, poncho, socks, underwear, a "shelter-half" pup tent, a T-handled entrenching tool, and personal items which, in Bill's case, included some art supplies and a pistol.

On command, they clambered over the gunwales and awkwardly gripped the vertical net ropes so that the men above them would not stomp on their fingers. Their craft bobbed forty feet below. Fumes from the idling engine wafted up, mixing with the smell of sweat, vomit, and feces. The landing craft caught a swell and rose until it practically knocked the soldiers off the nets before descending again into the trough. The men waited for another wave to rise, and then jumped backward into the boat.

Some of the division's soldiers hadn't made it into their landing crafts that day. Some fell or mistimed their jumps. A few drowned. Others, seemingly secure in their boats, had been knocked overboard by falling men and equipment. Bill held the net for those who followed, and then crouched down against the others, half of them vomiting from fear and seasickness.

As the landing craft zigzagged its way to shore, Bill looked up into a sunny sky, catching a glimpse of the war raging around him: black columns of smoke, geysers of water, flashes of cannon fire, and aircraft swooping down, shooting, and crashing into the sea. His eyes bulged uncomprehendingly, as if all of it were projected on some immense movie screen. Unnatural thunderclaps booming one after another momentarily deafened him. The noise reminded him of the metallic screams logging trains made back home, descending the mountain, brakes locked.

The landing craft thudded to a stop several yards offshore and lowered its steel ramp like a great metal jaw. Bill disgorged with the others, fighting the undertow with his pistol drawn. Stumbling onto the beach, he joined the largest amphibious invasion in history.[9]

---

LANDING 181,000 MEN on its first day, July 10, 1943, Operation Husky brought more troops to shore more quickly than would the Normandy invasion almost a year later. After being delayed for two months for lack of landing craft, the operation, almost miraculously, achieved a measure of surprise. The Allies had floated a corpse off the coast of Spain carrying phony invasion plans for Greece, a ruse that fooled no one but Hitler. The Führer overruled his advisers and kept Sicily underdefended, with only 50,000 combat-ready German troops. The 315,000 Italian soldiers on the island had antiquated weapons, little ammunition, scarce training, and almost no will to fight their Allied liberators.[10]

In the Allies' two-pronged attack, General Montgomery's British Eighth Army was to lead the way up Sicily's eastern coast (see figure 20). The drive would be for Messina on the northern tip, just two miles by sea from the toe of the boot-shaped Italian peninsula. As part of General Patton's American Seventh Army, the 45th Division would assist in protecting the British left flank. They were to capture three towns, two airfields, two pieces of high ground, and one highway before going north over the island's central mountains. From there, decisions would be made ad hoc, often according to the whims of field commanders like Patton. There was no larger endgame in mind, other than to take the island.

This plan's simplicity contrasted with the chaos surrounding Bill on the beach near Scoglitti. War's detritus lay all around him. Swamped, capsized, and blown apart landing craft sat in the water while twisted hulks of jeeps, trucks, crashed airplanes, and artillery bore witness to the enemy's "light resistance" to the invasion.

Bodies and body parts washed ashore, along with packs, weapons, and pieces of clothing. More orderly in their arrival were the 45th's barracks bags. They sat piled on the sand awaiting distribution, easy prey for supply soldiers who searched them for valuables. The division's payroll, at least, was secure from thieving shore parties. It lay at the bottom of the sea. During the landing, someone

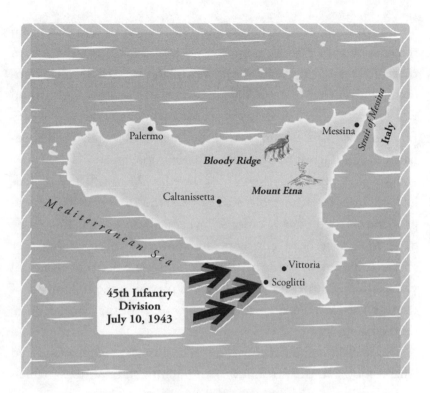

**FIGURE 20** Sicily, where Bill spent two months as part of Operation Husky.

had inexplicably thrown overboard the six field safes containing two million dollars.[11]

Onshore, men swarmed in confusion. Officers grabbed soldiers at random and assigned them to various tasks: tending the wounded, burying the dead, and guarding Italian soldiers who were surrendering in such numbers the Americans used them to unload supplies. About three dozen Italians tried to give themselves up to Bill and Don Robinson, who simply pointed them to the nearest crowd of prisoners. A nervous warrant officer commanded Bill and some other men to dig foxholes. Some unknowingly dug in a neighboring minefield. When the holes were dug, the officer ordered the men to march inland.

As if waking from a daydream, Bill, Tapscott, and Robinson remembered their mission and wisely separated themselves from their boat team. They made their way inland toward Scoglitti hoping to find a printing press, only to learn that the nearest printshop was miles away in Vittoria, still in enemy hands. They also heard from some combat engineers that their fellow reporters Fred Sheehan and Bill Barrett had died during the initial assault.

As dusk approached, the staff of the *45th Division News* dug shallow slit trenches under olive trees near the division's command post and opened their K rations. The trenches shook from nearby explosions. Overhead, enemy planes appeared, followed by tracer shells. Someone in a nearby trench raised his rifle to the sky and vainly squeezed off some shots. It was probably the only night of the war Bill did not spend writing, sketching, or otherwise working on the paper.

The next morning, as those in the headquarters area wondered what to do next, the three newsmen hitchhiked to Vittoria, which had been liberated overnight. Bill headed straight for the newly opened civil affairs office, presided over by a harried lieutenant colonel. "In addition to the hundreds of Sicilians who stormed the doors to have their problems of twenty-one years of fascist rule solved," remembered Don Robinson, "the colonel had Mauldin to contend with." Jumping to the front of the line, Bill badgered the officer into assigning him an interpreter and the right to commandeer a printshop.

On their way to the shop, the three men saw two members of the 45th celebrating the town's liberation by waving around their M-1s, a bottle of local wine, and two flaccid penises poking through their open flies. Townspeople, whose ancestors had endured countless foreign invaders over the centuries, peered out from shuttered windows. The division's provost marshal stepped forward, deputized Mauldin and Robinson as MPs (Tapscott having ducked around a corner), and ordered them to place the belligerents under arrest. Bill's first thought was of running away; his second was of the wonderful, if unpublishable, cartoon the scene would make. Don somehow threatened and cajoled the soldiers into surrendering to the provost martial, who promptly laid the drunken men out with open-handed slaps to the face. Bill and Don discreetly placed their MP armbands on a wall and slipped away to find their printshop.

By four o'clock in the afternoon, the team was already setting type for the first Allied newspaper published on Axis soil. The Sicilian typesetters, unsure what they might be paid for their efforts, shrugged at the American soldiers' dismay at the lack of *w*'s, *k*'s, and *y*'s in their type. The Italian language had no use for them. Don began to hand-print copy for the typesetters, trying to avoid the missing letters.

The staff retired after dark. Then, around midnight, they awoke to the drone of distant airplanes. The sound grew louder until, suddenly, the earth quivered with the explosion of five thousand antiaircraft guns fired almost in unison. Rumors of a German parachute drop designed to sever the 45th's supply lines had circulated all day. Ack-ack crews and machine gunners had been waiting for them.

But these planes were not German; they were American C-47s delivering the 82nd Airborne to assist in fighting an elite Panzer division up the coast. Under assault, the planes began dropping paratroopers. Hundreds were shot before they hit the ground. By the time the barrage ended, friendly fire had brought down almost two dozen C-47s and caused hundreds of casualties.

After sunrise, Bill ventured out to find silky swatches of parachutes and the bloody remains of American soldiers hanging in olive trees. The scene, Bill recalled, confirmed his "first practical lesson about war: nobody really knows what he's doing."

Holding firm to his own sense of purpose, Bill made his way through the grotesque festoonery toward the beach, in search of war news that would serve as copy. On the road he met two Italian soldiers who beseeched him to accept their surrender. He did so in exchange for their bicycle and carbine, using the former to ride to the beach and the latter to bribe a navy coxswain to ferry him to a ship anchored offshore. There, in the radio shack, Bill secured a sheaf of press reports, then returned to his waiting landing craft to find that the deck officer, also eager for souvenirs, had confiscated the carbine.

"That thieving son of a bitch," the coxswain groused before a Messerschmitt swooped down and strafed their boat.

Safely onshore, Bill pulled his stowed bicycle from some bushes and headed back to Vittoria. The road was empty now, and for a moment he enjoyed an almost leisurely excursion in the Sicilian countryside. Hearing an engine approach from behind, he steered to the edge of the road to let the truck pass, only to notice the dust in front of him dance as if pelted by hail. A large shadow appeared on the ground, and a quick glance upward was enough to identify the predator. It was a slow, low-flying gray and black Stuka dive-bomber returning to base with an empty bomb rack and a lethally playful rear-gunner. The gunner swung around as the plane passed overhead, firing at the GI bicyclist now sprawled on the road and rolling toward a ditch. When the plane disappeared, Bill dusted himself off, abandoned the wrecked bicycle, and hitchhiked the rest of the way to the printshop.

That night, the print crew finished setting type and turned out three thousand copies of the *45th Division News* by hand on an old flatbed press. A three-column two-page edition printed on a single seven-by-ten-inch sheet with upside-down *m*'s substituting for *w*'s, the paper conspicuously lacked cartoons and photographs. Sicily's only engraving equipment still belonged to the Axis. Nevertheless, the men celebrated with a bottle of Sicilian wine, against orders, which the paper itself had just printed, not to drink the ubiquitous beverage. The staff also toasted the return of Fred Sheehan and Bill Barrett, alive after all, not the last American soldiers Bill would know to defy their rumored demise.[12]

BILL'S FIRST CARTOONS in occupied Europe were so forgettable that he himself didn't mention them in his accounts of the war. They appeared on D-day plus seven and nine in two mimeographed issues of the *45th Division News* produced after the printer took ill. Bill had himself hand-cut rough stencils, as he'd done aboard the *James O'Hara*. The result was a poorly printed, barely legible cartoon of a soldier dismantling an outhouse, in reference to a story in the paper's first Sicilian issue about a German sniper being blown apart in a privy. "Yessir, Major," the soldier says, "ole K comp'ny is on the ball! Not a sniper left between here and Ragusa!"

The second cartoon featured one Wehrmacht trooper remarking to another: "Vot good iss it for Der Fuhrer to tell us God iss on our side? Der Americans haff got all der Indians." Only rarely would Bill again satirize the enemy, and never again in such a flippant manner.[13]

Bill grew increasingly frustrated by the lack of engraving equipment as the staff followed the rapidly moving 45th northward to Caltanissetta near the center of the island. The city had been virtually leveled by Allied bombing and reeked of human corpses decomposing beneath the sun-hot rubble. The five newsmen took up quarters in a partially-demolished opera house. Bill stripped the walls of its portraits of Benito Mussolini and King Victor Emmanuel III. He would go on to similarly loot official buildings throughout the Sicilian and Italian campaigns, almost as a ritual, using the backs of the high-quality double-weight paper to draw some of his most famous cartoons.

In Caltanissetta, Bill also rooted through the remains of a police station, fishing out a Moto Guzzi motorcycle in working order. When the police chief approached him for the bike, Bill typed out a receipt, signed it "George S. Patton," and plotted his course to Palermo, the capital of Sicily, where he hoped to find an engraver.[14]

The night before Palermo fell, Bill pulled out his brush, ink bottle, and portrait paper and composed his first well-illustrated cartoons since landing in Sicily. The drawings' dark atmospherics, distressed figures, and detailed renderings of Sicily's war-torn land-scape suggested why he was so eager to find an engraver (see figure 21). The shooting war had sharpened Bill's vision, as it does for most soldiers. Combat gives men new eyes, observed war correspondent Eric Sevareid. "Every scene is a vivid masterpiece of painting," he wrote. "The tree and the ditch ahead are all the trees and ditches of creation, informed with the distillation of sacred *tree*ness and *ditch*ness." More understated was Bill's recollection that Sicily had stimulated his senses like maneuvers, only "with live ammunition."[15]

At daybreak on D-day plus twelve, Bill rolled up his illustrations, carefully placed them in his musette bag, and started on the sixty-five-mile journey to the northwestern coast. He figured Palermo would probably be in Allied hands by the time he reached it.

He arrived around midday covered in the fine white Sicilian dust kicked up all over the island by the advancing and retreating armies. Palermo had fallen, but had yet to awaken fully to its liberation. The colonel in charge of civil affairs there was Charles Poletti, a former lieutenant governor of New York who was solicitous toward the press. He assigned Bill an interpreter and directed him to one of the city's few engravers, Signore Fastrelli. Fastrelli's shop had suffered a direct hit by a bombshell. So Bill took off for the engraver's house, which, he discovered, consisted of two walls and part of a roof. In the yard by a chicken coop, he found the shell-shocked Fastrelli tinkering with his ancient engraving equipment.

Even in such straits, the Sicilian agreed to help, if he could some-how get hold of zinc for the plates and nitric acid for the etching. With Fastrelli riding the fender, the two fastidious craftsmen motored about Palermo in search of supplies. They found acid in a warehouse brimming with items reserved for the black market and zinc in a coffin maker's shop. For the latter, Bill had to buy one of the coffin maker's finest pieces. Bill ripped the metal lining out of the casket, rolled it up, and tied it to the motorcycle's handlebars.

Bill and Fastrelli returned to the chicken yard, where, in Bill's

*"Stop shootin' at him, ya idiot!*
*Wanna give away our position?"*

**FIGURE 21** Inspired by an incident Bill witnessed his first night in Sicily, this cartoon, appearing initially as a halftone in the July 29, 1943, issue of the *45th Division News*, was Bill's first engraved drawing in occupied Europe. While the action and caption express the absurdities of combat, the rubble, tiled roof, exploding house, and distinctive inverted gull wings on the Stuka dive-bomber are evidence of Bill's heightened visual sense. Bill had always enjoyed drawing machinery and architectural details. Now it was destruction that caught his eye. In many of his cartoons, demolished buildings substituted for human corpses, which army censors would never have allowed. "Bomb-blasted houses," Bill explained, "are constant reminders of the war, long after the dead are buried."

words, the engraver "showed himself to be a genius at improvisation." Lacking an arc light or solvent to coat the zinc, Fastrelli used the sun and brewed his own chemical bath. He had no gas to heat the plates, so he built a wood fire. Without a frame for holding the engraving on the block, he nailed the picture down.

The plates Bill bundled into his shirt later that night for the long ride back to Caltanissetta bore the marks of Fastrelli's ingenuity. They were coarse halftones with nail holes in the corners, but the last Caltanissetta issue of the *45th Division News* contained engraved Mauldin cartoons. The entire expedition, including interpreter's and engraver's fees, had cost Bill fourteen dollars and some canned rations.[16]

BURDENED BY the challenges of printing the paper in Caltanissetta, the *45th Division News* staff had physically lost touch with both its readership and its sources. The 45th had moved quickly to the north-central edge of Sicily and had begun its final drive eastward along the coastal highway toward Messina. General Patton, irked by his mere supporting role in the invasion and concerned lest his rival Montgomery capture all the glory, pushed his Seventh Army to reach Messina first.

Bill and the four other newsmen rushed to catch up. They packed their belongings into a jeep—the division had recently assigned it to them in recognition of their efforts—and relocated to Palermo. There, at last, they had the luxury of electricity, a fully-equipped engraver, and a modern printing press. Bill cartooned again and revived his "Quoth the Dogface" column. He also began his practice of traveling to the front for material. In the last days of July, Bill visited his old outfit, Company K, just in time to see the worst fighting of the Sicilian campaign.[17]

Company K's riflemen were stalled along the coast at the base of a rocky, thistle-covered mountain mass that would soon become known as "Bloody Ridge." The 45th was discovering that the

Wehrmacht could be just as deadly retreating as it was advancing. The Germans had decided to abandon Sicily, but Hitler's army rarely yielded ground without punishing its attackers. What Allied generals had taken as a brilliant offensive on their part was actually a series of well-calculated rearguard actions by the Axis. The Axis evacuation would be slow and deliberate, organized behind defensive lines that took advantage of Sicily's rugged northeastern corner. German command had even brought in two extra divisions for the occasion. With the British Eighth Army driving from the south and the American Seventh Army from the west, the Germans took a temporary stand along the craggy peaks that guarded the approaches to Messina.

Elements of the 45th approached the strongholds from different directions under full German observation. At the moment of their choosing, the enemy poured fire from their pillboxes, machine-gun emplacements, and fortified artillery positions. Shards from exploding rock and steel ripped into the attackers as they struggled up slopes so steep that pack mules died from exhaustion during the climb. Mines and trip wires, snipers and booby-trapped bodies everywhere lay in wait. "The mountains are the worst I have ever seen," wrote Patton. "It is a miracle that our men can get through them but we must keep up our steady pressure. . . . [W]e must beat the Eighth Army to Messina."

Americans responded with artillery barrages of their own, as well as chemical mortars and even fire from navy gunships offshore. Well-trained German defenders held their ground until the last minute, then moved on to the next peak. On Hill 335 west of the town of San Stefano—the most notorious of the many "Bloody Ridges" in the area—the Germans refused to budge even when American soldiers came within yards of their positions. Throughout the day on July 28, German and American fighters lobbed grenades back and forth and fell virtually next to each other. That night, at least one pair of enemy combatants unknowingly shared a single foxhole.[18]

FIGURE 22 Although its target was the highly unpopular military police, who had a knack for banning combat soldiers from the towns they'd just liberated, this panel inadvertently expresses the hubris of the American Seventh Army before the bitter fighting of Bloody Ridge. It is one of the few cartoons Bill ever drew of men actually firing their weapons in combat.

*Copyright 1943 by Bill Mauldin. Courtesy of the Mauldin Estate.*

FIGURE 23 Bill entered this drawing of Bloody Ridge in an army art competition held in Sicily after the German evacuation. Note the dead mules among the rocks. The judges were unimpressed by Bill's composition, and he came away without a prize.

*Copyright 1943 by Bill Mauldin. Courtesy of the Mauldin Estate.*

Bill had seen some tough firefights in Sicily, but nothing like Bloody Ridge. With few exceptions, most of the 45th's engagements had been quick and decisive as the division sliced through the northern coastal towns. One of Bill's Sicily cartoons even depicted impatient MPs waiting to post OFF LIMITS signs as American soldiers fought in the streets (see figure 22). Little at Bloody Ridge suggested a cartoon. The spectacle of men fighting in groves of splintered olive trees and up stark, bald hills did, however, inspire furious sketch work. Bill submitted one drawing titled simply "Bloody Ridge" to the *Daily Oklahoman,* which noted the odd lack of a funny caption (see figure 23).[19]

After Bloody Ridge, Bill found it harder to repress his feelings of guilt over escaping from the infantry. "I had been conniving for several years to end up with a sketchbook in my hand instead of a weapon," he explained. The conniving, if that is the word, had continued in Sicily, until Bill and the *45th Division News* had attained a measure of recognition and stability. Indeed, back on D-day, the sight of wounded men from his regiment had sobered Bill and focused him on the newspaper. Bill's sense of destiny and conviction that his talents were best used at the drawing board had also mitigated the guilt. The carnage at Bloody Ridge, however, suggested the hollowness of such justifications. "I knew that nine out of ten guys getting killed out there were also better at doing something else than getting killed," he deadpanned. Flying shrapnel did not discriminate.

The tipping point in Bill's psychic conflict came when he heard a false rumor that Rayson Billey, the Medicine Man, was dead. Bill believed a story he'd heard about Billey, who, suffering from an acute bout of "battle fatigue," had supposedly died in a suicidal one-man charge. The story made sense to Bill. Rayson Billey had excelled at hand-to-hand combat and hated the long-range impersonality of modern warfare. A rumor circulated that he had charged a German foxhole with his bayonet drawn and flushed out its inhabitant. Laughing hysterically, he'd chased the German back and forth until finally skewering him in No Man's Land between the two lines of astonished soldiers. The German side of the audience then allegedly ended the ghoulish performance by opening fire on Billey and cutting him to ribbons.[20]

The apocryphal tale taught Bill that even highly trained soldiers had their breaking points. None could know when they would reach it. The lesson was true enough, but Billey hadn't yet gone over the edge. The Medicine Man was not dead, but merely missing in action. His death was but one of the many dark rumors, or macabre "folk narratives," that circulate in war to explain the unexplainable, release unbearable tension, and express the creeping sense of madness that combat engenders.

The truth of Rayson Billey's wartime service—that he had twice gone missing, had once been captured by the Germans, had escaped after killing his captors, and had been officially listed as killed in action, though he had only been wounded and sent home—was as improbable and instructive as his supposed spectacular death. But Bill would not learn this truth until decades later. And the Medicine Man would grow old suffering from survivor's guilt while unknowingly serving as the focus of Bill's own enduring sense of remorse and shame.[21]

AFTER THE BATTLE of Bloody Ridge, the Germans fell back. They had inflicted great damage, leaving over a thousand Thunderbirds dead and wounded. Most important, they had delayed the Allied advance long enough to allow 60,000 German and 62,000 Italian troops, and most of their equipment, to escape to the mainland. A stiff resistance was sure to await the 45th in Salerno.

As the division rested and prepared for the next invasion, Bill Mauldin rushed to produce a souvenir book of the Sicilian campaign. His primary motive was money. The twenty-one-year-old cartoonist was now a father. Bill learned of his son Bruce's birth on September 8, the very day Sicily exploded in celebration at the news that Italy had officially withdrawn from the war. Bill wandered the streets of a coastal village accepting garlicky hugs and kisses as personal congratulations.

In addition to Bill's home-front family, the *45th Division News* also needed cash. Prices in Sicily had skyrocketed during the Allied occupation, and the paper had racked up large printing and engraving bills. Bill's solution was to peddle 5,000 copies of *Sicily Sketch Book,* a twenty-four-page collection of his drawings, cartoons, and "Quoth the Dogface" columns. The printer in Palermo accepted Bill's promissory note for $243 only after two of the division's lieutenant colonels cosigned it. The 180th Infantry Regiment bought the entire run of the twenty-five-cent booklet immediately. With the profits, Bill ordered 12,000 more copies, which also quickly sold out. By late September, Bill had sent almost $2,000 home to Jean, and the *45th Division News* had accumulated enough funds to keep its operation going well into the Italian campaign.[22]

*Sicily Sketch Book* and the three-week layover before the Salerno invasion spread Bill's fame throughout the Seventh Army. The cartoonist especially attracted the attention of *Stars and Stripes,* which opened up shop in mid-August at the *Giornale di Sicilia* offices in Palermo. Originally a combat soldiers' newspaper in World War I, *Stars and Stripes* was revived in 1942 as an independent unit of the headquarters of the Allied commander in chief, General Dwight D. Eisenhower. The newspaper's head, Colonel Egbert White, was an advertising executive who had worked on the original *Stars and Stripes* back in 1918 and had started up *Yank.* Like Walter Harrison, White fiercely defended his paper's journalistic independence, resisting all attempts by the army brass to dictate its contents.

Neither the *45th Division News* nor *Stars and Stripes* accepted advertising, and for the most part, both remained committed to the enlisted men's point of view. The longer the war dragged on, the bolder the paper became in its defense of the frontline soldier. Highly decentralized, the amoeba-like *Stars and Stripes* also became harder to control. It split and spun off new offices and editions wherever U.S. occupation forces landed, except in the Pacific where General Douglas MacArthur squelched attempts to establish independent soldier tribunes. By 1944, over a dozen outfits were putting out their own versions of *Stars and Stripes,* which outshone the *45th Division News* as a big-city daily would an alternative news weekly.[23]

Within days of reaching Sicily, the *Stars and Stripes* staff bought up virtually all the zinc on the island, most of it from funeral parlors. Bill came to the *Giornale di Sicilia* offices looking to barter for some of it. *Stars and Stripes* combat correspondents Jack Foisie, Ralph Martin, and William Hogan knew of Bill's popularity in the 45th and had seen his cartoons. Ralph Martin had even clipped a few and sent them to Lieutenant Robert Neville, his editor back in Algiers. "You've got to get this guy," Martin told Neville.

When Bill entered the office, the newspaper staff reacted like many who knew the work but not the man: how could such mature, almost world-weary art be produced by such a callow-looking artist? "I don't think he even shaved when I first met him," recalled Ralph Martin.

Staff artist Stanley Meltzoff had taught art and art history in New York City. The first time he saw Bill's cartoons, he judged them the most important illustrations of the war. Mauldin reminded him of Bruce Bairnsfather, the great British soldier-cartoonist from World War I whose grim humor from the trenches had scandalized the military establishment and won the acclaim of frontline soldiers (see figure 24). "This guy Mauldin's better than Bairnsfather or any American military artist anywhere," gushed Meltzoff. "We ought to get his stuff in the *Stars and Stripes*."[24]

Stanley Meltzoff was not the only person to see the similarities between Bairnsfather and Mauldin. George Patton, commander of the Seventh Army, had personal memories of Bairnsfather from World War I. Mauldin's cartoons incensed him. "He's the Bairnsfather of this war," Patton groused, "and I don't like either of them." Before the Sicily campaign was even over, Patton began complaining to the commander of the 45th Division, General Troy Middleton, about the "damned bad example" his renegade cartoonist was setting with his "unsoldierly" characters. Patton, a spit-and-polish man, bristled as much at Bill's disheveled soldiers as at the subversive nature of the humor.

Fortunately, Bill's division commander was a fervent believer in the independence of the soldier press. Middleton, like his predecessor William S. Key, had championed the *45th Division News* back home. In Sicily, he protected Bill and the paper against Patton's tampering. Avoiding conflict, Middleton made it a habit to warn Bill away from the headquarters area when Patton was approaching. When pressed by his three-star superior, the two-star general also defended Mauldin's work, arguing that the cartoons were worth more in terms of morale than all the overseas entertainers combined. "Better to have the men work off their complaints vicariously through a Mauldin cartoon," he believed, "than to have them store up their grievances."

*"Well, if you knows of a better 'ole, go to it."*

FIGURE 24 In 1915, while recuperating from wounds and shell shock in an army hospital, British lieutenant Bruce Bairnsfather began submitting grim cartoons of trench warfare to a British magazine. Their popularity among combat troops compelled an initially disapproving army establishment to award Bairnsfather the title of "Officer Cartoonist." His cartoon about the "better 'ole" famously captured the common British values of irony and sufferance in war.

Patton was not convinced. After several go-rounds with Middleton, Patton pulled rank: "Get rid of Mauldin and his cartoons."

Playing his last card, Middleton asked Patton to put his order in writing.

If Patton planned on issuing a written order, he never got the opportunity. Soon he was embroiled in a scandal that far outweighed any disturbance caused by Bill's cartoons. In separate visits to field hospitals in Sicily, Patton cursed and slapped two privates he suspected of malingering. He even waved his famous ivory-handled revolver in the face of the second quivering soldier and threatened to execute him on the spot. News of the incidents leaked out, and some members of Congress began calling for a Patton court-martial.

General Eisenhower issued a reprimand, but in the end refused to dismiss his talented subordinate. Instead, he sent Patton to England, where the temperamental field general was assigned a decoy army made of cardboard. Patton's phantom First United States Army Group would fool Hitler into expecting an Allied cross-Channel invasion at Pas-de-Calais.

George Patton would eventually return to the field after the real invasion of Normandy, and he and Bill would again cross paths. When they did, the three-striped sergeant would have much more protecting him than a mere division commander.[25]

BILL ALMOST missed the Salerno invasion when a bout of "sand flea fever" landed him in a Messina field hospital for three days. Upon his release, he learned to his "unbelieving horror" that he was no longer a member of the 45th Division. He was being transferred to a replacement depot where, in accordance with the army's method for keeping units at full strength, he would eventually be reassigned somewhere else. Bill had become a "casual," an interchangeable part that could be slotted anywhere in the vast army machine.

He began to plot his escape. The stockade-like "repple depple,"

as the replacement depot was nicknamed, was filled with casuals like himself desperate to get back to their outfits. They'd seen
enough of combat to know how important group belonging was
to survival. Men in established units usually shunned replacements
and assigned them the most hazardous duties, perhaps even sending them out to draw fire to reveal enemy positions. Besides, as Bill
put it, in his case, "there was a fine, budding career at stake." So,
in defiance of the replacement depot's guards, who shouted and
waved their weapons but did not fire, Bill and twenty other casuals
rushed the high walls and scattered in search of their original units.
"As far as I know," Bill wrote toward the end of the war, "they still
have my name and I'm still AWOL from a repple depple."[26]

Bill caught one of the last landing crafts out of Messina. To pay
for his transit to the mainland, he remained in the cargo hold offshore and helped to unload upwards of five hundred tons of artillery shells, mortars, and grenades. A steady procession of DUKWs,
or amphibious trucks known as "ducks," rumbled out of the sea
onto the ship's ramp and back again while enemy shells, including new remote-control glide bombs, rocked the ship from every
direction. Finally, at dawn, after a long, hot night of heavy work,
Bill came ashore at Paestum, just south of Salerno.

What he saw on the pebbly beach dwarfed what he'd witnessed
in Sicily two months earlier. The picturesque shore with its dunes,
hills, and mountains rising behind it had been transformed into
one vast battlescape. Torsos, severed limbs, detached heads, and
pieces of vehicles and equipment bobbed in the oil-slicked surf.
The beaches were so crowded with debris and supplies that landing craft could hardly pull ashore. As he worked his way inland, Bill
encountered the grisly remains of close-pitched battles. Burned-out
tanks and jeeps, bullet-riddled packs and helmets, bloody scraps of
uniforms, unused boxes of ammunition, and mounds of spent
shells littered the roads and fields. Grotesquely twisted and bloated
dead Germans in gray uniforms lay scattered about, already smelling of decay under the hot September sun. American corpses, yet

unclaimed, were also rotting. Bill stumbled upon one heavy weapons company from the 36th Division that had been slaughtered, some members literally crushed under the tracks of Panzer tanks. Their swollen bodies and blackened faces were now crawling with green maggots.

The fight for the beachhead had been intense. The Germans had come close to throwing the combined British and American Fifth Army back into the sea. Two days earlier, commanders would have handed Bill an M-1 and ordered him to join the fray, as they had the division's cooks, clerks, and members of the regimental bands. In the end, overwhelming firepower from sea- and land-based artillery, along with critical German miscalculations about Allied force strength and movements, had saved the invasion. At home, American newspapers trumpeted the breakout of Operation Avalanche, as the assault was code-named. Following the ouster of Mussolini and the surrender of the Italian army, most American observers predicted a quick march up the boot. Even the Fifth Army's commander, General Mark Clark, boasted that he would capture Rome by mid-October at the latest.[27]

The Germans, however, would not yield the peninsula so easily. Their success during the Sicily evacuation emboldened German field marshal Albert Kesselring to attempt a similar rearguard action on the mainland, now defended only by the Wehrmacht after the Italian surrender. Italy's mountainous spine includes some of the most rugged terrain on earth, ideal for defensive operations. Moreover, the lines of defense could be steadily moved northward, almost mile by mile, compelling attackers to drain their forces in a bloody war of attrition. Conducted on a vastly larger scale over a longer period of time than the stand in Sicily, the German defense of Italy would soon render Bloody Ridge a mere footnote in the murderous chronicle of the European war.

The Wehrmacht was inadvertently aided by a divided enemy that lacked a coherent campaign plan. The Joint Allied Forces Headquarters settled upon Avalanche almost by default after the Sicily invasion. The Allies went into Italy because, in the words of one military historian, "no one, least of all on the American side, could think of anything better to do." Franklin Roosevelt and George Marshall conceded to Winston Churchill that the great hammer-blow against the Axis, a massive cross-Channel invasion of France, would not be possible in 1943. Churchill promoted the Italian campaign as a convenient alternative that would tie down German forces, build Allied momentum, and generate positive publicity on the home front. The Americans reluctantly agreed to slog on in the "soft underbelly" of Europe. In return, they insisted on peeling off seven divisions from the Mediterranean and redeploying them to England in preparation for next spring's Operation Overlord, the Normandy invasion.[28]

A smaller military presence in the Mediterranean might have worked if the Germans had decided to cede Rome, or if the Allies had imposed stricter limits on the Italian campaign. As it happened, the piecemeal commitment to Italy—the Americans derided it as a "sideshow"—virtually ensured a slow-moving front at best. High Allied casualty rates condemned Allied forces to advance only with the help of added divisions and a steady infusion of replacement troops. Italy turned into the battle the Allies did not want, tying down their own forces as much as the Germans'. By its end, the Italian campaign would become for the British and the Americans, in John Keegan's words, "the bitterest and bloodiest of their struggles with the Wehrmacht on any front of the Second World War."[29]

The Allies had defied history. "Italy is like a boot," observed Napoleon. "You must, like Hannibal, enter it from the top." Mountains and rivers twist across the peninsula east to west, perfect for dugouts, bunkers, artillery sites, and machine-gun posts.[30] In addition, Mother Nature, as one U.S. corps commander put it, seemed "to be fighting on the side of the German," offering as much resistance as the enemy. Autumn brought record rainfall to southern Italy, turning streams and rivers into swollen torrents and roads into impassable bogs.[31]

Italy was, in fact, a slow, punishing grind quite unlike the mobile, mechanized forms of warfare championed by Patton and modeled on the German Blitzkrieg attacks of 1939–41. The Allies took three months to move thirty miles to the Gustav Line, as the most fortified Axis stronghold was termed. Six months later, the Allies were still fighting to get to Rome, another seventy miles up the boot (see figure 25). The Germans never relinquished all of Italy, holding on until after Berlin fell in May 1945. By then, over a half million belligerents and civilians would be dead or wounded from the fighting, 114,000 of them American troops.

ONCE AGAIN, Bill struggled to establish the *45th Division News* in the midst of a war zone. The crew put out two issues in Salerno before moving on to Naples, which the Germans abandoned at the end of September. Bill entered a city in ruins. "Naples was like a whore suffering from the beating of a brute, teeth knocked out, eyes blackened, nose broken, smelling of filth and vomit," observed filmmaker John Huston, who had been rushed to Italy with the U.S. Signal Corps to capture the expected triumphant entry into Rome. "The souls of the people had been raped. It was indeed an unholy city."[32]

Naples also had no infrastructure. German demolition experts had dismantled the water, sewer, and gas lines, destroyed the electrical grid, barricaded the streets with rubble, and scuttled 130 vessels in the harbor. Every piece of equipment, including typewriters and adding machines, had been smashed. Searching the wreckage, Bill and the news staff found a habitable building on Via Roma near a small printshop. Somehow they got the paper back in business, though it would take a month to find an engraver for Bill's cartoons.[33]

The 45th's infantry, meanwhile, spent forty days in continuous combat, a record for Europe. For the last twenty-two of those days, rain fell in sheets. Lines of exhausted men trudged northward along

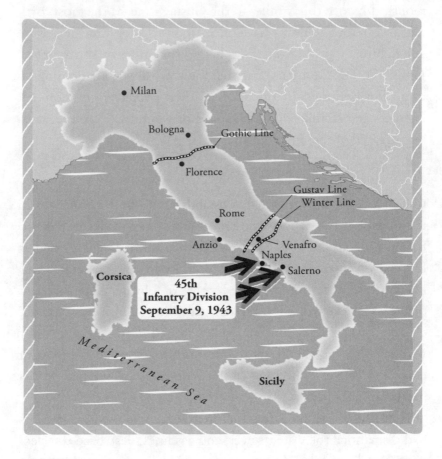

**FIGURE 25** Bill Mauldin spent most of the war in Italy, following the slow Allied progress up the boot.

the banks of the Calore and Volturno rivers toward the enemy's mountain entrenchments. Every now and then a six-barreled rocket mortar called the *Nebelwerfer* broke the silence with a rapid succession of piercing shrieks. The haunting cries of the "screaming meemie," as the troops nicknamed the weapon, "could damn near make your blood turn solid," in the words of one former Thunderbird. "I never drew pictures about 'screaming meemies,'" Bill later explained, "because they just aren't funny."[34]

Mortar, artillery, machine gun, and sniper fire sent the men sprawling instantly to the ground facedown. They made themselves as flat as they could, trying to muscle their spines through their stomachs, inching deeper into the cold wet earth. The soil was so heavy with rain that a few soldiers escaped flying shrapnel only to have heaps of mud thrown on top of them by exploding shells. If no one dug them out in time, they could drown in the slime.[35]

After its first forty days in Italy, the 45th Division had lost thirty percent of its men from illness, accidents, and enemy fire. They had yet to reach the so-called Winter Line, where the Germans would make their first determined stand.[36]

ON NOVEMBER 1, the 45th Division attacked a German army dug in along peaks surrounding the town of Venafro. The Germans were protected from Allied artillery and air bombardment by a network of underground bunkers. At one point, American batteries fired over 200,000 shells at a string of enemy positions just west of the 45th near the town of San Pietro. The bunkers were so insulated that a party of German soldiers played cards through the onslaught without even rising from the table.[37]

When the big Allied guns failed to dislodge the enemy, the Fifth Army turned to small patrols to probe and infiltrate German lines. The ridges were so steep that men risked not only enemy fire but falling off cliffs. Those patrols that did reach their objectives often found the strongholds abandoned. "No matter what hill you run 'em off, they run across a valley and into another hill a little higher and wait for you," said one veteran of the 179th Infantry. "It was damn rough." Many patrols never made it back.[38]

By mid-November, the Allied offensive had ground to a stalemate. While high command searched for a way out of the impasse, the men of the Fifth Army struggled just to hold their positions. The weather deteriorated, and supplies became scarce. Faced with mud, ice, and rugged terrain, the army resorted to mule teams purchased from neighboring peasants to deliver food, water, ammunition, and equipment to its frontline soldiers. The mules cost five dollars a day, more than twice what the men were paid. The 45th Division alone required a pool of three to five hundred of the animals just to keep its troops eating and firing their weapons. The Germans killed so many of the beasts that soldiers began hauling supplies on their backs. One officer who requested "pack animals" for his unit received a Mauldinesque reply from a weary supply sergeant: "If you want pack animals, sir, you'd better teach your men to crap when they walk." "Venafro wasn't miserable," recalled one veteran of the 45th, "it was a son-of-a-bitch."[39]

When the 45th was finally pulled out of Venafro during the first week of January, the division had spent over sixty days in the line. Bill Mauldin, who had returned to cartooning after a two-month hiatus, was there for about half of those days. For all its misery, the stalemate allowed Bill to establish his working routine of traveling back and forth to the front. He spent four or five days at a time up front for what he called "inspiration." Then he returned to Naples for the "perspiration," laboring an equal number of days to translate his observations into cartoons.[40]

All cartoonists struggle with ideas. But few have tried to turn the unremitting misery of primitive mountain warfare into something funny. Invariably Bill came back from each trip, as he put it, "feeling both grateful and guilty about being spared from those freezing-wet foxholes and those deadly accurate German 88s and mortars."[41]

Still, there was humor in the line; morbid, angry, compulsive humor born of the realization that few would survive the war with anything less than a life-altering wound. Dirty jokes and wisecracks proliferated, growing more graphic and vicious as the days wore on. Underlying the humor was a glaring gap between civilized conventions, such as the use of a toilet, and the line's animal existence, where men either kept "their assholes tight" or simply defecated in their trenches.

This life up front stood in stark contrast to the official sanitized picture promoted by the War Department and the media back home. In newsreels, morale was always high, and soldiers, motivated by skilled leaders, hurtled forward toward victory. No mud, no shit, no fear.

Behind every joke up front lay a growing storehouse of grievances against all who were not in the lines with them. Jokes at the front, observes combat veteran and literary scholar Paul Fussell, "operate like midget satires. They represent the spontaneous overflow of powerful feelings—toward civilians, especially 4-Fs; officers; optimists and euphemizers; and the Great in general. They are the sole weapon of the troops against the Others—all who have victimized them."[42]

Like a zinc plate in an acid bath, Bill soaked in the ambiance of the lines, allowing the sights, sounds, and smells to engrave themselves on his senses. He assimilated the men's grievances into his own. Bill's powerful ambivalence toward the world of combat revealed itself in his work. Still striking a delicate balance between representing his readership—the men of the lines—and fulfilling his official charge to bolster morale, Bill's panels during the late fall and winter of 1943 and 1944 virtually dripped with insinuations and veiled meanings. Unable as yet to voice the men's grievances directly or apportion human blame for the misery, Bill focused on nature. No one at headquarters could be faulted for the rain and cold.

Mud had an irresistible fascination, one Bill had long exploited during training and maneuvers. But now the sodden earth wasn't even earth, but a preternatural slurry of water, dirt, shit, and ground human and animal remains all churned together by tires, tracks, exploding shells, and tens of thousands of booted feet. The sludge, so thick it could pull the sole off a soldier's boot, collected in trenches, gullies, and foxholes. In heavy rain, these holes sometimes collapsed, burying infantrymen alive. Days and weeks of exposure to the slush could swell a man's foot to almost twice its size, turning it red, then blue, then black. Nearly seventy percent of all nonbattle injuries in Italy came from "trench foot." To depict such conditions, a cartoonist's most reliable tool, exaggeration, was almost useless.[43]

Still, Mauldin's mud cartoons captured an essential truth of the Italian campaign: the men, having regressed to near-total helplessness, were mired in filth. One early observation from the front, a simple but daring cartoon published in the *45th Division News* on December 4, suggested another truth: many officers, especially those operating in rear areas, were ignorant of the men's suffering or, worse, indifferent to it.

The cartoon features a major or lieutenant colonel in a covered jeep passing two weary dogfaces as they slog through the calf-deep mud under leaden skies. "Have your men tried Dubbin, Sergeant?" the officer asks, referring to a common water-resistant boot wax (see figure 26).[44]

Bill had never struck so directly at those responsible for the debacle in Italy. Shuttling back and forth between Naples and Venafro and depending heavily on the goodwill of army brass, Bill understood more than most the growing gulf between those few condemned to combat and the many safe in their rear supporting roles. Over the next several months, Bill would sorely test this goodwill as he exploited the tensions and contradictions within an army at war to become the leading spokesman for the American combat soldier. The role would make him rich and famous. By then, most dogfaces who had shipped with him overseas would be dead, wounded, captured, or deemed psychologically unfit to continue in combat.

*"Have your men tried Dubbin, Sergeant?"*

FIGURE 26 Bill Mauldin's increasingly jaundiced attitude toward military authority comes through in this early cartoon from the "Mud, Mules, and Mountains" campaign of 1943–44. The soldier on the right, bearing a striking resemblance to Emmett Kelly's "Weary Willie," is the first to exhibit the sad, tired eyes Bill would make famous in his Willie and Joe cartoons several months later.

*Copyright 1943 by Bill Mauldin. Courtesy of the Mauldin Estate.*

Chapter Four

# Doing Battle

*Never think that war, no matter how necessary, nor how
justified, is not a crime. Ask the infantry and ask the dead.*

—ERNEST HEMINGWAY,
CORRESPONDENT AND COMBATANT,
FRANCE, BELGIUM, AND GERMANY, 1944–45[1]

ON DECEMBER 11, 1943, Bill Mauldin carried his sketchbook
once more into the mountains above Venafro. It was an unusual
visit. The 45th Division had long peered up at the Germans, who
virtually rolled their grenades over the cliffs. Company I of the
179th Infantry Regiment, however, had somehow secured the
high ground overlooking several German positions on the slopes
below. Moreover, the enemy had no good view of I Company's
ice-covered supply trail. Instead, they listened for hoof and boot
steps, using their knowledge of the mule path's twisting route to
lay down harassing mortar fire.

Bill climbed to the sandbagged machine-gun emplacement

undetected. There he discovered just how close the enemy was. He could actually hear each mortar round drop into the short tube. Eventually he would have to dodge those rounds going down the mountain.

Bill and his hosts scoured the mountainside with binoculars. An artillery observer, thinking he'd spotted the enemy mortar position, called in howitzer fire. A few minutes later, a geyser of rock and ice erupted no more than a couple hundred yards away. Bill cocked his head as the dust cleared, straining to hear signs of enemy life. Convinced that the howitzer had done its grim work, he and another visitor, the 45th Division's artillery chaplain, thanked the machine-gun crew, jumped out of the hole, and started sliding down a steep grade on the seats of their pants. Their boots dislodged some stones. They probably never heard the metallic whomp of the mortar round being loaded.

The mortar followed a steep arc, whistling past Bill's head, bouncing near his heel, maybe even off of it, and then exploding into a white flash three feet below his boots.

For the next few minutes, Bill saw and heard nothing. The concussion, the likes of which had killed plenty of soldiers without leaving a mark, had temporarily paralyzed him. Eventually his hands began involuntarily groping his body. In such situations, Bill explained, "an old man thinks of his eyes and a young man grabs for his balls. I was young, and besides I was sure I was blind anyway."

His balls were intact, and his dirt-filled eyes slowly regained their sight. He was now terrified to search himself further. Most grievously wounded men, he knew, discovered their missing limbs, severed jaws, and uncoiled intestines only through deliberate self-examination, so numb were they to pain. Bill screwed up his courage and glanced downward, probing himself bone by bone. He was in one piece, everything in place, with only "three barber's nicks, the worst in the shoulder." "The wound hardly bled," he recalled.

Bill's companion on the trail was not so fortunate. A fragment had badly mangled the chaplain's arm, who had managed to stop the bleeding with a tourniquet made from his handkerchief. The two men continued sliding down the hill, the chaplain refusing Bill's help as his face turned ashen from the loss of blood.

At the battalion aid tent, a surgeon quickly plucked a tiny fragment from Bill's shoulder, slapped on a bandage, and told him to get checked through the division's clearing station on his way back to Naples. Bill did so almost as an afterthought. A medic there gave his right shoulder a final dressing and then pressed a green leatherette box into his hand.

Bill hesitated. The shard had hardly left a mark. "I had been cut worse sneaking through barbed-wire fences in New Mexico," he recalled.

"Take it," snapped the aid man. "The rules say if the enemy draws blood, you get one. Besides," he added, "it might get you discharged earlier at the end of the war. That case fits real neat in an empty K-ration box if you want to send it home to your wife."

That night, Bill mailed his Purple Heart to Phoenix, where Jean and his son Bruce now lived. Perhaps the medal would help his career. But he never could have dreamed that the "barber's nick" would become, quite literally, his million-dollar wound.[2]

NINE DAYS before his harrowing visit to Venafro, Bill had launched a new daily feature, published exclusively in *Stars and Stripes* under the bold title of "Up Front . . . with Mauldin." The 45th Division had put Bill on detached duty with the big paper; his transfer would not be final until February. Until then, he was still drawing "Star Spangled Banter" separately for the division's newspaper. Indeed, Bill was frantically raising money for the paper by selling 100,000 copies of a division Christmas card for two cents each. The proceeds went to produce a full-color Christmas edition of the newspaper as well as *Mud, Mules, and Mountains,* another self-published cartoon collection that funded the *45th Division News* and allowed Bill to send more money home to Jean. The venture would be Bill's swan song with the division he'd called home for over three years.[3]

Bill adjusted quickly to his new cartooning assignment. On the advice of Ed Vebell, a fellow artist with *Stars and Stripes,* Bill discarded his fine-point pen in favor of a thicker ink brush, which showed up better in reproduction. The cheap newsprint, the antiquated engraving equipment, and the poor quality of the ink, which was often cut with wine and used motor oil, called for bolder brushstrokes. The thick lines and two-column size of "Up Front," reduced from the half page he'd enjoyed on the *45th Division News,* meant that Bill often had to surrender the background detail that had deepened "Star Spangled Banter." "Up Front" was starker and more focused on the immediate circumstances of the characters.[4]

"Up Front" raised the stakes of Bill's career. He was now drawing for the entire American Fifth Army in Italy, opening himself up both to greater rewards and harsher criticism. It took only two installments of the new cartoon to spark reader protests. To Bill's dismay, the first complaint to his *Stars and Stripes* editors came from a combat soldier in the line.

*Stars and Stripes'* Mediterranean edition ran a lively "Mail Call" section, commonly referred to as the "B-Bag," where enlisted men spoke out on everything from postwar planning to the quality of lemonade packets in K-rations. The letters from frontline soldiers were brief and bitter. In late November 1943, for example, a special "combat edition" of *Stars and Stripes* ran an editorial arguing that experienced combat troops should not be sent home, but rather kept fighting until Germany fell. Outraged soldiers swamped the editors with angry handwritten responses. "Who in hell elected you to voice every opinion for the veteran?" asked one combat corporal. "You are a noncombatant tool," charged another infantryman. "Why don't you come up and ask the combat soldiers if they want to go to Berlin before they go home?"[5]

Private First Class E. H. Blankenship thought a new cartoon series titled "Up Front . . . with Mauldin" enough to cause "a feeling of nausea." "Mauldin has never seen the front and probably never will," the private alleged in a letter received by the paper the day after Bill's mortar wound. "I and many others enjoy Mauldin's cartoons, but don't let him think for a moment that he makes us believe that he draws them in a foxhole."[6]

The criticism stung. Bill already suffered from survivor's guilt. He had not only dodged the infantry but was actually gaining recognition as the war heated up. The mortar attack especially chastened him. He knew in a deeper way just how easy it was to die in those mountains. "Suddenly," he recalled, "the war became very real to me. . . . I really sobered up and started realizing there were some things bigger than me and my ambition."[7]

Blankenship's letter in *Stars and Stripes* was answered by an editor's note saying that Mauldin had been awarded a Purple Heart just the week before. "This award was granted for injuries he sustained from mortar shell fragments while at the front with Co. I of Pfc. Blankenship's own regiment," the editors tersely explained.[8]

Blankenship's letter opened Bill's way to wider fame. *Stars and Stripes* could hardly report on staff casualties without appearing to call attention to itself. By mentioning Bill's Purple Heart, the paper polished its image for intrepid reporting and gained credibility with frontline soldiers.

Bill accepted the role of daring frontline journalist, though he also made it a point henceforth to tell all who would listen that he never sketched in foxholes and was strictly rear-echelon. At the same time, Blankenship's letter had tuned him to the peculiar petulance of the frontline soldier. "Combat men are high-strung and excitable," he later explained, "and unimportant little things can upset them."[9]

After the Blankenship affair, Bill subtly altered the title of his feature; with the December 22, 1943, issue of *Stars and Stripes* Mediterranean, the feature was called "Up Front . . . *by* Mauldin."

All now fell into place for Bill. Two of the war's most influential American combat correspondents, Will Lang of Time-Life and Ernie Pyle of the Scripps-Howard newspaper chain, read the Blankenship letter and editor's note and sought Bill out for interviews. Within a month, Bill Mauldin's cartoons and life story would appear on newsstands throughout America.

No REPORTER of the war was more beloved than Ernie Pyle. Over two decades older than Bill, he'd roamed the United States during the Great Depression, filling his syndicated column with idiosyncratic stories of ordinary Americans surviving in hard times. Seeking out the marginal and down-and-out, Pyle drew a noble, dignified essence from his hard-bitten subjects, whether hoboes, sharecroppers, or waitresses. Mixing the mundane with the sublime, Pyle's style was direct, colloquial, and distinctly American.[10]

It was natural that the avuncular Pyle would take a liking to Bill. Bill's humble rural origins—in Pyle's beloved Southwest, no less— quirky looks, and well-earned expertise about soldiering endeared him to the senior correspondent, whose dispatches appeared in over two hundred newspapers. Pyle also saw reflected in Bill's cartoons his own fascination with the front, as well as his profound, almost pathological identification with those who fought there.

On Saturday, January 15, 1944, Ernie Pyle's readers learned of a young cartoonist whose central character "looks more like a hobo than like your son."

"Sgt. Bill Mauldin appears to us over here to be the finest cartoonist the war has produced," the 4,400-word column began. "And that's not merely because his cartoons are funny," Pyle continued, "but because they are also terribly grim and real. Mauldin's cartoons aren't about training-camp life, which you at home are best acquainted with. They are about the men in the line—the tiny percentage of our vast army who are actually up there in that other world doing the dying. His cartoons are about the war."

Grimness. Authenticity. Realism. War as an alien world made bearable only by the native goodness and strength citizen soldiers brought with them from home. These were what readers came to expect from Ernie Pyle's column. Now, Pyle promised the same in Bill Mauldin's cartoons. "Unfortunately for you and Mauldin both," Pyle teased his readers, "the American public has no opportunity to see his daily drawings."[11]

Two days later, *Life* magazine published a layout of seven Mauldin cartoons drawn in Naples. A brief introductory note, written by Will Lang, echoed Pyle's assessment. Mauldin's work represented "genuine war humor," unlike "Sad Sack" or "G.I. Joe," and was far removed from most popular depictions of America's fighting men. Lang even quoted Bill at length in order to explain to home-front readers the beards, vacant stares, and ragged look of his characters. "I was 18 when I joined the Army," Bill said, "I knew a lot of these kids then. Now, after they've been through a couple campaigns, after being in the line for weeks, they're old men. The poor guys have changed so that I hardly recognize them."[12]

The attention was electrifying. George Carlin, a manager at United Features Syndicate, immediately cabled Pyle: APPRECIATE ANYTHING YOU CAN DO URGING MAULDIN SIGN [STOP] UNIFEATURES BELIEVES DUE YOUR COLUMN WE CAN DO BIG JOB. Next, Bill learned that Eleanor Roosevelt, herself a syndicated columnist, had taken a personal interest in bringing Bill's work to the home front. An avid reader of Ernie Pyle, the first lady predicted that if Mauldin signed with Unifeatures, his cartoons would appear next to Pyle's column throughout America.[13]

Perhaps most gratifying were the telegrams and letters from those who had all along rejected his work. Russell Hall, the editor at Scribner's, wrote to apologize for being out of touch since Bill shipped overseas. A paper shortage, he explained, had forced him to pass on Bill's cartoon book in 1942. Could Bill please send him some drawings to review?[14]

By the end of January, so many book, magazine, and newspaper offers were pouring into *Stars and Stripes* that Colonel Egbert White, the paper's officer in charge, practically ordered Bill to hire an agent. Colonel White grew especially alarmed on learning that Melvin Ryder, the Washington, D.C.-based publisher of the *Army Times* with whom Bill had contracted the previous May to produce a cartoon book, was representing himself as Bill's agent to Unifeatures. A former advertising executive, White had his own contacts in New York. He asked literary agent Ann Watkins to step in. Watkins was skeptical. "I am too old to walk the streets peddling cartoons with a portfolio under my arm," she replied.

White had to explain that selling Bill's work was not an issue. Rather, she need only say "yes" and "no" to the right people. Further, White also assured Watkins that the army and *Stars and Stripes* would not stand in the way of "Up Front's" syndication. They wanted only first publication rights.[15]

Watkins' main problem as Bill's agent was tracking down precisely which cartoons could be offered on an exclusive basis, since so many had already appeared or were contracted to appear in print. Three Mauldin cartoon books already existed, and Army Times, Inc.'s long-awaited *Star Spangled Banter* was in production. In addition, Don Robinson planned to include nineteen of Bill's overseas cartoons, for which he paid a grand total of forty dollars, in his forthcoming book about the *45th Division News*. Finally, Bill had continued to submit select cartoons to newspapers and magazines back home. Watkins scolded him about "sending your stuff around indiscriminately."

Unknown to George Carlin was that several of the thirty-one drawings Bill mailed to United Features Syndicate in advance of his scheduled April debut had been published months earlier in the *Daily Oklahoman*. "I don't want to take down your young pants and spank you," the fifty-eight-year-old Watkins wrote to Bill when she found out, ". . . but if there's anything else you haven't told us about, shoot the works now, and quick, and we'll see if we can clean it up with as little bloodshed as possible."[16]

After a flurry of legal correspondence, Watkins arranged a contract with Unifeatures for six cartoons a week. Bill and the syndicate would split the fees down the middle. The contract guaranteed the cartoonist $150 a week, ten times his army pay. When several dozen newspapers signed up for "Up Front" the first day, Bill realized he would be earning at least $350 a week. "Now I was not only successful," Bill recalled, "but rich beyond my wildest dreams of avarice."[17]

In early February, during his final days as a member of the *45th Division News,* Bill checked into an army hospital in Naples with pneumonia and a 106-degree fever. The doctor on duty kept Bill waiting for hours (he later heard the doctor had been busy having sex with a nurse). Delirium set in, and Bill started entertaining dark fantasies about dying in the wretched hospital. Wouldn't that be perfect, he thought, the army killing me just as I'm hitting the big time.

Later, he was roused to consciousness by a motherly nurse. From his cot, he could hear her talking about him.

"Poor little shit," she said to someone nearby. "They're drafting them out of high school now."[18]


IN STEERING Bill Mauldin to syndication, Colonel Egbert White was not merely being a good mentor. He was also using Bill's success and Ernie Pyle's endorsement to insulate *Stars and Stripes* against growing pressure from the United States high command in Naples. Major General Arthur R. Wilson, commander of what was called the Peninsular Base Section (PBS) in the city, was especially angry at the paper's attention to disgruntled combat soldiers. Since November, each issue of *Stars and Stripes* seemed to carry more complaints from the front lines than the one before. By early 1944, infantry troops' grievances could be found in articles, the Mail Call column, and, of course, the upstart cartoon feature.

These were not ordinary army gripes about KP, inspections, or run-of-the-mill chickenshit. Rather, they were sharp critiques focused on the war's poor logistics in Italy and draconian base-area policies that eroded morale.

General Arthur Wilson headed up the Naples PBS. Its mission was twofold: to police the city's base area and to transfer the twenty thousand tons or so of supplies arriving daily by sea to half a million Allied troops in Italy. Clearly the PBS did a poor job of both.

Cargo pilferage in Naples attained levels unprecedented in the history of warfare. Food, clothing, fuel, medicine, blankets, cigarettes, and vehicles disappeared in such large quantities that by December 1943, Allied infantry were receiving only two-thirds of the supplies earmarked for them. Neapolitans had been starving. Even the city's countryside had been stripped of dandelions and other edible weeds. Such eye-bulging quantities of American goods, seemingly there for the taking, were like a gift from heaven.

Vehicles were stolen at a rate of sixty or seventy a night. Miles of telephone wire were routinely cut and hauled away, their copper openly sold in city markets. Nothing, noted one intelligence officer, was "too large or too small—from telegraph poles to phials of penicillin—to escape the Neapolitan kleptomania." One symphony concert audience used a five-minute intermission to steal the orchestra's instruments. Other ingenious thieves somehow lifted a few small supply ships out of the water and spirited them inland. There they sat, bereft of their contents, as if swept in by a great tidal wave.

By the spring of 1944, pilfered Allied supplies accounted for sixty-five percent of Naples' per capita income. It was the largest black market in history.

The Neapolitans could never have pulled this off without cooperation from thousands of U.S. troops. "Hard-working American boys under Neapolitan guidance," recalled Bill sardonically, "achieved miracles":

Long convoys of trucks, manned and guarded by crew-cut youngsters from such places as Brooklyn and Broken Elbow, led by jeeps bearing U.S. lieutenants and majors with personal papers and requisition forms in order, relieved freshly-arrived ships of comestibles, dry goods, or both. . . . Sometimes these convoys had MP escorts. The procession of trucks would take a shortcut through a side street or alley, emerge empty within a few minutes, and go back for more. Sometimes the vehicles themselves disappeared, having been dismantled on the spot for future sale as spare parts.

Nor were the railroads forgotten. One trainload of supplics bound for the front vanished entirely, locomotive and all.[19]

Bill Mauldin rarely made direct mention of such theft in his cartoons. Nor did he chastise participants. Hardly a person in the entire city, civilian or military, did not turn to the black market for food, alcohol, clothing, or cigarettes. In January 1944, Bill himself put out 30,000 copies of *Mud, Mules, and Mountains* printed entirely on paper stolen from U.S. supply ships and sold to him by Neapolitan dealers.[20]

Enchanted by the warm, generous residents of Naples whose "larceny," he said, "had a lilt, like the local music," Bill could hardly pass judgment on poor people struggling to survive. He focused instead on hardships suffered by troops in the mountains. They were enduring subfreezing weather without heavy overcoats or blankets, ankle-deep mud without boots, and close combat without adequate ammunition. "The [artillery] battery is outta HE [high explosives]," reports one Mauldin dogface to another in a December 22 cartoon. "Kin you use a couple tons of leaflets?"[21]

Food was scarce too. C- and K-rations lacked the nutrition necessary to sustain troops. After weeks or months of living on "meat product," hard crackers, bouillon powder, dextrose tablets, and chewing gum, a lot of soldiers began to exhibit signs of malnutrition: abscessed teeth, stomach ulcers, skin diseases. Cigarettes helped to settle sour stomachs. The smell of sweet Virginia tobacco and vomit pervaded the front wherever Americans went. One of Bill's final "Star Spangled Banter" cartoons depicts three soldiers wielding bayonets like carving knives as they size up a mule loaded with K-rations. "Honest, fellers—next trip I'll bring the 5-in–1's," says the mule tender, referring to the more palatable, nutritious— and rare—packages of food designed to sustain one soldier for five days.[22]

This horrendous supply situation, however, was not primary in putting Bill Mauldin and *Stars and Stripes* on a collision course with PBS commander Arthur Wilson. Rather, it was the rough treatment combat soldiers often received when they came to Naples on a four-day pass.

Bill had never cared for garrison MPs; he considered most of them bullies. But the ruthlessness of the base section's military police inspired special fury. Bill fumed over the way MPs, overlooking brazen thievery on the docks, kept vigilant watch on Naples' ubiquitous restricted zones. Most clubs, bars, theaters, and whorehouses were off limits to all but military government and base section staff. Soldiers on leave from the front were corralled into fortress-like "rest centers," which contained neither alcohol nor women. Most had been given the pass because they were near catatonic after weeks of trauma in the lines. "He was a mess," Bill recalled of the average GI coming down from the mountains. "His shoes were muddy, his clothes were filthy, torn, and often bloody, he needed a shave and a haircut, and you could smell him from a block away."[23]

Those who looked particularly unkempt or exhibited deranged behavior were whisked away to jail to preserve a façade of order and decorum in the American sector. Small infractions—beard, long hair, unshined shoes, unpressed trousers, a missing button or insignia—were enough to prompt arrest. MPs usually detained men for the duration of their pass, releasing them just in time for their return trip to the front.

Two cartoons in particular raised hackles within the PBS staff. The first, published in December 1943, features an immaculately dressed MP standing outside a rest center surrounded by three soldiers on leave (see figure 27). The scruffy dogfaces stare fascinated

*"Th' yellow one is fer national defense, th' red
one wid white stripes is fer very good conduct, and
th' real purty one wid all th' colors is fer bein' in
this theater of operations. . . ."*

**FIGURE 27** This cartoon from December 29, 1943, launched what
Bill called "The Battle of Naples." In order to buoy morale during
the Italian campaign, the War Department distributed ribbons and
medals to troops, few of which, however, made it to those in the lines.
Eventually a special Combat Infantryman Badge was handed out to
soldiers at the front. At least one infantryman wearing such a badge
was promptly arrested while on a pass to Naples. The MP had never
seen the decoration and cited the soldier for being out of uniform.

at the MP's blouse, festooned with ribbons for "Good Conduct," "National Defense," and "European Theater." Few combat soldiers had ever seen these decorations, hollow honors in a grossly unequal world.

A second cartoon was even more cutting. An enlisted man and his captain, equally bedraggled, arrive in a jeep to a base area plastered with signs and guarded by a scowling MP. Without base section credentials or clean uniforms, the men realize they have no place to go. "Th' hell with it, sir," says the driver to his superior. "Let's go back to th' front" (see figure 28).

This cartoon caused General Arthur Wilson to "hit the gold-leafed ceiling of his baroque office," as Bill put it. Beleaguered by the groundswell of complaints in *Stars and Stripes,* Wilson lambasted Colonel White, as well as chief editor Captain Robert Neville and managing editor Sergeant Dave Golding, for allowing such insubordination. The general came close to ordering the cartoonist off the paper.

Wilson's campaign against Mauldin received a boost when Lieutenant General Jacob L. Devers, deputy commander of the Mediterranean theater, learned of the controversy. Devers, also in charge of the Services of Supply, agreed that Mauldin's drawings were harmful to base section morale and briefly curtailed distribution of the offending issues.

Bill himself didn't know of efforts to censor him until he met a Women's Army Corps (WAC) stenographer. By chance, she'd just taken minutes at a conference of Fifth Army brass.

"I'm not at liberty to tell you everything that went on," the WAC teased Bill, "but your name came up."

General Wilson, she went on, had raised the issue of his cartoons, as well as the Mail Call letters, and recommended that the senior officers stand together "to purge the Italian campaign of the cancer of insubordination."

"Guess who stood up for you?" the WAC asked the thoroughly

*"Th' hell with it, sir. Let's go back to th' front."*

FIGURE 28 By early January 1944, Bill had grown quite bold in his attacks on Peninsular Base Section authority. By shrewdly including a captain in the passenger's seat above, Bill makes clear that his problem is not with rank, but with the policies of base section command. All combat soldiers, officers and enlisted men alike, suffered from the restrictions.

*Copyright 1944 by Bill Mauldin. Courtesy of the Mauldin Estate.*

riveted Mauldin. "General Theodore Roosevelt Jr. He got up there and said your cartoons were saying what was on everybody's mind about the way infantrymen get treated in Naples."

Roosevelt, the eldest son of Teddy, the twenty-sixth president, was a World War I veteran. Though slowed by arthritis and a heart condition, he held field commands in North Africa and Europe and had grown a reputation for his fierce devotion to foot soldiers. When Wilson charged that Mauldin's cartoons could incite mutiny, Roosevelt responded that the cartoonist "might be preventing it by blowing off a little steam for the boys."

"Did they take a vote or anything?" an enthralled Bill asked the stenographer.

"No," she replied dryly, "they had a few other things to worry about, like the war."

The generals' deliberation over Bill's cartoons climaxed a day or so later when the Fifth Army commander himself, General Mark Clark, called to request the offending drawing, signed if Bill could manage it. No need to bring it to HQ, the commander said. He would send his staff car to pick it up.

"Do you realize what this means?" an excited Captain Neville asked Bill. "Clark is giving you the Good Housekeeping Seal of Approval. It is his way of telling PBS to screw itself."

General Clark started a trend. Other field generals wanted originals of cartoons. Major General Geoffrey Keyes, commander of the U.S. II Corps; Major General Lucian Truscott, commander of the U.S. Third Division; and several regimental commanders all asked for signed originals.[24]

Perhaps the gesture was meant to show solidarity with their men, who, after months of punishing combat, were losing heart. As many as 20,000 American troops had deserted their units, not returning from leave. Infantry commanders were desperate to fan the dying embers of esprit de corps. Lashing out at the rear echelon might firm up unit cohesion. "Soldiers who are in danger," Bill explained, "feel a natural and human resentment toward soldiers who aren't.

You'll notice it every time you see men wearing muddy boots meet men wearing clean ties."[25]

The commander who championed Bill's work most was Lucian Truscott. Like Theodore Roosevelt Jr., Truscott had earned a reputation as an advocate for the infantry soldier. He spent half his time at the front with his troops, going over maps with company commanders on the hood of his jeep. He'd accidentally swallowed carbolic acid as a child, corroding his vocal cords. His gravelly baritone, as Bill put it, "made other strong men quail."

Truscott wanted a drawing delivered personally to his headquarters. When Bill showed up, wearing a mismatched uniform and hair longer than regulation length, the general greeted him warmly.

"How's your battle with the rear echelon progressing?" he asked.

A stunned Bill stammered that he "had nothing against the rear echelon—only some of its generals," who were now accusing him of undermining base section morale. Truscott then offered valuable consolation.

"When you start drawing pictures that don't get a few complaints," he said, "then you'd better quit, because you won't be doing anybody any good."[26]

So long as he continued to irritate the right people, Bill Mauldin would be an important part of morale building in Italy. He didn't know that back in Washington, D.C., events were afoot to give him a bigger role—on the home front.

IN EARLY SEPTEMBER of 1943, officers in the War Department's Bureau of Public Relations pulled out a classified file dubbed the "chamber of horrors" and carefully selected several dozen photographs of American war dead for release to the public. No such pictures had ever before been made available to the press. Military and civilian censors had removed photographs of dead Americans and every other image and written word that might be construed as negative about the American war effort.

Such wholesale censorship reflected the painfully slow progress of that war effort through 1942. Bogged down for fourteen months, Allied authorities feared the erosion of public confidence. Graphic representations of violence and suffering would surely demoralize the home front. Such candor might increase sentiment for a negotiated peace with Germany, a position shared by nearly a third of Americans in mid-1942. Many military leaders no doubt agreed with Admiral Ernest J. King, who thought the government should tell the American people nothing until the end of the war, and then announce who won.

By the summer of 1943, however, President Roosevelt, Secretary of War Henry Stimson, and Chief of Staff George C. Marshall faced a new problem: success. Guadalcanal had fallen; the Soviets had won at Stalingrad; German U-boats no longer terrorized the Atlantic; and successful campaigns in North Africa and Sicily had some on the home front thinking that the war would soon be over. Indeed, Bill Mauldin recalled that most of the men he landed with in North Africa in June "assumed the enemy was now on the run everywhere and that we had arrived barely in time to pick up a few souvenirs as we mopped up in Europe." A few "gung-ho types, especially in the rear echelons," griped that the 45th Division would get only "a little piece of the action before the armistice."[27]

The Roosevelt administration knew better. Plenty remained to be done. It would not do for the public to grow impatient with wartime rationing, bond drives, housing shortages, family dislocations, and wage and price controls. Scenes of suffering and dying American troops might sober the American people and make them mindful of sacrifices being made overseas.

Also, by emphasizing difficulties to come, Roosevelt would shield himself from the political fallout of a military setback. The press corps, too, would applaud looser restrictions. When fighting for democratic ideals, government candor had propaganda value in its own right.

On September 1, 1943, General Marshall sent a radiogram to his commanding generals expressing the president's unhappiness with the sanitized visual coverage of the war. The material thus far forwarded to Washington was "entirely unsatisfactory." Commanders were to support photographic units and other correspondents attempting to capture the front's gruesome realities. The president, he emphasized, wanted material that would "vividly portray the dangers, horrors, and grimness of War." Over the next several months, Marshall underlined this message, always stressing a need for images depicting "the tragic aspects of battle."[28]

Bill Mauldin's rise to renown as a combat cartoonist coincided with this liberalized censorship policy. What Ernie Pyle called Bill's "terribly grim and real" illustrations were in keeping with the government's new public relations campaign, which one historian equates with "playing the death card." Mauldin did not depict death, but his cartoons did suggest, as he put it, "that there were bodies just offstage." More important, the cartoons showed war as a slow, painful slog, and the enemy as efficient and lethal. If Roosevelt wanted grimness, he needed to look no further.[29]

Americans knew surprisingly little about their frontline troops. In the war's early years, the infantry received virtually no publicity, official or otherwise. Magazines and movies preferred dashing sailors, "gung-ho" marines, glamorous fliers, and members of elite units, such as the Rangers and the Airborne.

Hollywood loved all of them. The Marines had William Bendix in *Wake Island* (1942); the navy countered with Cary Grant and John Garfield in *Destination Tokyo* (1943). The air forces recruited Garfield for *Air Force* (1943) before landing Spencer Tracy in *Thirty Seconds Over Tokyo* (1944). Even naval construction battalions and the Merchant Marines had John Wayne in *The Fighting Seabees* (1944) and Humphrey Bogart in *Action in the North Atlantic* (1943). Overwhelmed by these well-publicized rivals, a humble army rifleman could only remove the stiffening grommet from his garrison cap, slip on sunglasses, and hope to be mistaken for Air Corps (see figure 29).

FIGURE 29 In this gag from the April 28, 1943, issue of the *45th Division News*, Bill lampoons the army fad for all things Air Corps. The soldier on the right, in fact, is the only true Air Corps officer, the rest mere dandies aping the fashions made popular by Hollywood and Madison Avenue. A little over a year later, Bill would be stunned when such image-conscious troops discarded their "glamor rags" and adopted the disheveled look of the combat infantryman, largely because of the popularity of his cartoons.

*Copyright 1943 by Bill Mauldin. Courtesy of the Mauldin Estate.*

The Marines had been smart in anticipating the interservice rivalry. Before any shots were fired, they retained a public relations specialist from the J. Walter Thompson advertising agency. The other branches soon followed suit, creating a new military occupation: the public relations officer. Public relations became so critical that about a third of all wartime correspondence between high-ranking officers concerned publicity—who would get the credit (or the blame) for what. World War II, as Paul Fussell asserts, was the first "publicity war," fought with as much a view to public opinion as to politics, morality, or even military expedience.[30]

No one understood publicity better than General Mark Clark.

His incessant quest for favorable news coverage led one observer to remark that Clark had misread Clausewitz's famous dictum and instead considered war "the pursuit of publicity by other means."[31]

A protégé of Dwight Eisenhower, Mark Clark led the Army Ground Forces' belated publicity charge. To do so, he had to overcome a war plan prejudiced against ground forces. Military experts never expected foot soldiers to play much of a role in Europe or the Pacific. The Joint Victory Program presented to Roosevelt in late 1941 called for 215 army divisions to fight a global two-front war. When the war came, only 89 divisions materialized. Most of the nation's human resources had been shifted to industrial production, especially the building of ships and planes.[32]

The navy required thousands of new vessels a year to take on the U-Boat terror as well as the Japanese. Airpower advocates like General Henry "Hap" Arnold, meanwhile, had sold the administration on strategic bombing. War plants operated around the clock fabricating the aircraft that would supposedly render massed infantry obsolete. In the United States, war mobilization, as pundit Walter Lippmann put it, consisted "basically of Navy, Air, and manufacturing."[33]

Even within the Army Ground Forces, the infantry remained something of a neglected stepchild. Armor and artillery claimed pride of place, promising swiftness, versatility, and awesome firepower. In addition, the army adopted a centralized bureaucratic management structure that required large administrative staffs to handle everything from training and supply to intelligence and operations. As a result, the United States Army had the most white-collar and officer-laden fighting force in the world. Winston Churchill called the American army "the peacock," so big was its showy tail.[34]

For every man at the front, the army needed at least three men, and normally several times that number, to maintain the long lines of supply and communication, police and entertain the troops, track soldiers' performance, and preserve the chain of command. Little more than five percent of the over 16 million Americans to serve in uniform during the war ever saw extended combat. The infantry accounted for only fourteen percent of those sent overseas, yet suffered seventy percent of the casualties.[35]

Recruits to the infantry landed in it largely by default. The best, most highly motivated men joined the Marines, the navy, the air forces, and the elite divisions. The rest, mostly draftees, went into the army. A perfunctory screening process, relying heavily on standardized testing, then sorted recruits into various job classifications. The better-educated usually received desk jobs, or even a chance at officer candidate school. The others filled the ranks of the "footsloggers." With women and most African Americans barred from combat, those selected for the front lines tended to be white working-class men, along with a smattering of Mexicans, Native Americans, and other minorities.[36]

Derived from a largely poor, subordinated population, the infantry suffered the lowest morale and the highest rates of alienation of any branch of the military. A survey conducted in 1944 revealed that most combat soldiers disdained the army, especially its officers and rear echelon. They never became disillusioned about the war, because they had little idealism about it to begin with. Only a tiny fraction of frontline troops could name even one of the Four Freedoms for which President Roosevelt said they were fighting (freedom of speech and religion and freedom from want and fear). Most soldiers admitted they would desert if given the chance, though they didn't want to abandon their buddies in the line, nor deprive their families of the pay and benefits they would lose in a court-martial. The best-case scenario they envisioned was a nonmutilating wound severe enough to get them out of battle.[37]

Upon this dispirited and cynical group of soldiers, whom Bill Mauldin said "gives more and gets less than anybody else," the American war effort devolved in the winter of 1943–44. By early January, the exhausted Allies had thrust themselves beyond the

Winter Line only to stall along the Gustav Line. There German engineers had created a defensive masterpiece. Anchored on its western end by the towering massif known as Monte Cassino, the Gustav Line was a complex network of caves, dugouts, tunnels, and other fortified positions. Parts of these could be abandoned in case of assault and then retaken in a counterattack. Fronting the mountain fortress were the raging Garigliano and Rapido rivers and behind them lay a floodplain of minefields planted among heaps of barbed wire up to four hundred yards deep. The only route to Rome was through the Liri Valley, situated directly under Cassino's imperious gaze.[38]

Here the American war plan all but collapsed. Allied air superiority, which Dwight Eisenhower thought would be "worth ten divisions" in Italy, was virtually nullified by the terrain, poor weather, and close quarter fighting. Artillery, though fired in almost unimaginable quantities, had little impact. Someone in Italy guessed it cost twenty-five thousand dollars' worth of shells to kill one German. With American armor stuck in mud beneath Cassino, the infantry would have to go to Rome one bootstep at a time.[39]

The War Department's new publicity campaign, meant to dampen expectations for a quick victory, now had to explain another stalemate. Enter the footsloggers, previously all but invisible in the media, now brought forward to embody America's fighting spirit. On the surface, the infantry in Italy appeared almost wholly resistant to the kind of image-burnishing that had made heroes of marines and bomber pilots.

It was Bill Mauldin's great talent to transform the infantry's surly alienation and disaffection into the stuff of pride and respect. Further, he did so with disregard for conventions that had governed earlier publicity about American fighting men. In their ragged appearance and sardonic attitude, Mauldin's soldiers appeared to be everything the heroes of the glossy magazines were not.

Bill embraced the role of infantry publicist, though not without ambivalence. He learned that success could be chastening. By the summer of 1944, for example, Bill noticed that some rear-echelon troops, who "were too far forward to wear ties and an' too far back to git shot," were beginning to look like Mauldin's foot soldiers. They had stopped dressing like pilots and started battering their shoes, growing their beards, and paying top dollar for worn combat jackets. These "garritroopers," as Bill called them, behaved the way they imagined battle-hardened soldiers should: they drank, raised hell, and harassed tie-wearing, khaki-clad clerks. Meanwhile, genuine frontline soldiers on four-day passes continued to be found, if not in jail, then drinking in silence or obsessively scrubbing themselves clean.[40]

ON JANUARY 22, 1944, the Allies landed three divisions, including the 45th, and some elite battalions behind German lines thirty miles south of Rome at the resort town of Anzio. Winston Churchill had championed the seaborne flanking maneuver, arguing that the landing, coordinated with a massive assault in the Cassino sector, could crack the Gustav Line and clear the way to Rome. The American high command wanted none of this. They had all but given up on Italy and turned to preparations for the invasion of France. But a persistent Churchill had cabled President Roosevelt on Christmas Day, 1943, pleading to save the amphibious maneuver, even though it meant delaying the Normandy invasion by a month. What, he asked the president, "could be more dangerous than to let the Italian battle stagnate and fester on for another three months?"[41]

That the operation would fail to break the stalemate should have been apparent to Allied leadership. A day earlier, the Germans had easily turned back an Allied assault on the Gustav Line. General Mark Clark, eager for the breakthrough to Rome to be an exclusively "American show," had assigned only one American division to the Gustav Line task: the exhausted, undermanned 36th.

On January 20, 1944, Clark ordered 6,000 infantrymen to wade across the flooded Rapido River under a storm of fire from Monte

Cassino. Within thirty-six hours, the 36th had been whittled down by almost a third. Only strenuous protests from the division's commander stopped Clark and II Corps commander General Geoffrey Keyes from ordering another advance. Carnage was so great that survivors of "Bloody River" demanded and received a congressional investigation into what one military historian calls the "virtual encyclopedia of mistakes" made by Clark and Keyes in planning and executing the assaults.[42]

Meanwhile, at Anzio, VI Corps commander Major General John Lucas lost any initiative he'd won with the surprise landing. Hitting the beach unopposed, Lucas ordered his men to dig in and prepare for a counterattack, rather than strike inland at German supply lines. The hesitation allowed German general Albert Kesselring to reposition forces on the Alban Hills overlooking Anzio, sealing off the beachhead while maintaining his defense of the Gustav Line. By the end of January, 70,000 British and American troops occupied a shoreline seven miles deep and fifteen miles wide, almost every inch of it within German artillery range. The Allies would remain stuck there for four months, losing almost 30,000 men from enemy fire and twice that from illness, trench foot, and psychological breakdown.

While a nightmare for the Allies, the two-front stalemate was a boon to Bill Mauldin. He could now commute both to Anzio and the mountains from his base in Naples. Anzio especially offered ample material for "Up Front." "If you liked ironies," Bill said, "that beachhead was a cartoonist's gold mine for ideas." Always under enemy surveillance, everyone at Anzio, from the docks to the front lines, came under fire. "A man would earn his Purple Heart at the front, get evacuated to the hospital, and pick up an Oak Leaf Cluster to his medal while lying on his cot," Bill recalled. The Allies had put their headquarters in a wine cellar on the south end of the beach, in clear sight of the Germans, who seemed to delight in knocking out officers' latrines. "When you deprive field-grade brass hats of their leisurely morning bowel movement," mused Bill, "you have created a serious morale problem." The lower the morale, Bill knew, the more valued his cartoons.[43]

Bill finally left the *45th Division News* about a month after the Anzio invasion. Don Robinson paid tribute to the celebrated cartoonist in the February 22 issue of the paper, describing Bill as a "thin, intense, pale fellow who could use three haircuts in quick succession." "He has apparently lost three pounds a week for the last three years," joked Robinson, but still "has energy in quantity" and remains "as brassy as the courthouse Civil War cannon."[44]

Privately, Robinson admonished Bill about joining *Stars and Stripes.* "Those bastards will ruin you," he warned. "They'll corrupt you."[45]

Bill was already wary about joining the big paper. He'd earned a remarkable amount of latitude on the *45th Division News,* and the *Stars and Stripes* was a lightning rod for controversy. Even so, Bill liked the relaxed style of his new employers. No one ever saluted, and everyone was on a first-name basis, including officers White and Neville. Bill knew that editors liked control. They might put him on assignment, request cartoons on certain topics, or even employ him as an art editor. So Bill studiously avoided the newsroom, and for the first time removed himself from the day-to-day operations of a newspaper.[46]

Since he worked best in solitude late at night he got permission to sleep in his studio instead of at the *pensione* with the other staff members. The studio, a third-floor room in the Galleria Umberto Primo, contained nothing but a chair, a table, and a canvas cot, but it served him well as he worked into the early morning hours crafting the cartoons that soon captivated home-front readers.

The Galleria's surreal, carnival-like atmosphere stimulated Bill's senses almost as much as the front. Completed in 1890 in a baroque fin de siècle style, the Galleria was once the world's largest shopping arcade, occupying several city blocks in the heart of Naples. In its heyday, the iron-and-glass-domed Galleria had been a virtual temple to the European faith in material progress.

Now, the glass panes lay shattered on the polished marble floors. Destitute Neapolitans scoured the building for discarded cigarette butts. Rain poured through the roof's twisted iron ribs down onto the broad promenades and sidewalk cafés, where visitors drank ersatz coffee brewed of roasted grains, herbs, and nuts. Despite its empty shops and dismal surroundings, the Galleria attracted swirling, ever-shifting crowds. Bill's Neapolitan neighbor, novelist John Horne Burns, called it "a cross between a railroad station and a church. . . . Everybody in Naples," Burns wrote, "came to the Galleria Umberto."[47]

They came for the liquor, mostly vermouth, which was consumed in vast quantities at all hours, day and night, and for the thriving sex trade and black market which made Naples, in the words of one French soldier, "a vision of a den of iniquity where everything was for sale."[48] In 1944, Naples' officially registered prostitutes numbered 80,000; it seemed, in addition to that, almost any Neapolitan woman could be bought for a price. "The place was jammed with Allied soldiers of every description," Bill recalled.

Aussies with their pinned-up sombreros, Free French troopers bargaining with boys for their big sisters while Moroccan Ghoums [or *Goums* or *Goumiers*: Moroccan soldiers attached to the French army] in striped robes bargained with the girls for their little brothers, Poles from the famous 10th Corps drinking rotgut cognac and trying to top each other's tales of personal woe and injustice, and American paratroopers looking for black market jump boots—items of issue which they should have received free but which fetched $100 a pair and somehow never got to the front.[49]

With the liberties of a civilian, the resources of a prince, and little to divert his attention from the war except drinking, gambling, and womanizing, the twenty-two-year-old cartoonist joined Galleria's kaleidoscope of humanity. Later he gingerly approached the subject of soldierly behavior while at war. "They all feel a certain freedom from the conventions they would observe in their own countries," he tactfully put it.[50]

One freedom Bill embraced while in Italy was heavy drinking. Bill was a teetotaler during his army years back home, a reaction to his family history. He turned to alcohol overseas, especially in the winter of 1943–44. It would have been very odd had he not. Virtually every soldier, especially those stationed near the front, drank copiously when given the chance. Many combat correspondents like Bill drank simply to help them sleep, so that, as Ernie Pyle explained to his wife, "you wouldn't hear the guns and planes." Bill's drinking was episodic, marked by great binges and prolonged sobriety. In this, he was probably saved by his instinct for self-mastery and control. At any rate, he never permitted the drinking to interfere with his work.[51]

Bill also kept his womanizing discreet. "Most of the time I was a clean, reverent, faithful, devoted young American husband, who wrote to his wife practically every day," he testified twenty-five years after the war. Of course, what passed for clean living in sordid, war-torn Naples would have made for scandal back home. To be sure, Bill did not "whore around" like most other rear-echelon soldiers with money, and he took pride in his comparative self-restraint when it came to women. But he did enjoy the company of Italian girls, not simply for sex, but also for comfort and companionship. "It just isn't possible to take millions of American men and shut them off from love for years on end," offered John Horne Burns by way of explanation. "We started casting our eyes on the Neapolitan girls."[52]

Following a convention that European soldiers found puzzling, Bill usually double-dated with *Stars and Stripes* artist Ed Vebell, a man with a strong libertine streak and, like Bill, an urge for independence. For a while the two went out with a pair of sixteen-year-old cousins, enjoying the beach, shows at the San Carlo Opera

House, and no doubt time at the girls' homes, where they made regular deliveries of black-market food, clothing, and other wares. After the Pyle interview, Bill, not wanting to jeopardize his marriage or budding career, had Vebell destroy photographs he'd taken of the girls at the beach and elsewhere. This romance was neither intense nor long-lived, but it was genuine. Sentimental as he was about the Neapolitans, Bill probably found something akin to love, as well as pity, compassion, and desire, in his relationships with these displaced girls of liberated Italy.[53]

Bill credited his play for another girl with saving his life. Across the hall at the Galleria lived a shopkeeper's family, including a beautiful teenage girl with dyed blond hair. Her little sister said she'd been "the toast of the Wehrmacht" during the German occupation. In any case, Bill cozied up to her immediately. One night as Bill lay sleeping on his cot during an air raid, the younger sister knocked on his door and asked him to accompany their family to the basement. Her father was out of town, she said, and her mother had become hysterical. In those days, the Luftwaffe's raids were mostly desultory affairs; German pilots normally dropped their payloads perfunctorily, far from the Galleria's location near the harbor; heretofore Bill had remained in his cot during the raids. Now, however, Bill saw his chance to make it with the blonde—and a good thing, too, for this time the Luftwaffe meant business.

Panic swept the crowded, stifling cellar as the entire building rocked from explosions. The blonde clung tightly to Bill as bombs narrowly missed the Galleria. When the raid ended, Bill led the girl to his room only to find his window blown out and shards of glass embedded in the opposite wall. His cot had been torn to ribbons. According to Bill, the girl's mother soon appeared at the door and escorted her daughter home. "I went to sleep musing that if I hadn't been trying to mess around downstairs I'd have been killed upstairs," recalled Bill. "There must be some sort of murky moral to all this, but it has always escaped me."[54]

As much as he enjoyed the wartime charms of Naples, no girl or black-market delicacy meant as much to Bill as the jeep General Clark awarded him in March of 1944. Until then, Bill had largely relied on the press motor pool to ferry him to and from the fronts. He hated his dependence on army chauffeurs, who tore carelessly over shell-pocked roads, often striking animals and civilians alike, and getting a lot of GIs hurt in the process. The drivers, he felt, had no respect for what he considered that most delightful and noble of machines, the jeep.

So in February of 1944, Bill entreated some ordnance men in Naples to allow him to rummage through their junk pile of wrecked vehicles. Having learned about vehicles from Pop, Bill fished a bent Harley-Davidson out of the boneyard, and with some borrowed tools got the machine in working order. Now, Bill was the one tearing up the southern Italian roads—until he crashed the motorcycle into a water-filled bomb crater two weeks later.

Approaching his buddies at the ordnance depot once again, he asked for a broken jeep this time, but they told him he needed written permission from Fifth Army headquarters for that one. On a long shot, Bill wrote a letter to the G-4 Section in charge of supply, explaining his need for independent transportation. Two weeks later, on returning from his first trip to Anzio, Bill got a message saying that his request for a "wrecked jeep" had been approved.

The sight of his jeep, a brand-new one freshly delivered from the States, sent Bill literally yelling for joy. He circled the vehicle in astonishment, lovingly examining it from top to bottom. On the front bumper was a license plate bearing his name and a portrait of his cartoon dogface. On the front seat lay a manila envelope containing stamped and signed papers attesting to Bill's rightful possession of the machine. Since jeeps were never assigned to soldiers for personal use, the registration papers named Bill Mauldin as an army unit in his own right, performing the functions of "pool officer, dispatcher, driver, and passenger." To top it off, a stack of trip tickets was also included, permitting him access anywhere in the

European theater of operations. He was now a free agent operating within an otherwise tightly regulated army structure.

"Congratulations," wrote Pop when he heard the news. "Do you realize that is the first new car our family has ever owned?"

For the boy from New Mexico, nothing—not his promotion to the *Stars and Stripes,* his celebrity, nor even his syndication—symbolized success more than that jeep. With the help of his friends at ordnance, he immediately customized the vehicle, installing leather seats cannibalized from a Lancia and building an elaborate locker and mini studio in the back, complete with electric light and drawing board. He also fashioned collapsible sides so that he could black out his jeep at night and work on the road. Finally Bill plastered the interior with photographs of his wife and child and christened the machine "Jeanie." Knowing that the vehicle would fetch a high price on the black market, Bill made it a habit to lock the hood, chain the steering wheel to the chassis, and carry off select parts of the motor every time he parked it.[55]

Once, as he was climbing behind the wheel, two burly GIs cornered him demanding that he turn over the vehicle. Then one of the men caught sight of the license plate and yanked his buddy's sleeve. "We don't want to take this guy's jeep," the soldier said, and the two toughs took off down the road.

Bill told this story often during the war, perhaps to reassure himself that the ultimate approval for his many perks came from the ranks. It was a privileged status he worked hard to preserve.[56]

ON FEBRUARY 29, 1944, shortly before the jeep's arrival, Willie and Joe were born. That, at least, was the day Bill first used the name "Willie" in an overseas cartoon. In fact, he hadn't paired Willie, originally a stocky straight man, with Joe, the wisecracking Indian, since before the Japanese bombed Pearl Harbor.

Meanwhile, the name "Joe" had become generic. Italian children, it seemed, knew no other. They routinely called out, "Hey,

Joe! *Caramella?* Cigarette?" to any passing American infantrymen. All of Bill's Joes resembled each other, but they truly coalesced into the now-familiar pug-nosed soldier in February, after publication of Ernie Pyle's column and *Life* magazine's layout.[57]

Bill's contract with United Features syndicate and reassignment to *Stars and Stripes* prompted him to streamline and standardize his feature. Will Lang of Time-Life proved especially influential in this process. The layout Lang put together somewhat disingenuously promoted Bill's main character as "G.I. Joe." The name, of course, had already been used by *Yank* early in the war for its version of a David Breger cartoon that had originally run in the *Saturday Evening Post* under the title of "Private Breger." A strong advocate of the combat infantryman, Lang encouraged Bill to establish more regular characters and settings. Lang suggested that Bill do a weekly series of pictures and accompanying text for *Life* depicting "the continued experience of one guy."[58]

The "G.I. Joe" in *Life*'s layout was a more realistic prototype of the Joe that later emerged. Bill's earlier Joe wore a hardened, angry expression, at times even accusatory (see figure 30). By contrast, the Joe that entered *Stars and Stripes* in early 1944, limned in a more "big foot" style, had a softer, wearier look about him, especially around the eyes. Bill had replaced surliness with a kind of sadness and resignation, made all the more poignant by his relationship with Willie.

Bill considered Willie and Joe rather unimaginative characters, distinguishable only by their noses. The prominent arch in Willie's nose appeared in a batch of mid-March cartoons Bill sketched on his first trip to Anzio. Bill tried to draw Willie as ten years older than Joe, a bit wiser and more worldly. Both of them now spoke in a pidgin of slum dialect and army slang close to the urban ethnic working-class origins shared by so many infantry soldiers in Italy. Such group traits were far more important to the cartoon than the idiosyncratic characters themselves. The trauma of combat had blotted out personality, reducing men to laconic survivors. As a

**FIGURE 30** This full-page cartoon ran in the special four-color Christmas edition of the *45th Division News*. Three weeks later, *Life* magazine identified the center character as "G.I. Joe." This prototype's direct address and realistic facial features made him a more threatening and less comical figure than the Joe who later appeared in syndication.

*Copyright 1943 by Bill Mauldin. Courtesy of the Mauldin Estate.*

pair, Willie and Joe were fine comic foils, but it was their camaraderie that offset the material's grim reality.

Like Ernie Pyle, Bill found redemption from war's coarseness in "the sacred circle of comradeship." "Their nobility and dignity," Bill would soon tell home-front readers, "come from the way they live unselfishly and risk their lives to help each other."[59]

# Willie and Joe: A War Gallery

*(1944–1945)*

> *The real war will never get in the books.*

—WALT WHITMAN,
UNION HOSPITAL VOLUNTEER, 1863–65

THE SENSATIONS of modern warfare are so divorced from ordinary experience that they "burst the petty bounds of art," as Walt Whitman put it, resisting word and image. During World War II, news from the front was further thwarted by government censorship. When in 1943 General Marshall requested materials portraying the "grimness of War," he didn't want or expect true candor, but rather the *appearance* of it. Even after the loosening of press restrictions, citizens back home never saw a pool of blood surrounding an American body or a dismembered limb. Death had to appear purposeful, not random, as if each life lost marked a clear and deliberate step toward victory.

Ernie Pyle often tried to write of "battle fatigue" and was always blocked by censors, until he despaired of ever conveying to readers an accurate vision of combat. During a brief visit back home, Pyle was approached by a man asking "in complete good faith": "Tell me now, just exactly what is it you don't like about war?"[1]

Drawing on the skeptical, idiomatic humor of the troops themselves, Bill Mauldin came closest to representing the experience
of combat. "They tell the facts," Rayson Billey said of Mauldin's
cartoons. "They make it short, make it to the point. Willie and
Joe—they were real." But, Billey also added, even Mauldin did
not show the true war. "He sketched behind the lines," Billey
explained, "you know, I mean, he didn't show everything."[2]

Only three times did field censors hold up his cartoons. Each
of the offending drawings contained background sketches of
new, undisclosed equipment. Never did the army censor his
work for its themes or messages.

In truth, Bill effectively censored himself. At the age of
twenty-two, Bill knew what he could get away with. He adhered
to what he called the journalistic "common sense" of the day,
which meant never depicting Americans dying ignobly, com-
mitting war crimes, assaulting their officers, forgetting their
own names, or smiling as they were carried from combat on a
stretcher. Instead, Bill showed an unbandaged Willie sitting in
a hospital bed with a "thousand yard stare"; readers could imagine the rest.[3]

Though Mauldin depicted only a fraction of the real war, his
fans in the foxholes read the truth between the brushstrokes
and clipped caption lines. True candor would have meant a
lot of obscenity, the best of the dogface's rhetorical weapons.
"What was magnificent about the word *shit*," writes World War
II veteran Norman Mailer, "was that it enabled you to use the
word *noble*." In merely suggesting the front's obscene reality, Bill
Mauldin managed to portray the nobility of America's fighting
men.[4]

*"I'm beginnin' to feel like a fugitive
from th' law of averages."*

**FIGURE 31**    On November 2, 1944, Willie expresses a terrible realization that dawned on every combat soldier: they were victims of forces they could neither control nor escape. At this time, infantry casualty rates in Europe had soared to a point where the army virtually ran out of trained replacements. Entire divisions turned over in a matter of weeks. By late 1944, Bill began to feel like a fraud. "I should have killed them," he said of Willie and Joe after the war. The dogfaces they were based on "were really dead anyway, why not kill them?"

*"We'll go away an' stop botherin' you boys now.*
*Jerry's got our range."*

FIGURE 32 Infantrymen resented all who did not share their lot. They felt especially ambivalent toward tank crews, who brought firepower but also attracted enemy artillery. Outclassed by German Panzers and Tigers, American tanks often withdrew under fire, leaving ground soldiers behind. This ability to leave battle irked the infantry. Bill's tactful note at the top of the panel indicates his awareness of the dangers faced by tank crews, who commonly referred to their machines as "death traps."

*"Uncle Willie!"*

**FIGURE 33**  The air forces inspired a litany of grievances among Bill's dogfaces, beginning with the frequency of "friendly fire" incidents. American ground losses to Allied bombing in Italy perhaps exceeded those inflicted by the moribund Luftwaffe. The air forces had lavish base accommodations, and crew members were awarded Distinguished Flying Crosses (nicknamed Lucky Bastard Ribbons) and trips back home after twenty-five missions (later extended to thirty-five, and then fifty). Aviators earned higher pay and quicker promotions than foot soldiers. They also won fourteen times as many medals. Note the colonel's wings worn by Willie's young nephew in this cartoon from April 4, 1944. Unknown to most ground troops was that only a quarter of all air crews survived twenty-five missions, and that the air forces' casualty rates were second only to the infantry's.

*"Don't look at me, lady. I didn't do it."*

**Figure 34** American infantrymen such as the one in this cartoon from November 7, 1944, encountered devastation wherever they went. The Germans demolished cities and towns as they retreated, and the Allies did the same in advance. Despite early expectations for "precision bombing" campaigns and rapier-like thrusts of armor through enemy lines, the United States Army soon turned to "Brute Force." Frequently stalemated, the Allies employed an inexhaustible supply of bombs and shells, pulverizing every inch of enemy-held ground before sending in tanks and foot soldiers. The strategy saved American lives but destroyed Europe. Italy, observed Bill, "looks as if a giant rake had gone over it from end to end." "Let's paint the town red," says Willie to Joe amid the rubble of an Italian village in another cartoon from April 12, 1944.

*"Don't startle 'im, Joe—
it's almost full."*

*"Hell of a way to waste time.
Does it work?"*

**FIGURES 35 AND 36** Many troops on both sides drank heavily before entering battle. "In my outfit," recalled author James Jones of his 27th Infantry Regiment, "we got blind asshole drunk every chance we got." Unlike the British or the Germans, the more prudish United States Army did not issue a liquor ration to enlisted men, leaving troops to scrounge for it or brew their own concoctions. It was not uncommon for men to mix grapefruit juice with Aqua Velva, antifreeze, or buzz bomb fluid. During the war's last nine months in Europe, more American soldiers died from alcohol poisoning than communicable diseases.

*Both cartoons copyright 1944 by Bill Mauldin. Courtesy of the Mauldin Estate.*

*"By th' way, what wuz them changes*
*you wuz gonna make when you took*
*over last month, sir?"*

**FIGURE 37** Resistance to military discipline reached dangerous levels among combat troops from 1943 on. Enlisted men's anger over the numerous perks of rank—from segregated latrines to exclusive access to liquor—rose sharply in combat. Only platoon leaders and company commanders who bent the rules, like the one in this cartoon from November 23, 1944, prevented a possible mutiny. The most effective officers shared in the deprivations and dangers of combat and identified more closely with their men than with distant superiors.

*Copyright 1944 by Bill Mauldin. Courtesy of the Mauldin Estate.*

*"Must be a tough objective.
Th' ol' man says we're
gonna have th' honor of
liberatin' it."*

*"Don't mention it,
Lootenant. They might have
replaced ya with one of them
salutin' demons."*

**FIGURES 38 AND 39**  Of cold consolation to combat soldiers were the euphemisms propagated by American publicity organs. In home-front newspapers, American troops never invaded or conquered territory, but always *liberated* it. Willie and Joe saw through such terminology, as in the cartoon on the left from August 31, 1944. They also defied traditional notions of battlefield heroics, as in the panel on the right from June 2, 1944. The "lootenant" with the conspicuously ignoble foot wound is carried to safety by Joe, who wishes to avoid having to break in a fresh replacement.

*Both cartoons copyright 1944 by Bill Mauldin. Courtesy of the Mauldin Estate.*

*"Wish to hell I wuzn't housebroke."*

**FIGURE 40** Soldiers routinely defecated in their foxholes or risked exposing themselves to fire. This cartoon from May 5, 1944, is perhaps the only reference to this common indignity published in the American media during the war.

*Copyright 1944 by Bill Mauldin. Courtesy of the Mauldin Estate.*

# Chapter Five

# Breaking Out

ITALY—FRANCE—BELGIUM—
LUXEMBOURG—GERMANY
(May 1944–June 1945)

*Anzio. May 23, 1944.* At three minutes past dawn, the beachhead exploded with sound as over eight hundred big guns opened fire in history's largest concentration of artillery. Shells, quietly stockpiled in munitions dumps over the previous weeks, now hurtled through the gray sky, bursting with a flash a mile or two away. The earth quivered as concussion waves roared back over the beachhead, where 90,000 Allied soldiers were hunkering down in wet foxholes.

Great clouds of smoke enveloped the men as the enemy began answering with shells of their own. The sounds of outgoing and incoming fire were now met, reaching a crescendo so loud that soldiers could almost see the air vibrate. "It was like the world was coming to an end," recalled one infantry officer.

After forty-five minutes, the Allied bombardment abruptly stopped. In its place rose the sound of machine-gun chatter, airplane and tank engines, and commands shouted to temporarily deafened subordinates. Platoon leaders waved their arms in great arcs toward enemy lines and physically pulled soldiers out of their dugouts here and there, pushing them onward. Slowly, more men emerged. Hunched and flinching as shells screamed toward them, they looked like exhausted prizefighters coming out for the final round. Across the beachhead stretched a ten-mile line of olive drab making its way through the smoke toward No Man's Land. The great Battle of the Anzio Breakout had begun.[1]

The VI Corps' advance on May 23 was the second of a two-phase offensive designed by British general Sir Harold Alexander, commander in chief of Allied forces in Italy, to break the stalemate on the peninsula. Twelve days' earlier, fourteen Allied divisions from a dozen nations had assaulted the western sector of the Gustav Line for the fourth time in four months. The first three had failed, but this time German defenses had buckled. Despite heavy casualties, elements of the British Eighth Army had entered the Liri Valley, and Polish troops, aided by expert Moroccan mountain fighters, had evicted the 1st German Parachute Division from Monte Cassino. General Alexander now saw a chance to break through the Gustav Line and capture the German Tenth Army, whose only escape route lay in the path of the VI Corps advancing out of the beachhead.

From Fifth Army headquarters in Caserta, General Clark followed the offensive's progress with rising alarm. He had opposed Alexander's plan, convinced that it was a British plot to deny him the honor—and publicity—of entering Rome first. "Not only did we intend to become the first army in fifteen centuries to seize Rome from the south," Clark noted in his diary, "but we intended to see that the people back home knew that it was the Fifth Army that did the job and knew the price that had to be paid for it."

Defying his superior's wishes, Clark ordered Lucian Truscott, who had taken over command of VI Corps, to divert the bulk of his forces toward Rome, away from the trap Alexander had set for the retreating Tenth Army. Truscott protested to no avail. The route leading to Rome, in the words of one military historian, became a veritable "Italian Grand Prix, with every unit and every war correspondent racing to be the first to enter the Imperial City."

Vehicles of all sorts, from jeeps and tanks to staff cars and troop transports, jammed roads and fields southeast of the city. General Geoffrey Keyes, commander of II Corps, now jockeyed for position with Truscott, while the French Expeditionary Corps nipped at their heels. Two divisions within VI Corps itself clashed over which would take the lead on Highway 7. They reached a compromise to share the road, and then threatened to fire upon the usurping American 85th Division, coming up hard upon their right.

Clark didn't care who got to the city first so long as they belonged to GENERAL MARK CLARK'S FIFTH ARMY, as the press releases habitually termed it. The general warned Alexander to stay away from the prize, saying he would use force if necessary against any Eighth Army soldiers who tried to get in on Rome's liberation.

As the German Tenth Army escaped up the Liri Valley to defensive positions farther north, General Keyes won the race with an advance patrol of eighteen jeeps carrying sixty men, including a number of correspondents and photographers. The Free French had actually scampered first into the deserted city center, but had failed to bring along a film crew to record the event. On June 4, Clark got just close enough to city limits to have his picture taken next to a huge ROMA sign, which was promptly dismantled and shipped to his headquarters. The next day, Clark paraded in triumph through Rome as press tickers back home carried the news of the Fifth Army's glorious victory.[2]

Mark Clark, however, had less than twelve hours to savor the publicity. By the morning of June 6, 1944, wire machines chattered with more dramatic news. Indeed, it was the biggest news event of the twentieth century: the Allies had landed a massive force on the coast of France: the long-awaited cross-Channel invasion had begun.

On the home front, church bells pealed, factory whistles blared, and honking car horns told of the euphoria. New hope arose in the nation, replacing the public pessimism long associated with the Italian campaign. In the space of a morning, Allied troops in Italy, including one famed combat cartoonist, had been relegated to a "forgotten front."

BILL MAULDIN followed the breakout and the race to Rome from his base at Anzio. On June 5, he loaded his jeep with supplies and sped north with Fred Sheehan, his old colleague from the *45th Division News*. They were instantly mobbed when they entered the city, which had been spared the kind of devastation visited upon Naples. Throngs of madly cheering young women surrounded Bill's jeep, some clambering aboard and smothering the men with kisses.

"As far as the girls were concerned, we were Don Juan and Casanova in a Ferrari," Bill joked. The pair hauled around several groups of the revelers dressed in their Sunday best before finding their way to the offices of the newspaper *Il Messagero*, where an advance guard of *Stars and Stripes* had already set up shop. Then Bill and Fred headed out again in search of a hotel.

By this time, Bill had learned to detest hotel managers. They, along with the police, Bill claimed, were society's "real bootlickers," swearing allegiance to whatever conquering authority happened to be in town.

One such manager of a small hotel rushed out to greet Bill. Seeing the jeep and two men wearing no insignia, he assumed that Bill and Fred were important officers. Bill requested a large room with a good view, signed the register, and was led to a double overlooking the street.

After two nights, the manager knocked on Bill's door. The hotel was reserved for officers and Red Cross personnel only, he said. Bill was to gather his gear and vacate the premises.

As the manager trailed him through the lobby, Bill ran into two Red Cross girls and a major he knew from Naples. The latter happened to be a billeting officer. The new arrivals greeted the cartoonist warmly and then expressed dismay at the news that he was being kicked out of the hotel.

"But that's silly—there's plenty of room," one of the women said. The major agreed and told Bill he could stay at the hotel until *Stars and Stripes* found accommodations.

"Please, signore, please let me have your things," the now confused and repentant manager said. "You can have your same room if you like."

"No thank you," Bill snapped, snatching back his bags. "You said I wasn't welcome." He then smirked goodbye to his friends and turned out the door "with flags flying."

"The truth is that with the Red Cross coming in I wanted out," Bill later explained. Red Cross personnel were well known for socializing only with officers, and Bill wanted no part of any clubby atmosphere at the hotel. "I had learned the art of inverse snobbery," he said.[3]

Such conspicuous acts of plebeian pride had become an important part of Bill's effort to maintain a reputation as a spokesman for the common GI, but in truth, his celebrity had begun to separate him from the real Willies and Joes. Where he'd once been able to circulate among the troops without attracting attention, now soldiers shouted out "Hiya, Bill!" as he drove by, and high-ranking officers received him like a visiting dignitary. They invited him to special dinners, placed staff cars at his disposal, and hounded him for signed copies of this or that cartoon.

Bill liked the attention, and at some level believed it was his due. But he didn't like the thought that such privileges came at the expense of men in the lines. He was careful never to flaunt his advantages, nor give any cause for resentment. He routinely turned down relatively comfortable field billets in order to bivouac with the troops. He bucked enlisted men's chow lines for portions of goulash instead of dining with silverware in officers' messes. Like George Patton, Bill knew the value of being seen at the front sharing in the conditions of the men.[4]

To be sure, given Bill's background and looks, he had no trouble passing for an ordinary GI. That he could juggle these two sides of the war—the hardships and the perks—says a lot about his will for self-presentation.

In fact, Bill's fussiness and peppery disposition compelled him to spend a lot of time alone, but in social situations he possessed a fluid personality and uncommon powers of observation that allowed him to adjust to almost any environment. He fit in everywhere. "I can't begin to tell you how he was able to walk into a room and in an instant case people out and know how to handle them," remarks friend Jon Gordon. At the front, his "perfect pitch" for dialogue and attitude virtually turned him into Willie or Joe, and in the rear, key friendships with officers and correspondents fueled his remarkable rise to fame.[5]

After Rome fell, Bill feared his hour in the spotlight might be nearing an end. The Normandy campaign had drained the Italian front of publicity, true, but more critical, also of the men and supplies needed to evict the Germans from the peninsula. While the Allies in Italy planned their next move, the enemy dug in along the Apennine Mountains north of Florence, some 150 miles from Bill's base in Rome. Material for Bill's daily feature was drying up. "You ought to come up here," wrote Ernie Pyle from Normandy on June 30. Pyle would use his influence to get Bill transferred to France.[6]

George Carlin at United Features Syndicate also supported the move to a more inspiring locale. Under contract for six cartoons a week, Bill usually sent in four, sometimes less than that. The syndicate was drawing down heavily on the cushion of older stuff Bill had delivered in March. Bill objected to the syndicate's use of dated cartoons. He, like Carlin, feared that "Up Front" would grow stale.[7]

More bad news came from Ann Watkins. Some editors were turning the feature down. Paper and ink were rationed, making newspaper space scarce, and publishers didn't want to risk offending readers with Bill's sardonic humor. In a heavily censored media, "Up Front" had the power to shock, even alienate, civilian audiences.

One woman objected to seeing Bill's cartoons in the *Daily Oklaho-man*. She said Willie and Joe looked like "prehistoric monsters who had just come out of a cave to see what it was all about." Another complained directly to the cartoonist: "Our boys don't look like the way you draw them. They're not bearded and horrible-looking. They're clean fine Americans." Most readers, however, were probably like the man who told a reporter, "It took me some time and study to catch on to Bill's brand of humor, but now I feel I know him and the men over there."[8]

Book publishers were also cautious. Ann Watkins was having trouble getting a contract for Bill's proposed book of cartoons and running text. The first three firms she approached had passed, saying that *Up Front* the book had "an appeal that was limited to the G.I. boys rather than the general public." Simon & Schuster turned the book down because Dick Simon, cofounder of the company, preferred "Sad Sack," whose humor depended less on captions and needed no explanation to audiences.[9]

Bill found himself torn between his readers on the home front and GI's resting up in Italy after months of combat. On July 12, one corporal wrote in to the B-Bag complaining that Mauldin should have shaved his characters after the Battle for Rome. "Remember that there is a time when every combat soldier shaves, even if he hates to," the corporal wrote. Two weeks later, Bill complied with a clean-shaven Willie. The new look lasted two days. Fighting had subsided on the Italian front, but Bill couldn't go back to the garrison humor of "Star Spangled Banter." Willie and Joe were now established characters, even commodities, beards and all.[10]

All the action was in France, and Bill had friends who could ease the transfer. But Bill had no desire to work for the London-based *Stars and Stripes,* which began operations in Normandy in early July. *Stars and Stripes* in Italy had been an independent unit of the local Allied headquarters. London's edition, however, operated under the army's Information and Education Division. Notoriously restrictive and heavily biased toward the air forces, *Stars and Stripes* brass in France might not take well to Bill's freewheeling style. "I've been allowed a maximum of freedom in what I draw or do," he told Carlin. A move to France would put him in a straitjacket.[11]

For a while the Rome edition seemed to be moving away from Bill too. With London running *Stars and Stripes* in Cherbourg, the Bureau of Public Relations, with the blessing of Secretary of War Henry Stimson, took over the Mediterranean edition. Right away the bureau purged Italy's paper of magazine supplements from home and blocked the flow of news from independent wire sources like the Associated Press. They restricted coverage of politics and the larger war to whatever the skittish Army News Service saw fit to distribute to the troops.

The director of public relations soon relieved Colonel Egbert White from command and ordered him home. White's departure stunned the staff, but his replacement, Captain Robert Neville, provided some solace when he vowed to maintain the paper's independence. Neville's job was made a little easier when U.S. newspapers picked up the censorship story and took a dim view of it.[12]

At the end of July 1944, invasion plans were afoot involving elements of the old Anzio VI Corps. The spot of the landing was secret, but everyone assumed—correctly— that it would be southern France. Bill received permission from Neville to accompany the invasion force and remain with them for sixty days.[13]

Energized by the prospect of another amphibious landing, Bill's cartoons came alive again. Early in August, before he and his jeep were combat-loaded onto an LST (landing ship, tank) in Naples Harbor, Bill batted out twelve cartoons depicting the beach assault—in advance. "I figured I knew enough about amphibious invasions by this time to make authentic pictures," he explained. Bill planned to mark the invasion with a dramatic cartoon published on D-day plus one. It was a predawn scene, inked in heavy black. Scared men huddled in a landing craft. A flare exploded overhead (see figure 41). "Any dope knows you can't make invasions unless the dark of the very early morning hides your activities," remarked Bill. But

"Try to say sumpin' funny, Joe."

FIGURE 41 Obsessed with authenticity, Bill was chagrined when this drawing appeared throughout the home front, depicting a nighttime landing on the shores of southern France.

*45th Infantry Division Museum.*
*Copyright 1944 by Bill Mauldin. Courtesy of the Mauldin Estate.*

when the drawing appeared on August 16, the joke was on the cartoonist. The first waves had landed near Cannes in full daylight. By the time his LST approached the shore, Bill stood at the rail gazing at the fabled Riviera "in the blinding glare of a very high sun."[14]

WEHRMACHT FORCES positioned between Cannes and Saint-Tropez put up little resistance to the invasion before beating a hasty retreat to the north. One French and three American divisions chased after them, covering more ground in one day than they had in months of bitter combat in Italy.

Bill grew restless waiting along the coast for a *Stars and Stripes* crew to arrive. He wanted to see the liberation of a French city. So on the morning of August 23, he took off on his own toward Grenoble. French Resistance members reported the route to be clear. A special task force from the 36th Division had already left for Grenoble in a convoy. Bill loaded his jeep with extra cans of gasoline and started up the legendary Route Napoleon, Alpine trails the great emperor had taken on his return from exile in 1815.

The 140-mile drive between Cannes and Grenoble was the most spectacular of Bill's life, more impressive even than the twisting canyon roads of New Mexico. After crossing three passes below snowcapped peaks, Bill descended into Grenoble, a charming, bustling city tucked at the base of the French Alps. There he caught up with the task force just as it entered the city. Grateful locals poured onto the streets to greet them. The Germans had evacuated, but not before executing a number of Resistance fighters.

As usual, Bill needed a printing press and paper. Making his way to *Les Allobroges,* the city's daily newspaper, he found, to his astonishment, Don Robinson, Fred Sheehan, and the rest of the *45th Division News* crew already there preparing copy. Using Robinson's page forms, some BBC news copy, and a hastily drawn cartoon, Bill put together his own wildcat issue of *Stars and Stripes,* the first such edition in southern France.[15]

Bill spent late August through early October of 1944 roaming about southern France and the Alps, whose scenery inspired a famous cartoon. "Beautiful view," says an officer to a colleague. "Is there one for the enlisted men?"[16]

During one sojourn north of Grenoble, Bill spotted a monk with a Saint Bernard hauling a sled of firewood. The monk kept his silence, but waved Bill to follow him back to the gates of a spectacular medieval monastery. Disappearing briefly inside, the monk emerged with an older man and several colleagues; all turned out to be members of the Carthusian order and lived such hermetic lives that they knew little of the war and nothing of such modern conveniences as Bill's jeep. The brothers circled the jeep in fascination, "peering under it and doing everything but kick the tires," said Bill. "All I could think of was schoolboys looking at a new model convertible." In return for offering up his jeep for inspection, the elder monk handed Bill two bottles, one green and one yellow. "My God!" exclaimed one of Bill's *Stars and Stripes* colleagues when he returned to Grenoble. "That's Chartreuse! You get lost in the hills and you stumble over one of the world's fancy booze factories." The monks, it appeared, supported their monastery by selling the elixir made from Alpine herbs according to a recipe known to only three of the brothers.[17]

Such picturesque adventures contrasted sharply with the anguish and grit Bill had known in Italy. "There's darn little misery here," he wrote to George Carlin in early September. "Sometimes there's a fight, but most of the time the only discomfort is plenty of walking. So I'm leaving the beards and the sad look on Joe and Willie, but I'm bringing in other and fresher characters, and doing more local color stuff" (see figure 42).[18]

Bill's cartoons in September and early October seemed positively breezy in comparison to his previous work. One published on September 12 even went so far as to depict a squad leader holding down his command post at a sidewalk café. "Hell of a patrol," a dismayed Willie snaps to his sergeant, "we got shot at."

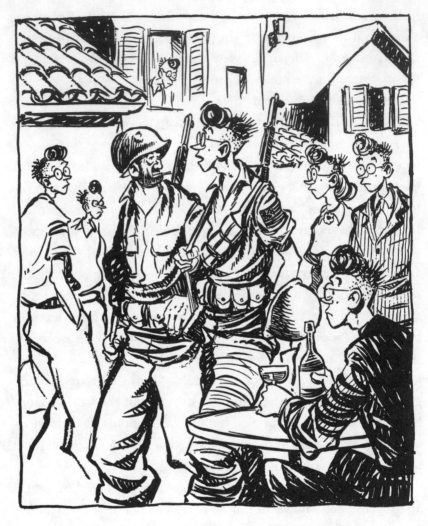

*"This is th' town my pappy told me about."*

**FIGURE 42** The relative calm of southern France encouraged lighter humor, including this rare sex gag from September 6, 1944.

*Copyright 1944 by Bill Mauldin. Courtesy of the Mauldin Estate.*

Bill later regretted the playful tone of these cartoons. Some troops fighting farther north and back in Italy had complained, convincing Bill that "anybody with picture-drawing ambitions shouldn't draw war pictures. He will go nuts trying to keep up with the right war at the right time."[19]

George Carlin, on the other hand, liked Bill's shift in attitude. It corresponded with the new mood at home. Optimism had been running high ever since the fall of Paris on August 25. The Wehrmacht seemed in full retreat, even on the verge of collapse. In mid-September of 1944, American patrols crossed into Germany. Allied high command now expected the war to be over by Christmas. In Grenoble, rumors bloomed that Hitler had surrendered and the United States would soon be invading Japan. Carlin requested a "V-day drawing" in advance, just in case the end came suddenly.

He also aggressively pursued new subscribers. Touting Bill's fresh outlook, he met with Roy Howard of Scripps-Howard to show him the new cartoons. He also took out a prominent advertisement in the trade journal *Editor & Publisher.* "Mauldin in France!" the ad's headline screamed. "The change from the intense misery of the Italian front has brought a new lift and sparkle to the Mauldin drawings," the copy read, "and a new feeling of buoyancy as the campaign advances."[20]

The prospect of a quick end to the war lent new urgency to Bill's book project. In late September, Ann Watkins finally closed a deal with Henry Holt and Company, which had published an Ernie Pyle collection and a book of army humor by Private Marion Hargrove. At first Bill Sloane, Holt's editor in chief, wanted a sort of illustrated memoir, chronicling Bill's early garrison career and rise through the ranks before creating the famous "G.I. Joes" of "Up Front." Introducing himself in a letter, Sloane made the almost fatal error of congratulating Bill on his growth and development since *Yank.* Marion Hargrove, on staff at *Yank,* had apparently passed along word that *Yank*'s editors had spurned Bill's work.

Bill countered, first, by setting the record straight: he had always detested *Yank*. Then he emphatically nixed any book about the "adventures of Mauldin." Rather, *Up Front* must tell the bitter truth of Americans who fought in Italy. The text and cartoons should tell the combat soldiers' story.[21]

Jean signed the contract with Holt on Bill's behalf, securing a $5,000 advance, and Bill immediately began writing. He was probably worried, as was Sloane, that the war would end before the book was even in production.

Ed Vebell recalls Bill holing up in a Grenoble hotel with an eighteen-year-old French girl for seven days, never leaving the room, not even for meals, writing all the while, taking breaks only to sleep, eat, relieve himself, and have sex. The telltale sounds of this last diversion were unmistakable to Vebell, who occupied the room below. Every few hours he would hear the desk chair scraping backward, then footsteps, murmurings, and the sound of bedsprings creaking. Then no more creaking, the feet padding back to the desk, and the chair scootched back into place.[22]

In mid-October, Bill packed away his 30,000-word manuscript and returned to Rome to finish some drawings and catch up on sleep. Reading over the draft, he found it too grim. "It seemed that I had overstated a few things," and had made the war in Italy sound worse than it was. "Sitting there in the warm room with the sun shining outside, I felt a little worried about the book."

Needing a break from the book, Bill decided to strike out once more for the Italian front, now two hundred miles north, near Bologna.

The Germans had settled in along a string of east-west mountain positions known as the Gothic Line. There the Fifth Army's offensive had flagged under a deluge of German artillery and machine-gun fire. The rains had come, too, and temperatures had fallen. General Mark Clark reported that "psychiatric breakdown" had reached alarming proportions in the Fifth Army, crippling any prospect for a continued offensive. American combat troops in Italy faced another long, cold, wet winter in the mountains, only this time, Bill remarked, "the Germans seemed to have more artillery."

Bill traveled to a battalion aid station located in a battered building under enemy observation about a thousand yards from the front. He introduced himself, saying he was looking for cartoon ideas. The medics pointed him to a chair by a small stove and invited him to play hearts and tell jokes until nightfall, when the wounded came down off the mountain. After sunset, they began to appear, a slow stream of young men with pneumonia, pulpy faces, missing limbs, black swollen feet, and gaping holes where their midsections had been. Bill attempted to assist the army surgeon, an irreverent young captain from Florida, but found, to his surprise, that he could not handle the job. He never knew why. The gore of combat was not new. At any rate, he retreated to a corner of the room, where he sat with his head between his knees trying not to vomit (see figure 43).

The following night, Bill sped his jeep down the mountain road as enemy shells exploded behind him and then went on to Rome, where he read over the draft of *Up Front* once more. Then he slipped into a warm bath and decided to send the manuscript off to Holt as it was, without any changes. Nothing in it had, in fact, been over-dramatized or made too dour.[23]


ALLIED OPTIMISM fell in the fall of 1944. The Germans had dug in behind the Siegfried Line, the Fatherland's last western wall of defense. A first Allied assault into the thick Hürtgen Forest on the Belgian-German border quickly bogged down. As in the mountains of Italy, the forest's terrain all but neutralized Allied superiority in artillery, armor, and air cover. The outnumbered Germans slowed the American advance with terrifying "treebursts," artillery fired into tightly packed treetops causing hot shell fragments and splintered timbers to explode downward onto prone American

*"Ya don't git combat pay 'cause ya don't fight."*

**FIGURE 43** Early in the war, infantry medics were often the butt of jokes. This drawing appeared in October 1944, after Bill's trip to the battalion aid station on the Gothic Line. Five months later, the War Department created the Combat Medic Badge for men working in direct support of infantry units. The badge carried a ten-dollar-a-month pay raise.

*Copyright 1944 by Bill Mauldin. Courtesy of the Mauldin Estate.*

troops. Soldiers learned not to drop onto the ground when under fire but to hug tree trunks instead.

Concurrently, the Germans counterpunched on December 16 against a weak eighty-five-mile section of the American line in Belgium and Luxembourg. A quarter million German troops smashed through the Ardennes forest south of the Hürtgen, taking the path Adolf Hitler had used for his Blitzkrieg invasion of France in 1940. The Führer hoped that history would repeat itself.

As thick clouds grounded American air forces, the Wehrmacht sped sixty miles into Allied territory, bending the broad Allied front on Germany's western edge. The "Battle of the Bulge" had begun. Heavy snow, frigid temperatures, and a lack of winter clothing recalled the Italian campaign. The Ardennes battle became the largest, deadliest battle in American history. Bill Mauldin's weary dogfaces once again seemed relevant, and the cartoonist grew itchy to join the soldiers holding the line in Belgium and Luxembourg.

Unfortunately, editor in chief Robert Neville had put him on assignment in Italy, and an odd one at that. Perhaps wanting some control over his pesky cartoonist, Neville had ordered Bill to cover a fact-finding tour of Italy by the House of Representatives' Military Affairs Committee.

Bill's first encounter with a committee member took place in a corridor of Rome's Grand Hotel. The unnamed congressman— Bill would never reveal his identity—wore only socks and an undershirt while "attempting a frontal assault on a chambermaid." The terrified girl had to "duck under and around the various folds of fat which he kept throwing in front of her." The man's triceps, Bill said, "hung down like hogs in hammocks." Bill didn't so much mind a man on the prowl for sex, but why did he have to "go about it like a slob," instead of getting it with good old American cash?

Another portly congressman proved equally outrageous a few days later while touring an evacuation hospital near Bologna. The men at the "evac" had survived initial treatment at frontline aid stations but were too unstable to be moved over rough roads to base area hospitals. Most were barely hanging on to life. Some were wrapped almost entirely in bloody bandages; others simply stared into space with mental wounds as severe as physical ones.

The congressman swaggered into the first tent trailed by a military aid, some medical staff, and a cartoonist. Strolling up to what Bill called "a torso with a great ball of red-and-white gauze for a head," the congressman demanded to know the patient's hometown. Learning that it was outside his district, the congressman continued down the rows of cots, searching among the wounded for one that was at least from his state. Finally he found a malarial patient from the right state. The congressman directed an army photographer to snap a picture with his arm around the soldier, ordered a hundred eight-by-ten glossies, and strolled back through the ward to his jeep.

Bill managed only one cartoon from the junket. The committee, he said, simply "defied caricature."

There was, on the other hand, the formidable Clare Boothe Luce, a forty-one-year-old Republican from Connecticut and the wife of media baron Henry Luce. Bill described her as "beautiful and frightening, with the fiercest eyes I had ever confronted." Fearless, tireless, smart, and curious, Luce saw more of the front lines than anyone else on the tour and kept copious notes of many talks with combat soldiers.

Bill had to endure a severe Luce interrogation about his postwar plans. Perhaps she saw in him the same ambition that had carried her to celebrity and power. Luce quickly saw that Bill had thought little of his future.

"Do you realize that you are going to be in a position to reach a lot of people?" Luce asked. "Don't you think you ought to be educated?"

Congress, she told him, had recently passed the Servicemen's Readjustment Act, commonly known as the G.I. Bill, which she had championed. Get yourself in college, she all but ordered. "Forget about being successful for a while."

"In retrospect," Bill said years later, "I think I probably should have taken her advice. At the moment, however, nothing was farther from my mind than forgetting about being successful."[24]

FINALLY, in January of 1945, Bill secured travel orders to the European theater. On an airfield in Pisa, Bill drove his jeep into the hold of a C-47 transport and settled back in his cushioned leather driver's seat for the flight to Lyons.

There he picked up a French edition of *Stars and Stripes* and discovered that the Battle of the Bulge was over. The Americans had finally pushed the Germans back to the pre-battle lines, at a cost of nearly 80,000 American casualties. Bill was supposed to be joining the American Seventh Army, but the Seventh was resting up before its assault on the Siegfried Line.

With nothing pressing, Bill headed for Paris. This, he said, "made me technically AWOL, but when you are driving your own jeep with a pocketful of trip tickets, Paris is within reach, and your original mission is blown, what can you do?"

What he could do was get arrested. MPs manning the Paris roadblock had never seen anything like Mauldin. First there was the customized jeep and the open-ended trip tickets, then there was Bill's fashion statement.

He'd dressed for a war zone, not Paris, and his getup bore no relationship to a complete uniform. On his head he wore a furry Russian-style rabbit hat unique to the 10th Mountain Division. He also wore a tank crew jacket and high-laced paratrooper jump boots. The combat fatigue pants were more common. Bill liked them for the patch pockets big enough to hold pencils and paper. And finally, in solidarity with the men of the lines, Bill's hair flowed longer than regulation length and, as always, he wore no insignia.

The MPs took him into custody without hesitation. The war in Paris, Bill decided, was a more formal affair than the one in Italy (see figure 44).

FIGURE 44  Bill and his Russian-style hat that so confounded
Paris MPs. While underappreciated at the roadblock, the hat got
him into an exclusive Paris sex club a few days later when Bill
impersonated a Red Army soldier who had been shot in the throat
during the Battle of Stalingrad.

*Prints and Photographs Division,*
*Library of Congress, LC-DIG-ppmsca-03235.*

*©Bettmann/Corbis.*

Bill did manage one concession. Instead of taking him to jail,
the MPs agreed to deliver Bill to the Paris offices of *Stars and Stripes*,
where the staff vouched for him. But if Paris had greeted Bill with
a frying pan, it also had a fire.[25]

Bill's cartoons had been running in the Paris *Stars and Stripes* for
a few months. A staff officer from de Gaulle's headquarters had
exploded over a gag batted out in Grenoble about the notorious
recklessness of French army truck drivers. The editors in Paris were
still dealing with diplomatic fallout.[26]

A steady stream of complaints had also filtered in from American brass. The European theater's quartermaster in chief, Lieutenant General John Lee, was campaigning to have Mauldin's cartoons removed from the paper.

Perhaps the most hated American general in Europe, Lee, defying Eisenhower's orders, had requisitioned the choicest hotels in Paris. His supply men lived in comfort, while combat soldiers on leave scrambled for barracks space at the Red Cross. A stickler for dress codes, Lee routinely walked the streets of Paris looking for uniform violations. On the other hand, under General Lee's command, pilfering and black marketeering in Paris reached almost Neapolitan proportions. The thousands of gallons of gasoline siphoned off each day led to a major fuel crisis for advancing American armies, inspiring a caustic Mauldin cartoon the previous September (see figure 45). Lee retaliated by threatening to cut off the paper's supply of newsprint.[27]

Every day brought a new anxiety at *Stars and Stripes*. Just as Bill reached Paris, General George S. Patton Jr., commander of the Third Army, wrote a letter repeating objections to Mauldin's grimy characters. If the editors refused to move "Up Front" out of the paper, Patton warned, he would block distribution of *Stars and Stripes* to his troops.

Though famously erratic and combustible, Patton was also a full-fledged national hero for leading the Allied counteroffensive in the Ardennes. The editors at *Stars and Stripes* immediately passed the delicate problem on to the Information and Education Division, directed in Europe by former White House aide Oscar N. Solbert.

A consummate fixer, General Solbert invited Bill to a meeting in his office. "The room reeked of good fellowship," Bill recalled.

"I hear you're having a little trouble with George," Solbert said with a smile after asking Bill about his time in Paris. "I'll be frank with you, son," he continued. "A lot of us around here are worried about the way he keeps getting himself into peculiar situations,

*"Sorry. Now we're outta charcoal, too."*

**FIGURE 45** This cartoon from September 15, 1944, satirizes the army's supply problem in France, especially the maddening fuel shortage. The contraption on the front of the jeep is vintage Mauldin, who delighted in detailed drawings of machinery. The engine resembles Pop's dual-drum apple sprayer that still sits in the junkyard on the Mauldins' Mountain Park, New Mexico, property.

publicity-wise. And this is just the sort of thing that might make a story."

The general then assured the cartoonist that most at Supreme Allied Headquarters, including Solbert himself, enjoyed Bill's cartoons and thought they were good for morale. But, he suggested, Bill might want to consider cleaning up his characters somewhat. Their appearance, he said, was affecting replacement troops who "think they've got to roll in a muddy ditch and grow whiskers before they're socially acceptable." Besides, he added, only a small portion of the army ever saw the front lines. Could Bill broaden his scope and include other characters besides combat infantrymen? Finally, playing his most reliable card, Solbert told Mauldin that a reformed Willie and Joe would do more for the "war effort" by easing Patton's unstable mind.

Solbert's "snow job" validated Bill's decision not to seek a transfer to France. But it also placed him in a familiar predicament—to sanitize or not to sanitize? Fortunately, Bill had friends in Paris who'd seen him through his troubles in Naples a year earlier. Reporter Will Lang from Time-Life and Sergeant Bill Estoff, the circulation manager at *Stars and Stripes,* now got together with Bill in an out-of-the-way bar around the corner from the *Stars and Stripes'* office. There they hatched a plot to take their cause all the way up to the Supreme Allied Commander in Europe, General Dwight D. Eisenhower.[28]

Estoff was the plan's indispensable man. Balding and heavyset, the middle-aged Estoff cut an unimpressive soldierly profile. Before being drafted, he'd been a bookie in Syracuse, New York, a history he eventually came clean about while languishing in a replacement depot in England. When the need arose for a circulation manager in the Mediterranean, the depot's officer in charge figured "bookmaker" meant "publisher" and sent Estoff to *Stars and Stripes.*

Now stationed in Paris, the streetwise Estoff put the situation succinctly to Bill.[29]

"The problem is that Patton got pissed and made a threat about you and it's all over town," he said. "He keeps sticking his foot in his mouth about politics and now it's freedom of the press that's involved. They're trying to figure out a way to cool it off before it becomes another episode, like him slapping that soldier in Sicily."

"I'm not looking for trouble with Patton," Bill said.

"That's not the point," countered Estoff. "The issue is a lot bigger than you are."

"You've got the army in a bind," he explained again a day or two later. "If they make you change your stuff, everybody will ask how come your dogfaces got creases in their pants all of a sudden. If they leave you alone, they've still got old Georgie chewing the rug and trying to push the paper around."

Estoff's solution was to approach navy captain Harry Butcher, General Eisenhower's aide and confidant who in civilian life had been vice president of CBS Radio. Estoff enjoyed ready access to Butcher through Butcher's mistress, whom Estoff had somehow met early on in Paris.

A discreet inquiry about the Mauldin affair quickly triggered a response. The Supreme Commander wished to have the dispute settled. Would Sergeant Estoff please escort Sergeant Mauldin to Butcher's office for a meeting?

Butcher greeted the little group warmly and asked Lang and Estoff outside while he spoke with Bill. The captain appeared just as friendly as General Solbert had been, but took a blunter approach. He explained the Patton situation as General Eisenhower saw it.

"We've all decided," he said flatly, "the best solution is for you to go have a talk with the general [Patton] himself."

Bill was scared, he admitted later. "I remember thinking that I had come a long way in a few years but that I had finally overplayed my hand." Clearly required to say something in reply to Butcher, Bill managed a weak promise to "think it over," while also respectfully questioning the value of a 180-mile drive to Patton's headquarters in Luxembourg just to have his ass chewed out. Then the shaken cartoonist left Butcher's office to consult further with advisers Lang and Estoff.

In the end, Lang and Estoff explained to Bill that Butcher's proposition wasn't optional, and Bill returned to Butcher's office saying, as the naval aide remarked in his diary, that "he had mustered up his courage and if I'd make the appointment, he would go to Third Army headquarters and see old Blood and Guts himself."

"Morning, General," Butcher chirped into the phone. "How's Willie?" he asked, referring to "William the Conqueror," Patton's pet bull terrier.

As the two men exchanged pleasantries, Butcher waved to Bill to pick up the extension and listen in. Coming out of the receiver was a shrill, squeaky voice Bill first ascribed to the antiquated French telephone system. As Butcher explained the reason for his call, a high-pitched voice on the other end took unmistakable form:

"If that little son of a bitch sets foot in Third Army, I'll throw his ass in jail."

Butcher was not Ike's aide for nothing. He merely shifted into the first-person-plural mode of address.

"General," he said plainly, "*we* feel around here that it might be a good thing to do."

The debate was over. Patton had to capitulate.

Before saying goodbye, Butcher casually mentioned the terms. The meeting would be private, face-to-face, man-to-man, no rank. Before the general could explode, Butcher wished him well and hung up the phone. Bill was bound for Luxembourg.[30]


BILL AND PASSENGER Will Lang approached Patton's Third Army territory on the afternoon of February 27. Pulling off the road, Bill prepared himself as instructed to meet the general. Both he and his jeep had to conform to the Third Army's strict code of appearance, Butcher warned, or the interview would go badly. Bill cleaned and standardized his jeep as much as possible, slipping a hood over his personalized license plate and, though it was cold and rainy, folding down and covering his windshield. The furry hat was gone, replaced by a helmet. He also wore a necktie, neatly creased shirt and pants, and a polished sidearm to match his regulation boots. It was like the ROTC all over again.[31]

As he entered Luxembourg there was the usual trouble with MPs, who took him down a muddy road to the provost marshal. Clearly not impressed with Bill's celebrity, the officer tried to make sense of Bill's papers. It appeared that Sergeant Mauldin, though from the Mediterranean theater, was now on detached duty with the Seventh Army in Alsace, that he'd stolen a jeep, gone AWOL in Paris, and was now in Luxembourg for some imagined meeting with the Third Army commander.

Thinking Bill deranged, the provost marshal ordered the MP to treat the "looney bastard" gently and humored Bill by calling Patton's public relations officer, Major James T. Quirk, who confirmed Bill's mission. The provost coolly apologized for making the sergeant late.

"Oh, that's all right," the equally nonchalant cartoonist responded, "the appointment was pretty well open, depending on when I got there."

Bill drove slowly to the ducal palace Patton had requisitioned for his headquarters. Upon entering, Bill got looked over by "a small task force of vitamin-packed MPs with mirror-toed shoes and simonized headgear," then was passed to Major Quirk and General Hap Gay, Patton's chief of staff, who subjected the guest to more scrutiny. "Undoubtedly Sgt. Mauldin is a great cartoonist," Gay remarked in his diary, "and much to the surprise of the Author, he is merely a boy." Quirk led Bill upstairs and down a corridor to the gilded throne room that served as George Patton's office.[32]

Down what seemed like a football field's worth of baroque carpeting sat the general behind his desk, "big as life," Bill recalled, "even at that distance":

His hair was silver, his face was pink, his collar and shoulders glittered with more stars than I could count, his fingers sparkled with rings, and an incredible mass of ribbons started around desk-top level and spread upward in a flood over his chest to the very top of his shoulder, as if preparing to march down his back, too. His face was rugged, with an odd, strangely shapeless outline; his eyes were pale, almost colorless, with a choleric bulge. His small, compressed mouth was sharply downturned at the corners, with a lower lip which suggested a pouting child as much as a no-nonsense martinet. It was a welcome, rather human touch. Beside him, lying in a big chair, was Willie, the bull terrier. If ever a dog was suited to master this one was. Willie had his beloved boss's expression and lacked only the ribbons and stars. I stood in that door staring into the four meanest eyes I had ever seen.

Then that high squeaky voice from Butcher's office broke the spell.

"Come in, Major," the general said in his soft upper-class south-ern accent.

Bill marched with his escort across the carpet, came to a swift halt, and flashed his smartest salute since basic training.

"Hello, Sergeant," said Patton, grinning weakly ("an impressive muscular feat," Bill noted, "considering the distance the corners of his mouth had to travel").

In defiance of the deal struck with Butcher, Patton told Quirk to stay and got down to business.

"Now then, Sergeant," he barked, "about those pictures you draw of those god-awful things you call soldiers. . . . You make them look like goddamn bums. No respect for the army, their officers, or them-selves. . . . What are you trying to do, incite a goddamn mutiny?"

If Bill had a reply in mind, he never got to use it. Like Pop, Patton brooked no interruptions while on an oratorical roll:

"The Bolsheviks made their officers dress like soldiers, eat with soldiers, no saluting, everybody calling everybody Comrade—and where did it get 'em? While they ran an army like that they couldn't fight their way out of a piss-soaked paper bag. Now they've learned their lesson. They put uniforms back on their officers. Some men are born to lead and don't need those little metal dinguses on their shoulders. Hell, I could command troops in a G-string. But in wartime, you're bound to get some officers who don't know how to act without being dressed for it. The Russians learned you had to have rank and if some comrade looks cross-eyed at a superior today he gets his teeth kicked in. . . . How long do you think you'd last drawing those pictures in the Russian army?"

Another rhetorical question, mere prelude to a lecture-cum-diatribe about the need for military discipline, larded with examples reaching back to antiquity.

Though clearly an object of scorn, Bill sat enthralled, actually feeling his old ROTC esprit, long dormant, awaken and rise like an ember fanned into flame. It was, Bill said, "as if I were hearing Michelangelo on painting."

Spellbound, Bill absently reached out with his drawing hand to pet Willie, then quickly pulled it back as the bull terrier poised to strike. Had he not done so, Bill mused years later, Willie "would have put me out of business, accomplishing in one snap what his master was trying to do the hard way."

Finally, winding down, Patton opened a desk drawer and pulled out a small stack of clippings from *Stars and Stripes*.

"I'm going to show you what I consider some prime goddamn examples of what I mean by creating disrespect."

On top of the stack sat a Mauldin cartoon drawn in Grenoble of Willie and Joe pelting their commander from behind with ripe fruit during a parade through a liberated French village (see figure 46). Another sample, which the general held up "by the tips of his thumb and forefinger as if it were contaminated," depicted soldiers lined up outside a theater before a USO show. Around the corner at the stage door stand neatly dressed officers waiting for the dancing girls to emerge (see figure 47).

FIGURES 46 AND 47 Two cartoons General Patton pulled from his desk drawer while meeting with Bill on February 27, 1945.

*Copyright 1944 (left) and 1945 (below)
by Bill Mauldin.
Courtesy of the Mauldin Estate.*

*"My, sir—what an
enthusiastic welcome!"*

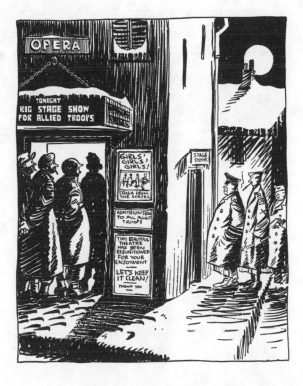

"Where are the words under this one?" roared Patton. "Somebody cut off the goddamn words!"

"Sir, there wasn't any caption under that one," Bill replied, starting at the sound of his own voice.

Bill tried to explain what the drawing meant—that enlisted men can only look at the girls, but officers get to take them out.

"You think the soldiers ought to get laid instead of the officers, don't you?" challenged Patton, managing a slight grin.

Then, in what was, for Patton, an astonishingly gracious move, the general sat back in his chair, and gave Bill the floor to answer a single question:

"Why did you draw this picture if it wasn't to create disrespect for officers?"

Bill responded with the "letting-off steam" theory of morale that had justified his career for four and a half years. Combat soldiers, he explained, stewed constantly about getting "the short end of the stick in everything, including women." They might not blame the women for the situation . . . or the officers, Bill hastened to add. But the inequity planted a powerful sense of injustice.

"Jesus Christ, Major, does this make any sense to you?" a bewildered Patton asked his public relations officer. Then he allowed Bill to continue.

Bill concluded his short speech by claiming that when the aggrieved soldiers open *Stars and Stripes* and see a cartoon that expresses their gripes, they feel validated and are thus less likely to cause problems within the ranks.

"I don't know where you got those stripes on your arm," Patton stated as if Bill had never spoken, "but you'd put 'em to a lot better use getting out and teaching respect to soldiers instead of encouraging them to bitch and beef and gripe and run around with beards on their faces and holes in their elbows. Now I've just got one last thing to say to you: You can't run an army like a mob."

"Sir, I never thought you could—" Bill started to reply. But the general just looked at his watch. The meeting was over.

Bill rose, snapped another sharp salute, and marched toward the door. Behind him, he heard Willie jump up and reclaim the chair.[33]

Back on the road, Bill told the story to Will Lang, who asked Harry Butcher's permission to publish an account of the meeting. Butcher approved the story so long as Lang "didn't embellish it with too much color." Ten days later, *Time* magazine ran a 165-word article titled "G.I. Mauldin v. G. Patton."

"After 45 minutes with Old Blood & Guts," the article said, "Young Gags & Grime emerged grinning, reporting last week: 'I came out with all my hide on. We parted good friends, but I don't think we changed each other's opinions.' Mauldin G.I.s remained unwashed, unsquelched."

Patton of course went nuts when Butcher read the article over the phone, threatening once again to throw Mauldin in jail if he ever ventured into the Third Army area.

But Eisenhower had had enough. Officers, Ike stated plainly in a letter sent throughout the European theater, are "not to interfere" in "such things as Mauldin's cartoons, the 'B' Bag," and other controversial materials published in the army newspaper.

"It looks to me," wrote Butcher in his diary, "as if General Patton . . . has lost the battle of Mauldin."[34]

BILL WENT BACK to Italy in mid-March on the first leg of what turned into a kind of personal victory tour. Awaiting him in Rome was a short stack of mail from Ann Watkins. His syndication orders were up sharply, his advance book sales were surging toward 100,000, and the Book-of-the-Month Club had made *Up Front* a selection for July. Bill's wife Jean was collecting so much money—almost $100,000 by April—that neither she nor Bill knew what to do with it. Bill asked Watkins for advice on investing. He also sheepishly requested a loan. With all the money going to Jean, Bill needed $300 to buy black-market cigarettes and pay off a poker debt to Bill Estoff, who had taken Bill's prized German officer's watch as collateral.[35]

Bill's final trip to the front in mid-April was even more gratifying. After over eighteen months grinding up the rugged boot of Italy, the Allies had breached the Axis' last major defensive line. By April 20, Bill was roaring in high gear across the Po Valley south of Milan, chasing the advancing Fifth Army. He motored into Milan one day after Italian partisans had strung up Benito Mussolini and six Fascist followers at an Esso gas station. Racing through the city's deserted streets, he almost ran over a German paratrooper holding a burp gun outside the Regina Hotel. Bill threw his jeep into reverse, hopped out, and ducked into a nearby bar, where he found Donald Downes, an intelligence officer from the Office of Strategic Services, the forerunner of the CIA. Over several drinks, Downes explained that the trooper belonged to one of the unsurrendered Axis contingents left in Italy, an SS battalion holed up in the hotel waiting for the Americans. They didn't want to surrender to the fanatically anti-Nazi local partisans.

"Let's both go," Downes said to Bill, and the two men, "full of fermented courage," strode up to the barricaded hotel. An SS officer welcomed them inside, where another American intelligence officer was already negotiating the surrender. As the SS battalion commander prepared to address his men in the lobby, a German captain approached Bill with a French blonde on one side and a German shepherd guard dog on the other.

"I realize that the girl must go with me to prison camp and I must leave the dog," the Nazi said with tears in his eyes, "but I wish it were the other way around. . . . Will you try to find a home for her? The partisans will shoot her if she is turned loose."

Bill walked out of the Regina Hotel with Anna the dog just as tanks from the American 1st Armored Division roared up the street to make Milan's liberation official. Bill would spend the next month touring balmy northern Italy with the windshield down and Anna in the passenger's seat.[36]

ON MAY 9, 1945, one day after Allied victory in Europe, Bill opened the *Stars and Stripes* and read that he'd been awarded the Pulitzer Prize "for distinguished service as a cartoonist" (see figure 48). "I wasn't even sure exactly what a Pulitzer Prize was," he recalled, "except that it had something to do with journalism and literature and was prestigious."

Bill quickly learned the value of a Pulitzer, as his syndication doubled overnight to over two hundred papers reaching perhaps 40 million readers. *Time* magazine requested a full-color portrait of Willie to commemorate the end of the European war and accompany a cover story on the cartoonist. Publication of *Up Front* had to be delayed until June because Henry Holt and Company couldn't find enough rationed paper to cover advance orders. Hollywood studios began bidding for the movie rights, NBC and CBS for the radio rights, and publishers for the reprint rights. Virtually every major national magazine wanted something—an article, an excerpt, a drawing, a photograph, *anything*—so long as it was Mauldin.

Clearly playing catch-up, the Allied high command in Italy hustled out an award of its own, the Legion of Merit, which was bestowed in a ceremony at Allied headquarters in early June.[37]

Like the desert turtles he'd so admired as a child in rural Arizona, Bill instinctively withdrew as the accolades piled up around him. It was almost as if he needed to shrink the terrain he'd so avidly pursued. Instead of satisfaction, he often felt bitterness toward the vile war that had catapulted him to fame.

The feeling went beyond survivor's guilt. His self-censored cartoons had degraded the traumas of combat, making its horrors palatable for mass consumption and, at worst, reducing the men of the front to a sort of patriotic commodity. Bill resented especially his role in coining the name "G.I. Joe," which he derided as "Tin Pan Alley's conception of every soldier" and "an advertiser's bread and butter." Almost as penance, he planned to sacrifice Willie, Joe,

**Fresh, spirited American troops, flushed with victory, are bringing in thousands of hungry, ragged, battle-weary prisoners.** *(news item)*

FIGURE 48　First published on October 13, 1944, this cartoon made the twenty-three-year-old Bill Mauldin the youngest Pulitzer Prize winner in history. Both he and his editors at *Stars and Stripes* were astonished by the selection, which did not seem to them particularly noteworthy.

or both men on the last day of the war. He would draw a panel of a blasted foxhole with their gear scattered about, he thought.

"Don't do it," said Robert Neville when he heard of the idea, "we won't print it."

Bill backed down and reluctantly decided to take his cartoon dogfaces home with him.[38]

On Memorial Day, 1945, Bill attended a ceremony at the American cemetery in Nettuno, just east of Anzio. He mused over the real Willies and real Joes buried there among the twenty thousand neatly arranged white crosses. "Normally," Bill said, "I am allergic to Veterans Days and Armistice Days and the like."[39]

This time, however, General Lucian Truscott was scheduled to speak. The gravelly voiced commander had supported Bill in his battle with General Arthur Wilson, taken over the dispirited VI Corps at Anzio, and moved on to head the Fifth Army in Italy. Bill admired him tremendously. "He could have eaten a ham like Patton for breakfast any morning and picked his teeth with the man's pearl-handled pistols," he said.[40]

Bill had long derided as "brass" those like Patton who used their positions of power to aggrandize themselves. Indeed, Mauldin became something of an expert on brass, defining it not as rank or office, "but a state of mind." "Brass," he wrote several years after the war, "is an alloy which knows it is not gold, and mistakenly tries to hide this fact by polishing itself to a high shine which removes it even farther from the true, mellow, dull, twenty-four-carat glow."[41]

By this definition, Lucian Truscott's Memorial Day performance was pure gold. Before a crowd of army luminaries and VIPs from the States, including several U.S. senators, General Truscott climbed onto the speaker's platform and turned his back on the audience; his address, he informed the crowd, was for those lying beneath the endless rows of graves in the sandy soil of the Anzio beachhead. "It was the most moving gesture I ever saw," said Bill.

The general's comments were brief and poignant. He apologized to the men arrayed before him for sending them to their deaths. It was his fault, he said, and the fault of all those commanders who order men into battle. He had made mistakes, the general admitted, and those errors had cost lives. He did not expect to be forgiven. Then, as if speaking for Bill, Truscott rejected the usual platitudes about the honor and greatness of dying for one's country. "Truscott said he would not speak about the glorious dead," Bill recalled, "because he didn't see much glory in getting killed in your late teens or early twenties. He promised that in the future if he ran into anybody, especially old men, who thought death in battle was glorious, he would straighten them out. He said he thought that was the least he could do."[42]

Ten days later, Bill left Italy to return to the States. This war was over, but another one, of a different kind, lay not far ahead.

# Chapter Six

# Coming Home

*(June 1945 — 1949)*

IN EARLY JUNE OF 1945, an exhausted and edgy Bill Mauldin boarded a C-54 transport in Casablanca and headed home after two years of war. While millions of other soldiers sweated it out in overseas replacement depots or, if they were lucky, sailed slowly back across the Atlantic, Bill flew with A-1 air priority aboard the premier four-engine airliner of the day, the same kind Franklin Roosevelt had adopted as the first Presidential aircraft (see figure 49). The honor was so rare that the three-stripe cartoonist was given the temporary rank of major general to expedite clearance and fend off any punctilious clerk who might boot him off during a stopover.

In Casablanca, Bill learned he'd been designated an official army VIP, which entitled him to lay over in a seaside villa reserved for his use, complete with orderly. Bill was tempted—perhaps he'd be assigned a valet who outranked him. At the same time, he was desperate to get home, back to Jean, Bruce, and a world without war and military regimentation.

*"I don't remember no delays gittin' us overseas."*

**FIGURE 49** On May 13, 1945, Bill shaved Willie and Joe and retitled his feature "Sweatin' It Out." When news spread of Bill's A-1 air priority, some foot soldiers called on Bill to abandon the new title because he was not, in fact, "sweating it out" with the men. Bill received one letter from a lieutenant preparing for the invasion of Japan. "If your Willie and Joe do not go [to the Pacific]," the officer said, "then they are not the Army's Willie and Joe."

He lay low on the flight, passing time playing hearts and stud poker with a few others from the lower ranks. As the airplane traced a great arc toward Nova Scotia, Bill reflected on the distance he'd traveled since shipping overseas with the 45th Division. Once an obscure technical sergeant grateful for having escaped the infantry, he was returning the most famous enlisted man in the United States Army.[1]

The prospect filled him with fear and wonder. "Even a little kid knows what the celebrity treatment is in America," Bill said later, "and I had a pretty good idea of what was coming in the next few months." Bill had experienced a taste of fame in Italy and enjoyed it. But the novelty had long since worn off, even become a burden. "I am not being a modest little boy when I say I want to go home and stay there, without any bother," he wrote Ann Watkins just before leaving Naples.[2]

But where, for Bill Mauldin, *was* home? Press reports listed it variously as Mountain Park, New Mexico; Phoenix, Arizona; Abilene, Texas; Lawton, Oklahoma; and various locations in California. Jean and Bruce, the son he'd never met, lived in Los Angeles, a city he'd never seen. Bill dreamed of doing "a fast disappearing act" to a quaint town in New England or upstate New York, away from friends, family, and publicity agents. He wanted to "get the hell out before the ballyhoo begins." He yearned to resettle into a quiet, comfortable life with his wife and child, as if the war had never happened. "But I'm in a spot now," he confided to Watkins, "where I can't think of many of my own preferences."[3]

Bill's reverie ended at La Guardia Field in New York. When the C-54 taxied to a stop, an army staff car approached, chauffeured by a neatly dressed WAC. A captain emerged and climbed aboard to escort his assigned VIP to the hangar several hundred yards away. A half dozen high-ranking officers on board, decked out in dress uniforms and gaudy decorations, stepped forward to accept the escort. The captain looked over their heads.

"*SERGEANT* WILLIAM MAULDIN!" he called to the back, placing special emphasis on Bill's rank.

Snaking his way up the aisle dragging his barracks bag, he met the captain, looked down onto the rain-swept tarmac, and braced himself.[4]

A phalanx of reporters greeted him in the hangar. "Are you glad to be home?" "How bad was the fighting?" "Will you go to the Pacific?" Mostly they wanted war stories. Bill stopped long enough to snap a quick answer.

"If you really want to find out about the war," he said, "talk to a real infantryman, not to characters like me."[5]

The next day, Bill faced even more questioning at a well-scripted press conference in lower Manhattan arranged by Army Ground Forces Public Relations (AGFPR). The red carpet had been engineered by AGFPR in order to deliver him back home in time for the publication of *Up Front* on June 15, Infantry Day. Bill was to be featured in a full schedule of celebration and ceremony, capped by a parade through Manhattan. It was all part of AGFPR's enduring campaign to convince the public that the air forces operated in support of ground troops, rather than the other way around.

Before his press conference, a public relations officer took Bill aside for a briefing.

"Lay off the subject of food," he ordered, instructing Bill to offer no complaints about army rations. Other taboo subjects: clothing, equipment, weapons, discipline, and, of course, morale.

Bill intended to make no waves. Despite his 131 "solid gold" demobilization points—forty-six more than were needed to secure a discharge—Bill knew he could be declared "essential to the war effort" and kept in uniform until the war against Japan ended. "If the army was going to treat me like such a prize package," he reasoned, "maybe it was going to be reluctant to turn the package loose."[6]

Bill had sensed trouble early on. Even before he left Italy, the army had begun investigating his use of military courier bags to deliver drawings to United Features Syndicate in New York. Perhaps the investigation, which soon involved the Treasury

Department as well, was part of a scheme to pressure him into re-upping.

"I'm more worried about the army than anything else," he told Ann Watkins. "The same army, which is very excited about how I sent my drawings back, is also full of characters with twenty-dollar collar insignia and ten-cent brains, who will possibly have ideas about selling propaganda or war bonds."

In a worst-case scenario, the army would ship him off to the Pacific, where he'd be put to work "doing the same old drawings, using palm trees instead of mountains for background." Bill dreaded the thought of another front. Ernie Pyle's death in April by a sniper's bullet on Okinawa was especially chilling. "One war is enough for anybody," he told Watkins. At the same time, he couldn't be glib about a role in the Pacific when many survivors of the Hürtgen, the Bulge, and the Gothic Line were soon to ship out to fight again.[7]

So when the question came up, Bill responded simply that he would go if asked.[8]

Bill did manage one cutting remark during the course of his grilling by New York's press corps. When asked, "what should be done for the veteran?" Bill suggested that returning soldiers be hired as consultants to advertising firms and national magazines catering to the patriotic public. Then the American people would get an accurate view of the war.[9]

After Bill's press conference, a sympathetic officer, *New Yorker* writer E. J. Kahn, quietly arranged for him to be discharged at Fort Dix in New Jersey, where Bill might escape the crush of publicity and anybody interested in recruiting him for further duty (see figure 50).

After a final physical—the doctor raised an eyebrow over the invisible wound that had won him his Purple Heart—civilian Bill Mauldin collected his $300 mustering-out pay and his discharge papers. It was one of the happiest moments of his life. "You're a mister, and you love the world," he said.[10]

**FIGURE 50** Bill at Fort Dix—paratrooper jump boots and all—on June 22, two days before his discharge. A reporter from the left-wing newspaper *PM* managed to infiltrate the separation center for an interview. Fearing controversy, Bill kept a reasonably tight lip. *PM* ran its full-length profile, this photo included, after Bill was safely returned to civilian life.

*Up Front* climbed rapidly to the top of the *New York Times* nonfiction bestseller list and stayed there for the next nineteen weeks. Its immense popularity baffled Bill. He had intended *Up Front* to disturb and even offend home-front readers. What he had to say about combat soldiers surely ran counter to popular perceptions of the war.

Unfortunately, much of Bill's shocking content had been removed by the War Department before publication. Field censors had passed the text almost intact, but "the fancy boys with razors and rank" in Washington, D.C., cut out the book's more trenchant criticisms of the army and eliminated most of Bill's account of his troubles in Naples. No naming of offending officers, including Arthur Wilson; no details of base section policies that had landed so many combat soldiers in jail. "I am a little sick to me stummick about what those monkeys in the Pentagon did to the book," Bill told Ann Watkins when he saw the changes. "They fairly took the teeth out, and I am going to fairly howl about it if the opportunity comes up." The 30,000-word text, he lamented, "now looks like a junior Pyle with a hangover."[11]

Still, Bill gives readers enough to make their own judgments, offering a kind of ethnography of the combat soldier, written by a participant-observer:

> Dig a hole in your backyard while it is raining. Sit in the hole until the water climbs up around your ankles. Pour cold mud down your shirt collar. Sit there for forty-eight hours, and, so there is no danger of your dozing off, imagine that a guy is sneaking around waiting for a chance to club you on the head or set your house on fire.
>
> Get out of the hole, fill a suitcase full of rocks, pick it up, put a shotgun in your other hand, and walk on the muddiest road you

can find. Fall flat on your face every few minutes as you imagine big meteors streaking down to sock you.

After ten or twelve miles (remember—you are still carrying the shotgun and suitcase) start sneaking through the wet brush. Imagine that somebody has booby-trapped your route with rattle-snakes which will bite you if you step on them. Give some friend a rifle and have him blast in your direction once in a while.

Snoop around until you find a bull. Try to figure out a way to sneak around him without letting him see you. When he does see you, run like hell all the way back to your hole in the back yard, drop the suitcase and shotgun, and get in.

If you repeat this performance every three days for several months, you may begin to understand why an infantryman some-times gets out of breath. But you still won't understand how he feels when things get tough.[12]

Such earthy descriptions, coupled with the 162 cartoons, did indeed offend some reviewers. Sterling North of the *New York Post* called *Up Front* "a travesty on humanity and the GI in particular." John Senior of *The Nation* concurred. "The cartoons are not funny, and the text is characteristically illiterate," judged Senior. "He has bad taste too," he added for good measure.[13]

Bill took perverse delight in such criticism. Rare as it was, it proved he had not exploited men in combat for humor or liter-ary inspiration. The praise, in many ways, was harder to handle, and it came down in sheets. Most influential was *New York Times* book reviewer Charles Poore. Formerly an army intelligence and civil affairs officer in Sicily, Naples, and elsewhere, Poore saw the genius in Bill's work. "Mauldin has told more people what the sol-dier really thinks about war than all our living poets," Poore wrote. Indeed, Poore habitually judged any subsequent war book against *Up Front* as the standard of measure. A few years later, he would declare Bill the most important artist of his age, one whose words and pictures had shaped the nation's wartime consciousness.[14]

In New York City, Bill reunited with Jean, who had flown from Los Angeles without Bruce. Several weeks earlier, the twenty-two-month-old toddler had fallen from a second-story window to a concrete porch and fractured his skull. He was not well enough to travel.

Ecstasy and anxiety must have overwhelmed the lovers after a two-year separation. The sudden flush of wealth and publicity intensified and complicated the reunion. Bill had sold the movie rights to *Up Front* to International Pictures for $50,000 plus ten percent of the gross, the biggest book deal ever made in Hollywood and one sure to net a quarter million dollars, plus another $50,000 if Bill acted in the movie.[15]

*Up Front,* meanwhile, was selling so fast that its publishers couldn't meet demand. Almost a million copies would be sold over the next six months. Offers from magazines, movie studios, radio networks, newspaper syndicates, lecture bureaus, and advertising firms were pouring into Ann Watkins' Park Avenue office. The agent had jammed Jean and Bill's schedule with lunches, dinners, parties, and business meetings so, she said, the couple could "meet the people who are going to make you rich."[16]

The twenty-two-year-old Mrs. Mauldin had just taken her first airplane flight. Now, she spent an afternoon with Bill sipping tea at Eleanor Roosevelt's Manhattan apartment, a meeting requested by the first lady, who called it "a great thrill." "Sgt. Mauldin looks so young and is so natural it made me feel as though I were talking with one of my own sons. How much we owe these young people—not only the men who fought the war, but the girls who stayed at home and had the babies and took care of them and kept their men's spirits up overseas, and who meet them now with love and joy shining in their eyes. . . . Sgt. Mauldin tells me he will go on with his work in civilian life, and I shall watch with interest his development."[17]

In truth, Bill had other plans. He needed a break from cartooning, he told George Carlin. He wanted to cancel his contract with United Features, or at least be given a sabbatical while he readjusted to his new life.

Carlin sat in silence behind his desk as Bill made his case. He owed his success, Bill said, not to some special talent easily transferred to the home front, but from an intimate knowledge of combat and a public hunger for compelling images of war. Since the war was over—his war at least—Bill had nothing special to offer. "All I know—grown up—" he'd told journalist Fred Painton back in Italy, "is Army life." He was a novice to the world of wives and babies, jobs and bank accounts, Republicans and Democrats, bosses and price controls. How could he pretend to understand the lives of Willies and Joes as they struggled to pick up the pieces?[18]

Bill's plea had little impact on the savvy Carlin. After offering warm words of encouragement, Carlin reminded Bill of how much money his feature earned. United Features was not about to forfeit that income over some youthful insecurities. He looked forward to seeing Bill's cartoon four days a week over the next two years and ten months when his contract ran out.

While overseas, Bill had sometimes imagined civilian life as a state of perfect freedom. Now, it seemed, he had traded one taskmaster for another.

BILL AND JEAN reached their rented Los Angeles home in the wee hours of June 26, accompanied by a *Life* magazine photographer. Ann Watkins had arranged for *Life* to capture Bill's first moments with his son Bruce. She considered the story almost as dramatic as his overseas adventures, one that might lead to another book, or at least an article in *Ladies' Home Journal*.

The *Life* photo spread told an ancient, comforting story with a modern American twist: the citizen-soldier, who had put down his plow to pick up a weapon, returns home to live a productive

**FIGURE 51** The Newspaper Enterprise Association syndicate sent a photographer to snap this picture of Bill having breakfast in bed his first morning home while puffing on a Bavarian pipe. Agent Ann Watkins thought it would make a fine magazine story. Mauldin declined.

*Prints and Photographs Division,*
*Library of Congress, LC-DIG-ppmsca-03237.*

*© Bettmann/Corbis.*

and peaceful life. But whereas Cincinnatus of the Roman Republic had been a stern patriarch in total command of his household, Bill Mauldin, like so many returning veterans, had to be taught all about domestic behavior by his wife. The photos depict young father, still in uniform, reaching out to wide-eyed toddler who looks back at a face seen only in pictures. A bemused Bill struggles with diapers, buttons, and the baby himself while Jean smiles patiently behind, ready to bail him out (see figure 51).[19]

For the Mauldins and millions of other families, postwar

reconversion was expected to be like "Bringing Up Daddy" and other stories about taming men who for too long had known only the rough camaraderie of barracks and bivouac. The nation was hunkering down to a new era of unbridled domesticity, and the Mauldins were on the front lines.

Not surprisingly, Bill's early postwar cartoons reflected domestic rubs, a feeling of being held captive. Bill had always identified more with the bachelor Joe than the older married Willie. Indeed, when Joe finally got a shave, he looked a lot like Bill.

By July, however, Joe had faded from prominence, replaced by the jaded Willie, who went from being a grizzled GI, alienated by war, to a clean-shaven family man, struggling to retain autonomy and independence (see figure 52).

Even casual readers of "Willie and Joe" inferred that trouble was brewing in the Mauldin household. One cartoon from August depicted Willie sprawled on the floor with a picture frame smashed over his head. His wife towers menacingly over him. "Come in, Joe," Willie says to his buddy, ". . . I'm bein' rehabilitated."[20]

Bill explained to Ann Watkins that he was still "getting adjusted to a gal who has as many ideas about things as I do—and most of them different." He had idealized Jeanie while overseas. "I have discovered," he told his agent, "that two people who have been living alone and apart for two years, doing pretty much as they damn please, have a hard time getting together." The couple fought constantly.[21]

Bill's first summer back home held other disillusionments. "Somehow a guy expects everything to be just like he left it," Bill said, "his bachelor friends still unmarried, his family no older, the malts just as thick, and the cars just as shiny." But three and a half years of war had frayed the home front. Most available labor and material had gone into war production. Everything needed repair. Peeling paint, pothole-filled streets, broken-down appliances, and tired, shabby clothes were the norm. Luxuries were scarce, and everyday goods expensive. Bill stood in line for hours at his local rationing boards, seeking permission to buy tires, a refrigerator, gasoline.[22]

"How's it feel to be a free man, Willie?"

FIGURE 52 At the time he made this drawing, published on August 8, 1945, Bill shared a common fear among returning vets: getting trapped in family breadwinning routines.

*Prints and Photographs Division,*
*Library of Congress, LC-DIG-ppmsca-03241.*

*Copyright 1945 by Bill Mauldin.*
*Courtesy of the Mauldin Estate.*

Housing was in short supply. The Mauldins counted themselves lucky to pay top dollar for a drab five-room bungalow in run-down East Los Angeles. The house's owner barred Bill and Jean from drinking, smoking, cooking aromatic meals, and, incredibly, having sick friends over to visit. After a month of searching, the couple finally bought a place of their own in upscale Westwood, near Beverly Hills.

The automobile market was even tighter. No new cars had been manufactured since 1942. Flush with cash and eager to buy the biggest, brightest sedan he could find, Bill paid $2,500 for a DeSoto with a rigged odometer, patched tires, worn engine, and a bad paint job covering the word TAXI on the sides. The DeSoto channeled Bill's frustrations, and he devoted much of the summer to getting it to run (see figure 53).[23]

Even more insufferable were the bullying servicemen Bill encountered everywhere he went. Many had never left the States, and yet they boasted of combat heroics in bars, jumped to the front of lines in stores, and harassed all those, like Bill, they suspected of "dodging the draft." Bill learned that if he wanted to avoid a fight, he'd better display his discharge pin prominently when leaving the house.[24]

That summer of 1945, Bill found reasons to go out alone as his relationship with Jean deteriorated. Jean seemed cold and distant, and at times voiced suspicions that her husband had been unfaithful while overseas. While Jean snapped about the "European bitches," Bill harbored his own doubts about Jean. In a cartoon from August 23, Willie wakes up next to his wife, whose brow is furrowed in anger. "Don't get so huffy," Willie says, "you talked in YOUR sleep, too. . . ."[25]

Press reports circulated that the marriage was on the rocks. "It's just because we have been apart for so long," he told a reporter in September. "Besides, we never really lived a family life. It's new and kinda tough. But we'll work it out."[26]

They did not work it out. The breaking point came on October 1.

*"Of course, the steering wheel costs $750, but we
knock off fifty bucks for ex-soldiers. . . ."*

FIGURE 53 High prices and poor quality vexed Bill, as did scofflaws
who evaded Office of Price Administration (OPA) regulations.
Bill supported price controls, even illustrating an OPA pamphlet
for returning vets. In 1946, he sold a Pontiac convertible for the
OPA price of $2,000, though he could easily have gotten almost
double for it.

In an unpublished story based on his homecoming, Bill recounts Jean's furtive behavior, the whispered phone calls and mysterious appointments. He also describes meeting a friend of Jean's named Alex who lived nearby and played so familiarly with the toddler Bruce. In the story, "the Kid," as Bill calls himself, catches his wife and Alex having sex in the front seat of the family DeSoto while Bruce sleeps in the back. "A great black cloud seemed to come over him, and to envelop him, and to hold him," the manuscript reads. Instead of lashing out, the Kid lifts the baby out of the car and walks away. "He had seen a world of hurt, and he was hurt, and perhaps he couldn't stand seeing any more hurting."[27]

In real life, a private investigator had made the fateful discovery, and the "correspondent" named in the divorce suit filed three weeks later was Elmer Gaines, a friend of Jean's who had not gone to war. When Bill learned that the relationship had been a lengthy one, he washed his hands of Jean and left for good. In decades to come, Jean, a victim of the era's sexual double standard, would never lose hope for an eventual reconciliation. Two marriages and over a half century later, her persistence would finally pay off.[28]

TENSIONS WITH JEAN, guilt over the war, and the distractions of celebrity stymied Bill's work in the summer of 1945. In Italy, such doldrums had lifted with trips to the front.

To find similar wellsprings at home, Bill went slumming. He hung around veteran centers and employment agencies, and even took a job in a shipyard days before Japan's surrender. The end of the war cost him the job and almost put the yard out of business. In a final desperate search for material, he took to haunting the bars of Los Angeles's skid row.[29]

Such expeditions yielded little but the chance to feed his rising alcohol intake. Under deadline pressure, he increasingly resorted to simple gags. In one early September cartoon, for example, an emasculated Willie admonishes Joe to wear his rubbers or "you'll catch yer death o' cold." "It was 'Willie and Joe' meets 'Family Circus,'" as Bill's son Nat refers to this work. Newspaper editors hardly noticed the slump. They'd bought "Willie and Joe" as entertainment, and most carried it on the comics page next to "Blondie" and "Li'l Abner." Several editors even congratulated Bill on keeping up his "entertaining wartime standards."

Bill, however, felt his craft slipping away. The postwar work, he said, was "atrocious stuff . . . half-baked in content and sloppily drawn. . . . It wouldn't have qualified for space in a mimeographed high school paper." *Time* magazine expressed faith that Bill Mauldin would once again show himself to be "something better than a gag man." Others speculated that the cartoonist was a "war baby," "used up by one great experience."

"You remind me of a kid who has fallen into a cookie jar, and can't eat the cookies," a frustrated Ann Watkins told Bill. "You have tremendous circulation for your cartoons but you don't know what to draw. You could sell an article to any magazine, but you don't know what to write. You are successful, but you can't relax and get used to living high, because it won't last and you don't want to let yourself in for too many disillusionments."[30]

The criticism coupled with the death of his marriage at last roused Bill from his torpor. He set out to prove that he *was* more than a flash-in-the-pan gag artist. He would transform his feature into a soapbox, and he would do it in New York. Back East, suddenly Bill was everywhere, accepting awards, giving interviews, speaking on national radio, and lending his name to dozens of committees and organizations.

Somehow, whether from his bitterness over Jean, the syndicate, the army, and the huge cost of the Allies' victory, his anger spilled out in a great wave, exposing "an honest angry core." He spoke out for public housing and price controls, for labor unions and a living wage, for a strong United Nations and a strategic alliance with the Soviet Union. He denounced racial segregation and poll taxes, the conservative control of the media, and the belligerent nationalism which, he believed, would only lead to another world war. But most of all, in cartoons and public pronouncements, Bill attacked the purveyors of a malignant anti-Communism—the new Red Scare—which threatened progressive social reform and the very civil liberties men had fought for.[31]

Bill's sudden radicalism gave him high visibility along the "cultural front," a broad collection of left-leaning artists, writers, and intellectuals who came together in the 1930s and early 1940s. Forged during the Great Depression by Communists, liberal New Dealers, and everyone in between, the cultural front was an unsteady but powerful force for change. During most of this period, the Communist Party in America eschewed narrow revolutionary dogma and embraced a "popular front against fascism." It cooperated openly with any antifascist cause, as well as supporters of labor, antipoverty, and civil rights. In 1945, the party was alone in disavowing racism. Communists were also prominent in the Congress of Industrial Organizations (CIO), which recruited millions of new union members concentrated in the steel, auto, rubber, and electrical industries.

Only a small fraction of those on the left actually became members of the Communist Party. Some, like Bill, distrusted Communists even while joining them in common cause. "Some of my best friends have been communists," he joked years later. "I don't mind them. I just think they're dumb."[32]

Mainly Bill Mauldin stuck to speaking for the returning veteran. Captain Ronald Reagan of the Army Air Corps Motion Picture Unit asked Bill to join the board of the American Veterans Committee (AVC). The AVC promoted "industrial democracy" by agitating for a strong CIO, civil rights legislation, and international cooperation. Joining a surprising number of combat veterans, Bill vigorously opposed the virulently anti-Communist American Legion, which had been born during the Red Scare of 1919. In articles for *Life* and *Atlantic Monthly,* Bill charged that old-guard Legionnaires, fearful of returning soldiers' radicalism, were denying new members voting rights. He especially disliked the Legion's view of veterans as "a separate and privileged part of society." Rallying to the AVC's slogan, "Citizens first, veterans second," Mauldin opposed special benefits for veterans, preferring the "Economic Bill of Rights" for all Americans, proposed by President Roosevelt in 1944.[33]

A lot of Bill's friends and fans were shaken by his new stance. Despite his bouts with army brass, few considered him political in any conventional way. His former colleague on *Stars and Stripes,* Ralph Martin, says Bill had no discernible politics whatsoever until late in the war. "He was just a kid. He didn't even shave. He knew nothing about politics. . . . But he kept his eyes and ears open."

Indeed, it was while on *Stars and Stripes* that Bill received his political education. "The *Stars and Stripes* was his university," says friend Norton Wolf. Unlike the London edition, which had a strong conservative bias, the Mediterranean *Stars and Stripes* was dominated by liberal and left-wing editors and reporters. Before the war, editor in chief Robert Neville had worked for *PM* in New York, a great left-wing organ. Managing editor Dave Golding had a socialist background. *Stars and Stripes* had no editorial page because, according to reporter Herbert Mitgang, "none was needed. Nearly all the staffers were on the same wavelength." They hated fascism, heartily supported the expansion of Franklin Roosevelt's New Deal, and cheered the Soviet Union's valiant struggle against Nazism. By the end of the war, the Mediterranean edition featured glowing articles about gallant Nisei and African American troops who braved enemy fire overseas and yet faced inequality and injustice at home.[34]

Unlike many of his colleagues, Bill never held an ideological view of the war. Willie and Joe never expressed any antifascist motives or lofty democratic ideals. Their Krauts were not Nazis but ordinary Krauts, quite a bit like the dogfaces they fought.

Now, however, Bill put aside his cynicism about wartime propaganda, and challenged America to realize its ideals and justify the bloodshed.

In a coast-to-coast broadcast sponsored by the *New York Herald-Tribune*, Bill delivered a talk titled "The War Isn't Won." Sharing the program with President Truman, General Eisenhower, and several cabinet members, Bill declared, "We were told that it was worthwhile for some of us to get killed, so that our kids could grow up in a world free from hate, prejudice, force, and intolerance. . . . Those of us who live still have that hope," he intoned in his southwestern drawl, "but the hope isn't being nourished by what a lot of us see going on in our own country."

The list was long, and much of it would have made Hitler proud: highly decorated Japanese American soldiers denied jobs and housing, black veterans returning to segregated towns, newspapers fomenting anti-Semitism, radio networks denouncing "the menace of organized labor," United States senators from Dixie promulgating racial theories of white supremacy. "If we were told the truth about the reasons why we went overseas and why some of our best friends were killed and crippled before our eyes," he concluded angrily, "then we have not won the war—we have only won the battles."[35]

As Bill went about giving speeches, he was also overhauling his cartoon feature. Like General MacArthur's old soldiers, Willie and Joe just faded away. Beginning in early November, the former dogfaces, now gas station attendants, slipped out of the cartoon, replaced by more politicized content, especially jabs at the rising tide of right-wing reaction (see figure 54).

One of Willie's final moments appeared on January 8, 1946. He stands on a darkened street, redolent of the betrayal, isolation, and bewilderment felt by many who fought for a better world. "Accordin' to you, mister," says Willie, "I spent th' last three years helpin' my worst enemy kill my best friends."

That same day, an FBI agent clipped the cartoon from the *Washington Daily News* and slipped it into a folder titled "Mauldin, William H." The file would fatten over the following months, and years later Bill would learn that his official status was "Security Matter—Communist" (see figure 55).

*"You have just heard our commentator read the Gettysburg Address. The opinions expressed do not necessarily reflect our sponsor's point of view."*

FIGURE 54 The Gettysburg Address deeply influenced Bill's "The War Isn't Won" speech. Attacking corporate censorship of liberal opinion on the airwaves, the cartoon also draws a shrewd analogy between World War II and the Civil War, when Lincoln called upon the nation to fulfill its democratic destiny.

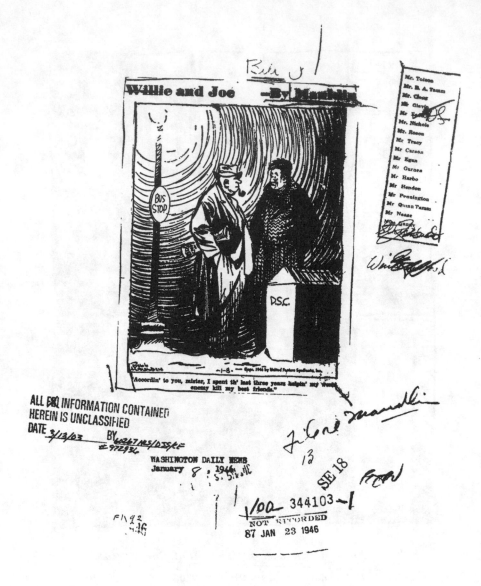

**FIGURE 55** This page from Bill Mauldin's FBI file includes a cartoon of Willie voicing dismay over the right-wing view that Nazi Germany was preferable to the Soviet Union.

*Copyright 1946 by Bill Mauldin. Courtesy of the Mauldin Estate.*

"You ARE TRYING to fall in love," said Jean from Los Angeles in mid-October. "You're the kind that falls in love."

Jean was right. Less than three weeks after filing for divorce, Bill met Natalie Sarah Evans at a Manhattan cocktail party and promptly fell in love.

The party was hosted by Natalie's stepfather Edgar Lewisohn Rossin, a mining executive, financier, and philanthropist. Bill found Natalie on the third floor, hiding out from the guests below. The two hit it off immediately. After several hours of laughing and playing cards with other young guests, the couple walked back to Natalie's apartment on Sixth Avenue. They stayed up talking until 5 a.m.

Natalie was unlike any woman Bill had ever known. Shy, intellectual, and darkly beautiful, she'd grown up in a cultured world amid the avant-garde. Her father, John Evans, was the only son of Mabel Dodge Luhan, the leading light of turn-of-the-century Greenwich Village. In 1916, Luhan had moved her bohemian salon to the northern New Mexico village of Taos. Natalie had spent her childhood romping in Luhan's "Big House." Over the years, she'd met Georgia O'Keeffe, Ansel Adams, Willa Cather, and countless other luminaries drawn to Luhan's mountain retreat.

Natalie's maternal grandparents, poet Alice Corbin Henderson and architect William Penhallow Henderson, had created a similar community in Santa Fe, founding the artists' colony that lives on as Canyon Road and the Camino del Monte Sol. The two families had helped to fashion New Mexico's "Land of Enchantment" mystique, an image far removed from rough-hewn Alamogordo and Mountain Park.

Six months before meeting Bill, Natalie had graduated summa cum laude from Sarah Lawrence College. Her mentor, mythologist Joseph Campbell, had suggested graduate school. Despite several fellowship offers, she'd decided to take a year trying to make it on her own as a writer. At the urging of her family, who worried about her moodiness and isolation, she worked part-time at a bookstore in Grand Central Station just to maintain contact with human beings.

The adventurous and irreverent Bill was, in many ways, a perfect foil for the bookish Natalie. Bill charmed her with his gentle demeanor and thoughtful conversation. "Mom couldn't believe that he never made a move on her the whole night, that he listened to what she had to say," recounts their son Nat. "That's why she agreed to see him again."

"He's a very special kind of person," wrote Natalie to her grandmother, "one of the most wonderful I've met in my young life. He's only twenty-four, yet tremendously wise, and with a wonderful sense of humour. . . . He's a crusader in the best sense of the word, loving all peoples, and wanting to do all he can for them. He belongs to the people, and particularly, he belongs to our time."[36]

The romance deepened quickly, though Bill and Natalie kept the relationship quiet due to complications in Bill's divorce proceedings. Jean was pregnant with their second child, and Bill was suing for custody of Bruce. Jean's attorneys fired back with a restraining order, and then the two sides entered into deliberations over custody and property. It would be late spring 1946 before the California Superior Court issued its interlocutory judgment of divorce, giving Jean custody of Bruce and allowing Bill and Natalie to plan their own wedding.[37]


IN THE MEANTIME, Bill returned to Los Angeles to work on the filming of *Up Front*. He'd long questioned the project, doubting that Hollywood could make a war film "that wasn't an insult to the soldiers it was supposed to portray." Indeed, Bill's initial demands were so extreme that his Beverly Hills agent, Bert Allenberg, had trouble selling the rights. Bill had insisted that the film involve no comedy, romance, or heroism. He simply wanted "plenty of war, of the gruesome variety."[38]

International Pictures' eye-popping offer, as well as studio exec-utive William Goetz's assurances that Bill would retain creative control, eroded the cartoonist's resistance. Bill was pleased when Goetz hired brothers John and Ring Lardner Jr. to write the screen-play. John had been a stalwart correspondent at Anzio, refusing to evacuate the beachhead in February 1944 even when the Germans seemed poised to throw invasion forces back into the sea. Ring had already won his first Academy Award for *Woman of the Year* and was a vocal proponent of left-wing causes.

With the help of several former *Stars and Stripes* staffers Bill man-aged to get on International's payroll, the brothers drafted a mas-terful screenplay in the spirit of Bill's cartoons. The script's comedy was sardonic and the romance grotesque. Joe, for example, pursues a beautiful Italian girl, only to be tricked into having sex with her Amazon sister. Willie and Joe (given the last names Wingfield and Cooper) spend much of the screenplay drunk, taking potshots at authority, running from MPs, and trying to avoid combat. The pair eventually escape prosecution for their various crimes and misde-meanors when they're mistakenly credited with capturing thirty-two Germans and awarded Silver Stars. In creating a narrative that defied all conventions of previous war movies, even comic ones, the Lardners' *Up Front* fulfilled Bill's vision.[39]

Unfortunately, Universal's acquisition of International Pictures in 1946 sidelined the film. Studio executives believed that the pub-lic's appetite for war movies had waned and shelved the project for a later date. The Lardners' screenplay was never produced, though Ring Lardner Jr. would revive *Up Front*'s black-comic vision of war twenty-four years later in preparing his Academy Award–winning script for Robert Altman's *MASH*.[40]

As the studio pondered the fate of *Up Front,* Bill wintered 1946 in his palatial office on MGM's sprawling Culver City lot. There, with a secretary to answer his voluminous fan mail, Bill scratched out four cartoons a week and did virtually no work on the movie.

Hollywood both fascinated and repulsed him. The average movie lot, he discovered, was as rigidly hierarchical as the army, and just as segregated by rank. As a bestselling author, Bill enjoyed something akin to general's status. He dined at the "executives' mess" and drank in the swankiest of night clubs. Bouncers and headwaiters routinely lifted the velvet ropes as they saw him approach. On Sam Goldwyn's lot, Bill rubbed elbows with Edward G. Robinson, Loretta Young, and Orson Welles, who all behaved as if *they* were honored to meet *him*. After several weeks of such treatment, Bill stopped feeling like an interloper and began, however tentatively, to accept his rank as his due (see figure 56).

In 1940s Hollywood, one reward of rank was access to the studio steam room. Here, stars and executives mingled stark naked, sipping top-shelf Scotch in canvas beach chairs while billows of steam boiled their skin pink.[41]

One afternoon while sweating in the fog, Bill struck up a conversation with Orson Welles, who was in town shooting *The Stranger* on International's lot. Like Bill, Welles was a prominent cultural-front personality who had taken on big shots and been proclaimed a genius at a young age. Now, five years after *Citizen Kane,* he was wrestling with editors and executives over creative control of his work.

He took to Bill immediately and, though only six years older, adopted a protective, almost paternal, attitude toward the cartoonist. In his weekly newspaper column, Welles called Bill "the ranking spokesman of the greatest army in the world" and expressed surprise that such a powerful artist should turn out to look like a scared little boy.

"Our problem, Bill," mused Welles through the steam, "is that it all came too fast, too soon for us." Like Merlin, he and Bill were living their lives in reverse, he said. Where else could they go now, except backward?[42]

FIGURE 56 Bill's introduction to Hollywood came on August 15, 1945, V-J Day. He spent the day with Orson Welles watching crowds of revelers on Hollywood and Vine before taking part in "Command Performance—Victory Extra," a special production of the famous Armed Forces Radio show. Pictured backstage are, left to right, Marlene Dietrich, Burgess Meredith, Bill Mauldin, and Jinx Falkenberg.

*Courtesy of the Mauldin Estate.*

BILL RETURNED to Manhattan in March of 1946 to a crisis that had been brewing for months. Newspaper editors, so pleased with Bill's output the previous summer, were furious over his increasingly strident politics. Some cartoons were so controversial, especially in the South, that newspapers simply refused to print them. Editors flooded the syndicate with letters and telegrams threatening to cancel their subscriptions unless Mauldin changed his ways.

The managers at United Features, who had inherited Bill's

account after George Carlin's death the previous fall, pressured him to tone down his commentaries. "If you're gonna do that kind of crap," one finally snapped, "you should stop doing syndicated work and ask for a job at the *New Masses* or the *Daily Worker.*"

Such complaints merely heated up the fight in Bill. He tasted blood, and he liked it. "Every time an editor bitched about my drawing a race-relations cartoon," Bill recalled years later, "I drew eight or ten of them in a row." Natalie grew concerned that Bill's crusading spirit had turned self-destructive. She looked to Ann Watkins for a moderating influence. "I'm sure she can help Bill find the most devastating way of making himself heard," Natalie wrote her grandmother, "without strangling himself in the process."[43]

Watkins had seen the crisis coming in early January when New York's *World-Telegram,* the flagship of the Scripps-Howard newspaper chain, unceremoniously dumped "Willie and Joe." Publisher Roy Howard accused Bill of "following the Communist Party line" in his attacks on red-baiting politicians (see figure 57).

Howard's action unleashed a stampede of canceled subscriptions. By spring, newspapers were dropping Bill's feature at a rate of one a day, cutting his syndication by over half. "I set two records in a very short period of time," joked Bill. "I rolled up more papers than anybody had, and I think I lost more than anybody had."[44]

In order to stop the hemorrhaging, United Features invoked a clause in Bill's contract, which he had not read, that gave the syndicate the power to edit his work as they wished. Copy editors altered drawings, rewrote captions, and simply withdrew cartoons from syndication if they were deemed too offensive to fix. Out of some two hundred cartoons Bill submitted in 1946, over forty were censored. What Bill called the syndicate's "blue-pencil operations" dulled his cartoons' political messages and sometimes subverted them altogether. One caption concerning racial segregation was butchered so badly that the new version scarcely made sense (see figures 58 and 59).[45]

Bill, of course, fought the syndicate's every change, while left-

"Whar's thet gol-durn sign painter?"

**FIGURE 57** This cartoon from January 3, 1946, was the last straw for Roy Howard, publisher of the *New York World-Telegram*. Despite his aversion to Communism, Bill detested the House Un-American Activities Committee, which he called a "congressional Gestapo." Syndicate editors placed white tape over a Nazi eagle and swastika on the door.

*Prints and Photographs Division,*
*Library of Congress, LC-DIG-ppmsca-13566.*

*Copyright 1946 by Bill Mauldin. Courtesy of the Mauldin Estate.*

wing tribunes like *PM* and the Communist Party's *Daily Worker* took up his cause. For a while Bill reveled in the controversy. He declared that General Patton had it right all along when Old Blood and Guts had accused him of drawing "seditious" cartoons that "incited soldiers to mutiny." His work had always contained "deep, dark meaning," he said, "and wasn't meant to be entertaining at all."

Typically, however, Bill's outrage eventually gave way to reflection and self-criticism. By late summer, he better understood his dilemma with United Features. The censorship was no conspiracy to silence left-wing opinion and preserve the "reactionary press in America," as the *Daily Worker* charged. The syndicate only wanted to make money. With a syndicate, "your stuff is a product, merchandised and sold like soap, with an eye to pleasing the greatest number of customers most of the time." To meet the syndicates' unrelenting production schedules, cartoonists began to take on assistants who assembled cartoons by lettering words, inking drawings, filling in backgrounds, and working on the gags and story lines. Such assembly-line techniques discouraged originality and craftsmanship in favor of, in Mauldin's words, "standardized and gutless comic strips . . . offered dirt cheap to all comers."

Bill's mistake, as he understood it, was to let fly with a "sledgehammer," by serving up blunt political statements as unsubtle and one-dimensional as the "gutless" comic strips he disdained. Eager to thumb his nose at United Features and their conservative client papers, Bill had turned preachy and "soapboxy" instead of insightful and thought-provoking. Good cartoons, he reasoned, should be like stilettos "thrust gently, so that the victim doesn't know he's stabbed until he has six inches of steel in his innards."

In an attempt to recover his sense of craft, Bill petitioned United Features once again to release him from his contract. The *New York Herald-Tribune* had picked up Bill's feature after the *World-Telegram* dropped it, and now offered Bill a job as political cartoonist if he could get free of the syndicate. But United Features refused to let Bill go. So he settled for an office at the *Herald-Tribune* which at least

*"About holding United Nations conferences in your home town, Senator—you may all be 100 per cent Americans, but you see,* United Nations *includes other 100 per cent nationalities too."*

*"About your home town's offer to let United Nations hold its conferences there, Senator—don't you think the Abyssinian delegation might object to riding the back seats of the busses?"*

FIGURE 58 These two competing captions from 1946 exemplify how United Features Syndicate sometimes sabotaged Bill's work by editing his more pointed cartoons. Regardless of its other merits, the second caption, Mauldin's original, at least has the virtue of making sense.

**Figure 59** Many newspapers refused to run this cartoon on December 20, 1945. For those that did, Unifeatures offered the alternate caption in typescript above the drawing.

*Copyright 1945 by Bill Mauldin. Courtesy of the Mauldin Estate.*

gave him the sense of working for an individual paper instead of a faceless mass market.[46]

As he struggled to regain balance as a craftsman, Bill also fought to separate himself from the left. "I was getting in enough trouble on my own," he joked, "without somebody else doing it for me." A break with the cultural front was inevitable. Impatient with theory, distrustful of formal ideology, and disdainful of hypocrisy, Bill refused to subordinate his own common sense to the needs of a movement. He regretted his radical speeches where he had struck a "phony attitude" that "smelled strongly of propaganda." The only worthy cause, one that trumped any narrow party or program, was that of independent citizenship. Each person must follow his or her own light. "I like free living," he said, "and I don't think there is a Messiah, a Leader, or a Planner alive whose system or regime gives the results worth the loss of personal freedom."[47]

No simplistic libertarian, he continued to support progressive principles and causes. He split with the Communists mainly over Russia's belligerent and imperialistic behavior. He believed powerfully in the new United Nations as a safeguard against future wars. He endorsed world federalism and looked forward to the abolition of all armies, save for an international peacekeeping force. He was outraged at Stalin's unilateral power grab in Eastern Europe and his declaration in 1946 that a war against the capitalist West was inevitable. "We're all wrong," he declared, "but Russia is wronger." Bill thought American Communists' defense of Stalin's repressive regime particularly craven, given their loud demands for free speech and civil liberty at home. "If you are going to snort about freedom and all that stuff," he carped, "it has to work both ways."[48]

In late 1946, Bill began withdrawing from Communist-led organizations like the American Youth for Democracy and the Joint Anti-Fascist Refugee Committee. He also published cartoons critical of the Communist Party and the Soviet Union, at the same time railing at the venomous anti-Communist right. "Every time I start work on a drawing about Russia's misbehavior," he said, "I shrink inwardly because I think of all the sons of bitches in this country who are doing the same thing for reasons of their own, and I often throw the drawing away."[49]

Nationally, the *Daily Worker* decried Bill's treachery, while conservatives gloated that Mauldin had finally seen the light and "converted" (see figure 60). Bill tried to steer the middle course, calling himself an "anti-anti-Communist" and steadfastly distinguishing between red-baiting and legitimate criticism. But such nice distinctions were lost in the din of Cold War rhetoric. The entire world, it seemed, had split into two deaf, hostile camps.

During 1946, a "year in cement," the United States and the Soviet Union hunkered down into opposing spheres of influence; by 1947, both countries had put their governments and their economies on a war footing. New bureaucracies—the Department of Defense, the Central Intelligence Agency, and the National Security Council—sprang up, gathering power in the executive branch and cloaking worldwide military operations in secrecy. Loyalty oaths, background checks, and political inquisitions—what would later become collectively known as "McCarthyism"—began to stifle public debate and curtail social reform. "It's very tough to live in this country and cling to young ideals," concluded Bill that year.[50]

In March of 1947, President Harry Truman declared the Cold War officially begun and instituted a Loyalty Security Program for federal employees. A month later, Bill started work on a book meant to salvage his ideals and stake out an independent ground between the frozen poles of left and right. As always, he wrote quickly—too quickly in this case—pounding out thousands of words a day while keeping up with his cartooning and awaiting the divorce decree that would allow him to remarry. In early August, while on honeymoon with Natalie in Maine, Bill sent the manuscript and 195 accompanying cartoons to Armitage "Mike" Watkins, now running the literary agency after his mother Ann's retirement.

"Two magazines are competing for exclusive serial rights, if we convert."

**FIGURE 60** No postwar cartoon caused more grief for Bill than this one, published on February 19, 1947. Bill intended it as a stinging commentary on the right-wing press's appetite for lurid "True Confessions" of ex–Communist Party members. But conservative Catholics mistakenly interpreted it as a criticism of Clare Boothe Luce's then-current series in *McCall's* about her conversion to Roman Catholicism. Catholic newspapers denounced Mauldin as a bigot. Bill considered suing, but then thought better of it "after sulking behind my drawing board for a few days."

*Copyright 1947 by Bill Mauldin. Courtesy of the Mauldin Estate.*

*Up Front* had been demure, but in *Back Home* Bill had placed himself squarely at the center, recounting his troubled homecoming, his battles with United Features, his views on everything from fraudulent auto repair shops to civilian control of nuclear energy. "Mauldin has a need and a gift for working in terms of character," remarked John Lardner, "but through no fault of his own he, himself, is the only character he has had much chance to investigate in the last two years."[51]

Moody and disjointed, *Back Home* has a choppy, unfinished quality, as if Bill were still "trying to figure out how to live like a democrat," in the words of one reviewer. "Seeing both sides is a passion with Mauldin," Lardner observed, "a fine, civilized passion, but you can see how it might get in the way of a crusader taking one side or the other of any question at all." The book doesn't so much explain or describe independent citizenship as model it, thoughtfully deliberating over such issues as rent control and the need to rearm for the Cold War. Finally, *Back Home* is the work of a disillusioned twenty-five-year-old veteran seeking to balance the integrity of his pure personal vision against a democratic imperative to compromise.[52]

Prepublication thoughts about *Back Home* were decidedly dour. Mike Watkins believed its strident criticism of the American Legion would alienate much of the reading public. *Collier's* found the text so rambling as to resist excerpting. The editor of the *Saturday Evening Post* took exception to Bill as "a heavy thinker" and advised him to stick to cartooning. Journalist E. J. Kahn called the book "a rambling introspective jumble of observations and comments," redeemed, however, by the "candid, sensitive, impulsive, impudent, progressive, idealistic, softhearted, perceptive and immensely likeable" author, whose engaging personality somehow held the text together. Nobody thought it would sell well, including its author.[53]

They were all wrong. *Back Home* became a bestseller after its release on Halloween of 1947; the Book-of-the-Month Club made it a main selection for November. Critics and readers responded powerfully to Bill's quirky belligerence and frank, self-deprecating humor. Christopher Morley called the book "one of the valuable confessions of our painful time," while the *New York Times* hailed it as "the most welcome testament liberals have come across in a long time." E. J. Kahn observed that the book had a large following among veterans like himself "who have sadly watched what they had hoped would be a rosy future turn into a present of heavy greyness." Travel writer Oriana Atkinson wrote Bill a letter to say, "You are what we need, an impertinent young squirt who will needle us in the most vulnerable and uncomfortable places. You are all the irritating adolescents of the world rolled into one prickly bundle and you are very good for us indeed. . . . Be careful crossing the streets."[54]

Two months later, Bill drove his big shiny Buick to a Manhattan auto dealer. Like the Pontiac convertible and the DeSoto sedan before it, the Buick was a great status symbol, but unreliable and expensive to fix. So, once again, he traded in his car. This time he roared out of the showroom in a Willys-Overland jeep, a virtual twin to the one he'd driven and maintained himself in Europe. He even had it painted olive drab—the only color, he said, for a jeep.

A few days after Bill bought the jeep, New York City was socked with over two feet of snow, the city's worst winter storm in recorded history. As the blizzard reached its peak, Bill dragged Natalie out for a ride around Manhattan. The couple motored along the deserted streets in four-wheel drive "like two kids on a lark," taking in the hushed beauty of the frozen cityscape.[55]

BILL'S CONTRACT with United Features ended on April 8, 1948. "We're tired and we're going fishing for a while," read the final cartoon's handwritten caption beneath a gallery of Bill's characters. "We hope to see you again soon."[56]

Bill did indeed go fishing, traveling to Ponte Vedra Beach, Florida, with the pregnant Natalie. There he started working on another book which, rumor had it, would not include cartooning. He also quietly signed on for $185 a week as a political cartoonist for the yet-unpublished *New York Star*. Slated to launch in June, the *Star* was a successor of the left-wing *PM*, which Marshall Field III had sold after eight tumultuous years. Unlike *PM*, the new paper would accept advertising and would shun the Communist-aligned left in favor of an independent liberalism.[57]

Bill's cartoons that fall included a few about the 1948 presidential race and a final Willie and Joe drawing. The newspaper's syndication deal with Bill stipulated that no one could alter his drawings or captions.[58]

On January 1, 1949, Bill flew to Fort Bliss, Texas, near El Paso, to write a series of articles on how the army had changed since his discharge three and a half years earlier. It was a particularly apt assignment. Bill's highly publicized complaints about the military "caste system" had helped inspire the creation in 1946 of an army investigative committee headed by the legendary air commander Jimmy Doolittle. Bill had testified before the "Doolittle Board," whose stated aim was "to make the army more compatible with a democratic nation."

The board's final report cheered Bill immensely. It strongly condemned the tyranny of the officer corps and called for better pay and treatment of enlisted men, racial desegregation, the integration of women, a reformed military justice system, new grievance procedures, and a clearly enunciated bill of rights for common soldiers. Desperate to attract volunteers to an institution many Americans viewed as a "Prussian" holdover, the army quickly adopted most of the Doolittle Board's recommendations and liberalized the officer–enlisted man relationship.[59]

In Texas, Bill liked what he saw of the "new army." Enlisted men now sat on courts-martial, black and white soldiers ate together, and inspectors general routinely investigated abusive company commanders and NCOs. Only the housing was worse than in wartime. He placed hope in a cooperative housing movement launched by the base's enlisted men. One soldier told Bill it all sounded "a little communistic" to him. Then, to Bill's delight, he added defiantly, "Who gives a damn?"[60]

But Bill's two-week stay at Fort Bliss had a dark, secret side: he was being closely watched. The army and the FBI considered Bill a security risk. Alerted to Bill's visit, Special Agent D. K. Brown of El Paso's FBI office asked his boss, J. Edgar Hoover, for instructions. Hoover told Brown to monitor Mauldin's activities and to make no contact with the army, which was already watching Bill.[61]

Bill returned to New York in late January, just as the *Star* was folding up shop after a dismal seven months of publication. Bill sold the remainder of his series on Fort Bliss to the *New York Post* before retiring from cartooning and the newspaper business altogether.

A shrewd reader of Mauldin's final cartoons for the *Star* might have guessed at what he would do next. Bill's work on the *Star* had featured a precocious "Brat" modeled on Bill himself. Dodging traffic, gambling in alleys, and fighting off bullies and cops, the scrappy Brat challenged authority without raising any hot-button political issues (see figure 61).

After the *Star*'s collapse, Bill fleshed out the Brat's narrative. Inspired in part by the birth of his and Natalie's first son Andy the previous September, Bill cast his memory back to the Southwest and his childhood under the sway of his ingenious, erratic father.

The memoir was the most difficult writing Bill had ever attempted. A master of essays and short humor pieces, Bill lacked the patience and organization for a sustained narrative. Further, unlike his "Quoth the Dogface" columns and various postwar musings, the new book had no ax to grind, no grievance to set right. Nevertheless, Bill stuck with it, determined to break out of cartooning and establish himself as a true writer.

The subject matter, he knew, was ripe. America's obsession with national security had chilled public debate, encouraging a new focus on private family life. Books like *Cheaper by the Dozen* (1948) and movies like *Life with Father* (1947) dealt with oddball family

"Beat it. I'm busy stirrin' up th' masses."

FIGURE 61 The embattled and sardonic street urchins of Bill's postwar work served as proxy for the war's wisecracking GIs. The boy "stirrin' up th' masses" is Bill as a child, while Bill's brother Sid stands to the right of the soapbox. Such cartoons allowed Bill to express his jaundiced views of authority without entangling himself in controversy.

*Copyright 1948 by Bill Mauldin. Courtesy of the Mauldin Estate.*

men in need of taming. Bill had the task of casting Pop as eccentric, but not frightening, and his family as sweetly adventurous, rather than dysfunctional.

Bill finished the manuscript in May of 1949 and hastily sketched its ninety-odd drawings. Mike Watkins immediately contacted Beverly Hills agent Bert Allenberg to say that the book had "the qualities of a *Huckleberry Finn*" and was worthy of a movie treatment.

The only problem was the title. Bill insisted it be *A Sort of a Saga*. Editors at W. W. Norton thought it too awkward. One of the *a*'s had to go. After a few weeks of arguing, Norton relented and released the book in October of 1949, bad syntax and all.[62]

Reviewers praised *A Sort of a Saga,* although Hollywood and the Book-of-the-Month Club passed. The cartoonist's charming, earthy style, said one critic, "falls somewhere between Mark Twain and Steinbeck or rubs shoulders with both." The *Saturday Review* concurred, saying that "if Tom Sawyer had been born in 1921, and if he had spent his boyhood in New Mexico and Arizona instead of Missouri, he would have lived this life and written this book." Charles Poore of the *New York Times* probed deeper, saying that *A Sort of a Saga* revealed the source of Bill's rugged independence, but not of "the magnificent chips he carried on his shoulder in wartime, chips that eventually came to blaze like insignia of unearthly rank."

Pop and Sid, out in Southern California, bristled at seeing themselves turned into near-cartoon characters, and Bill himself might have cringed at Lewis Gannett's remark in the *New York Herald-Tribune* that *A Sort of a Saga* contains "healthy memories of a healthy boyhood."[63]

After *A Sort of a Saga*'s release, Bill, Natalie, and Andy moved from their apartment on East Twentieth Street in Peter Cooper Village to a stone manse thirty-five miles north in Rockland County. The ten-acre property on South Mountain Road had belonged to Marion Hargrove, author of the huge bestseller *See Here, Private Hargrove*. Hargrove had bought it on the proceeds from the book and movie and soon nicknamed it "the Old Bailey" in reference to his unhappy home life. Bill had run into Hargrove in New York and learned of the place's availability. "I had too much land and Mauldin had too much money," Hargrove told a reporter, "so we swapped. Maybe in ten years we'll swap back."[64]

Years earlier, in Italy, Bill had talked with Ernie Pyle about the war's end. Both dreaded coming home. Pyle said he meant to disappear somewhere until people had forgotten about him. Then he would go back to doing honest work.

Now, Bill was finally making his own escape, starting life over with his new family.

Chapter Seven

# Starting Over

*(1950–1963)*

"Hell, this is ditch-diggin' work." Bill was lounging in the shade, blue kepi pushed back on his head and a cigarette holder jutting between clenched teeth. It was too hot even for cards. California's sun, scrubby hills, and clouds of dust kicked up by marching soldiers recalled his summer in Sicily.

Five years after leaving the army, Bill found himself back in it, playing Tom Wilson, the Loud Soldier, in John Huston's adaptation of *The Red Badge of Courage.* Huston's celluloid army resembled the real thing, not in the realness of battle scenes, but in the way the actors got treated on the set. While Huston and his crew planned the next shot, the cast sat like "silly little dolls waiting to be picked up and pushed around." As in the war, Bill passed the time rolling cigarettes, telling jokes, playing poker, and sharing stories about his civilian life.

"I'm just here raisin' scratch so's I can go back home and work on my play," he drawled.[1]

It was not Bill's first acting job. Four months earlier, in April of 1950, Bill had gone to Italy as a technical adviser on MGM's *Teresa*, a film scripted by Stewart Stern about a neurotic GI who marries an equally troubled peasant girl. Bill's wholesale script changes distressed Stern but pleased director Fred Zinnemann. On the set, Zinnemann asked Bill to play the easygoing American soldier named Grissom, a character Bill himself had created. He found the role agreeable enough, especially at $1,500 a week.[2]

A month later, John Huston had Bill up for martinis at Huston's Waldorf Tower suite. They'd met in 1944 when Huston was in Italy shooting a documentary called *The Battle of San Pietro* for the Army Signal Corps. Trudging through snow with a handheld camera, Huston had followed the 143rd Infantry Regiment into the mountains above the Liri Valley. Through smoke, concussions, and flying debris, Huston had captured the most harrowing footage of the Italian campaign.

Bill considered *The Battle of San Pietro* the greatest war documentary of all time. At a special screening before the House Military Affairs Committee in December 1944, the VIP audience howled in protest at the sight of dead soldiers being stuffed into body bags. The War Department froze the film's release, but General Marshall, after a viewing, ordered it shown to all recruits and promoted Huston to major.[3]

Bill didn't care for Huston's haughty manner, but he did like the director's script for *Red Badge*, which closely followed Stephen Crane's 1895 novel. Moreover, Bill shared Huston's rugged temper and penchant for rebellion. The film would have no standard plot, no romance, no female lead, and the protagonist, Henry Fleming, would distinguish himself mainly by running from battle. Nor would there be much action. *Red Badge* would focus on Fleming's thoughts and feelings, as well as on the "ironically thin line between cowardice and heroism." Huston also decided to cast no stars in the picture. "I'm going to prove I can make a movie without actors," he told Bill with his usual melodramatic flair.[4]

Bill agreed to play the Loud Soldier, Henry Fleming's friend, for $2,000 a week. The money, together with earnings from *Teresa*, would cover a year's worth of living expenses. Bill stipulated only that he be spared the Hollywood publicity treatment. He wanted no interviews with the likes of Louella Parsons and Hedda Hopper. He also insisted that the studio issue a simple statement that Bill Mauldin was *not* turning to acting for his career.[5]

Natalie, pregnant with their second child, traveled with Bill to John Huston's California ranch for the filming. The forty-nine-day shoot was the most chaotic and stressful of Huston's career. Working on a shoestring budget and compressed production schedule, the director also had to deal with lead actor Audie Murphy. The most decorated soldier in American history, the twenty-six-year-old Murphy was the son of an impoverished Texas sharecropper. He'd become a family breadwinner at age twelve when his father deserted him and his eleven brothers and sisters. The war offered an escape, but neither the Marines nor the paratroopers would accept the fragile, underweight boy. He ended up tracing Bill's steps in the infantry, traveling to North Africa, Sicily, and the mountains of Italy before fighting his way through France, Belgium, and Germany. In June 1945, still too young to vote, he returned from the war with 240 confirmed enemy kills and every combat decoration the army had to offer.

Huston was drawn to the contradictions of Murphy's character: viciousness wrapped beneath a soft, sensitive demeanor. On the set Audie was generally withdrawn, depressed, even unresponsive. Occasionally he broke his moody silence by picking fights with stuntmen. One day, Audie arrived to the set late with bruises and scraped knuckles. On his way to the ranch he'd seen two guys in a truck trying to run some kids off the road. Murphy had forced the truck into a ditch, pulled out its occupants, and pummeled them until an ambulance arrived. "He was a scrappy little sonofabitch," Bill said, "a wary little bobcat, lonely and angry."

Audie never punched Bill, though he probably wanted to. During a crucial concluding scene, inserted into the script by Huston, Audie's character Henry confesses to the Loud Soldier that he'd abandoned his comrades in battle. Over many takes, Audie stood strangely silent, glowering at Bill instead of speaking his lines. Bill quickly figured out the problem.

"I think Audie is having trouble confessing to a *Stars and Stripes* cartoonist that he ran from battle," Bill told Huston.

"You got it, Mauldin," mumbled Audie.

Bill offered to confess to cowardice first. Audie agreed but still could only bring himself to say that he had been scared "only for a minute" (see figure 62).[6]

Murphy clearly disdained Bill as a "rear-echelon inkslinger," but Bill instinctively understood the troubled war hero, sensing in Audie's rage a hardscrabble spirit of the Depression-era Southwest, "where we shot our meat and could never pay our bills," as Bill put it. "I shared his terrible need to feel respected, upright and important," Bill said. "However, I was lucky. My furies weren't as burning as his, and I was able to work most of them out on paper. Audie took the hard way, cutting a swath through the Wehrmacht and then trying to do the same in Hollywood."

Bill managed to keep his own demons at bay, and yet felt a twinge of regret at having reined in his temperament to get along in respectable society.[7]

In mid-October, *Red Badge* moved out of production just as the film version of *Up Front* was moving into it. Universal had brought it out of mothballs the previous fall, and Bill had spent a frustrating four weeks in late 1949 shaping the picture. The Lardners' script could not be used for political reasons. Ring Lardner Jr. was in prison for refusing to testify before the House Un-American Activities Committee. In 1947, the committee chair had asked Lardner, "Are you now or have you ever been a member of the Communist Party?" Lardner's response—"I could answer the question . . . but if I did, I would hate myself in the morning"—had earned him a spot on the Hollywood blacklist.

**Figure 62**   The Loud Soldier and the Youth as they appeared in *The Red Badge of Courage*. Audie Murphy derided Bill as a "faggot artist." Bill, on the other hand, identified with Audie's never-ending struggle to prove himself.

The Red Badge of Courage © *Turner Entertainment Co.*
*A Warner Bros. Entertainment Company. All Rights Reserved.*

Universal froze Bill out of any creative role in the film. The new writer, Stanley Roberts, and director, Leonard Goldstein, refused to put Bill's suggestions into the script. They wanted a mere B-grade slapstick comedy, marketed under the brand of Willie and Joe. Bill's Hollywood agent, Bert Allenberg, could do nothing. The studio had full control. Conceding defeat, Bill gave up his $10,000 advising fee and began to distance himself from the Hollywood version of his wartime characters. When the picture, starring David Wayne as Willie and Tom Ewell as Joe, opened in early 1951, Bill told reporters that he had not seen it. "I've just heard," he said cannily, "that it had a lot of jokes and everybody laughed."[8]

John Huston did more or less the same when *The Red Badge of Courage* opened later that year. MGM, always nervous about the unconventional film, had panicked in postproduction and cut it drastically, removing over an hour of Huston's cut and every hint of ambiguity and irony. MGM's publicist even nixed using Bill's drawings for promotion because they were "too grim." With McCarthyism in full swing and the nation at war once again in Korea, any hint of "antiwar" was anathema.

John Huston considered *Red Badge* his greatest movie, but no original cut of the film has been discovered. Rumor had it that executive Dore Schary himself had the excised sections destroyed for fear that someone would discover the studio's brush with subversion.[9]

The fates of *Up Front* and *Red Badge* fixed Bill's resolve to quit Hollywood. "Movie acting is like driving a locomotive," he said a couple of years later. "It's one of those things you want to do once in your life, and once is enough."[10]

SOME IN the press speculated that Bill might reenlist his ink brush for service in Korea. "If the war gets worse, which I imagine it will, we'll all be in it," he said evasively in April of 1951. "Right now I'm just biting my nails like everybody else."[11]

In truth, Bill wasn't eager to join another shooting war, especially one as wild and unpredictable as Korea. In the summer of 1950, Communist forces had swept south of the 38th parallel, capturing the South Korean capital of Seoul and all but pushing the American-led UN troops into the Sea of Japan. Then General Douglas MacArthur's surprise invasion at Inchon had cut off North Korean supply lines and sent the Communists fleeing back home. MacArthur's troops retook Seoul, then pursued the enemy to the Yalu River, North Korea's border with China. There the UN offensive collapsed when eight Chinese divisions reinforced the North Korean People's Army. Brutal mountain warfare followed that winter as the joined Communist armies evicted the Americans from the North and took Seoul again. By the time the film version of *Up Front* was released at the end of March 1951, a final UN counteroffensive had gotten Seoul back before stalling along the 38th parallel. The slaughter continued on a static line in the mountains, deaths rising into the hundreds of thousands. All in all, Korea was a mess.

Further, Bill now had two children and a third on the way. In terms of career, Korea would be a regression. He had no desire to "rehash" his wartime cartooning. His focus had shifted from the drawing board to the typewriter. Even his artwork had moved beyond pen and ink to oils and watercolors. In the summer of 1949, he'd spent several weeks at the Skowhegan School of Painting and Sculpture in Maine. He still cartooned occasionally, but kept this work discreet, submitting roughs almost exclusively now to *The New Yorker* (see figure 63).

In April 1951, book publisher and South Mountain Road neighbor William Sloane implored Bill to gather a collection of his best army cartoons, many never seen by the public. Bill rejected the idea out of hand, calling it a "step backward" and a cheap attempt "to cash in on the present war with old stuff." He wanted "to learn new things," to take on "something fresh."[12]

By fall, however, Bill had changed his mind about Korea and about the cartoon collection, which was rushed into print as *Bill Mauldin's Army* in December 1951. His various writing projects had not panned out, the war had stabilized, peace talks were under way, and both *Reader's Digest* and *Collier's* were offering big money for rights to Bill's Korean dispatches. With some reluctance, he prepared for a three-month tour of the Korean theater.

A couple of weeks before his departure date, however, Bill learned that his visa application for travel to Korea had been rejected. The Defense Department had refused him security clearance.

Bill immediately called a former aide to General Omar Bradley, Chet Hanson. He and Hanson had worked on a foreword to

**FIGURE 63** In March 1950, Bill submitted this rough along with several others to *The New Yorker*. The cartoon took its cue perhaps from Natalie's sister, Tish Frank, a graduate of Bennington College in Vermont. The genteel subject matter and more refined style contrasted with Bill's earlier drawings of soldiers, workers, and street urchins. The magazine returned the rough to Bill and never published any of his cartoons.

*Prints and Photographs Division, Library of Congress, LC-DIG-ppmsca-03246. Copyright 1950 by Bill Mauldin. Courtesy of the Mauldin Estate.*

Bradley's memoirs and Hanson, now at the CIA, said he would look into it. Half an hour later, Hanson called to say that the visa had been held up by the FBI, which had shown Bill's file to the Defense Department.

While Hanson worked to free up the visa, Bill got in touch with

*Reader's Digest* editor William L. White, who shot a letter off to J. Edgar Hoover. White knew Hoover, and Hoover, as Bill's friend Herbert Mitgang put it, "knew the power of the *Reader's Digest.*" White told Hoover that Bill had been "mixed up in some left-of-center journalism for which he has no reason to apologize," and that he was "as good a security risk as I am, if not better." Bill's visa came through several days later.[13]

Bill finally flew to Tokyo on January 11, 1952, and on to Seoul.

Seoul brought back memories. The city had changed hands four times in eight months and looked like several Cassinos heaped together. Most of the buildings were rubble. The ones left standing had been burned out or sheered off. At the airport, Bill climbed aboard a waiting jeep and headed north to the battle line.[14]

The line snaked across Korea's peninsula, with both armies hunkered down in weather so cold "you could spit and hear it clink when it landed." Bill's visit to the American 7th Division took him just west of the line's center, amid mountain peaks nicknamed Bloody Ridge, Heartbreak Ridge, and Old Baldy. The previous winter, supply lines were unstable, warm clothing scarce, and the fighting so fierce and fast-moving that the men didn't have time to dig out bunkers. Evidence of firepower that had raked the frozen landscape was everywhere. The mountains were completely denuded. Only stumps poked out of the snow, ice, and dusty red earth. Even rock outcroppings had been blasted into pebbles. Truce negotiations in October had ended the major offensives. Both sides now relied on an "active defense" of small patrols and raids carried out from well-fortified positions.[15]

Some of what Bill saw in Korea reminded him of the Gustav and Gothic lines in Italy, down to the bunker stovepipes made of used C-ration cans. But the differences were large. The enemy was just as lethal and the artillery as accurate, but Korea in 1952 lacked the grim hopelessness of Venafro or Cassino.

To bolster morale, the army had introduced a rotation system. After nine months on the line, combat troops went home. A veteran of the Mediterranean theater told Bill that in Italy, a dogface knew the only way home was "to get carried out of the hills feet first." In Korea, he said, a man has "something to look forward to, and I swear it makes a man a better soldier. He takes care of himself better, and he does his job right." The army gave combat troops priority in almost everything, keeping men in the bunkers supplied with dry socks, insulated boots, and two hot meals a day delivered by Korean conscripts.

The officers, too, were more professional and humane. When Bill flew back to Tokyo with an ear infection, he found medical facilities for enlisted men on a par with those for officers (Bill himself carried a temporary rank of major while embedded in the Eighth Army). Throughout his three-month tour, with the Marines in the mountains, the navy on an aircraft carrier, or in the rear in Tokyo, he found a remarkable lack of chickenshit. The integration of African American troops also seemed to work, with few signs of interracial conflict.[16]

All of this good news disarmed Bill. His dispatches for *Collier's* (which had won out over *Reader's Digest* with an offer of $21,000 for seven articles) were breezy, even, at times, light-hearted. They had little of the bite and horror that had dominated *Up Front*. Composed as letters from Joe, now a war correspondent, to Willie, a blue-collar family man, the articles contain only one reference to "dogfaces." At the end of his trip, while covering truce negotiations in the mud-hut North Korean village of Panmunjom, Bill happened upon two North Korean goldbricks smoking cigarettes behind a hill. The soldiers, in grimy quilted uniforms and sneaker-like combat boots, were supposed to be patrolling while their superiors talked truce terms in a nearby tent. Bill considered approaching the Red "dog-faces" and then thought better of it.

Outside the negotiating tent, Bill spied a high North Korean delegate stepping out of his staff car. He was a colonel in shiny boots, purple breeches, electric blue jacket, French Foreign Legion cap, and "shoulder boards as big as shingles." The colonel snapped his fingers, and a junior officer ran to help him into a topcoat. A second minion then got busy buttoning the coat up while the popinjay delegate puffed on his long cigarette holder. The scene defied caricature and dampened Bill's enthusiasm for satirizing his own army.[17]

Back in the United States, Bill hurriedly repackaged his *Collier's* articles into a 30,000-word book for W. W. Norton, published as *Bill Mauldin in Korea*. Bill hated the title, which suggested his mere presence in Korea justified the book. In the foreword, Bill tries to inject a note of gravity, calling Korea "a slow, grinding, lonely bitched-up war" with no possibility of victory in the traditional sense. The text's forty-five heavy-line drawings resemble his work in the Italian campaign, though Benday shading softens their impact.[18]

Reviewers of course drew contrasts with *Up Front*. "Not sardonic humor but an air of precocious respectability pervades these pages," noted Herbert Mitgang in the *New York Times*. "The men don't gripe very much here. Mauldin is more serious." One senses, concurred Martin Blumenson in the *Saturday Review,* "that Mauldin went to Korea to be brash and outspoken. But he couldn't get the feel of it. Times have changed." "Mauldin deserves to be remembered for the part he played in the change," Blumenson added, "but that was long ago and another story."[19]

At age thirty, Bill Mauldin was on the verge of becoming a has-been.

WITHIN DAYS of returning from Korea, Bill sold rights to the movie sequel of *Up Front* to Universal Pictures for $50,000. The studio put three writers on the script for quick action, eager to get the slapstick comedy about Korea, titled *Back at the Front,* into theaters before a truce was signed. Bill judged the script so bad, so far removed from anything in his books or cartoons, that he had no sense of being exploited, "no feeling of shameful association." The money would support his family for two years while he worked on his literary projects.[20]

FIGURE 64 The former Hargrove house on South Mountain Road, New City, where the Mauldins lived from late 1949 to 1958.
*Courtesy of the Mauldin Estate.*

The sale to Universal might seem cynical, but it answered the contradictory pressures of Bill's life on South Mountain Road (see figure 64). Twisting along the base of the Ramapo Mountains, "the Road," as residents called it, was home to a circle of very successful artists. It was a bucolic world of upscale bohemianism that included, at various times, lyricist Alan Jay Lerner, composer Kurt Weill, playwright Maxwell Anderson, cartoonist Milton Caniff, sculptor and painter Sidney Simon, singer-actress Lotte Lenya, actors John Houseman and Burgess Meredith, and painter, potter, and architect Henry Varnum Poor. "They had their own in-jokes, their own rivalries, their own histories, their own inbred snobbism, and they walked through the woods and in and out of each other's houses at any time of the day or night," recalls Maxwell Anderson's daughter Hesper.

Nobody on the Road was respected more than Bill Mauldin.

Hesper Anderson remembers him as "wiry, pugnacious, with a dev-
ilish grin and a Southwestern drawl. He was the sort of person that
when he told you he'd started smoking at age three, you believed
him." "He was the kind of a grown-up that you didn't think of as
a grown-up," explains actor René Auberjonois, who as a teenager
babysat for the Mauldins. Auberjonois remembers him as grinning,
joking, and down-to-earth, always at ease with the kids on the Road.
The neighbors teased Bill mercilessly for working on old jalopies
in his yard and ritually washing his cars every Saturday. "But then
there was all this aura around him," Auberjonois observes. "He was
one of the stars on the Road because of his drawings, which were
held in such reverence."

Seeming to put his work and his wars aside, Bill immersed himself in the community's active social life, spending most nights playing poker at the Caniffs', the Simons', the Merediths', or his own
house. The sound of his infectious laughter pervaded the room like
smoke from the players' cigarettes.[21]

Life on South Mountain Road encouraged experiment, often at
the expense of craft. Bill worked by day in a converted fieldstone
garage, "drifting aimlessly," he said, "between a drawing board and
a typewriter." He'd once viewed writing as a "pleasant avocation
to relieve the drudgery of drawing." Now, he subjected his prose
to the same scrutiny that had marked his artwork. Whereas *Up
Front* and *Back Home* had been published virtually as Bill first wrote
them, his manuscripts from the 1950s show painstaking revisions
and multiple drafts. He could dash off magazine essays and columns relatively quickly, but a book remained elusive.[22]

He and Mike Watkins shot book ideas back and forth. Watkins
proposed an illustrated Mark Twain anthology with commentary by
Bill. Bill countered with a handbook on poker, a collection of short
stories, or a novel about Willie and Joe as civilians. Eric Swenson,
Bill's editor at W. W. Norton, urged him to write a sequel to *A Sort of
a Saga* focusing on the war years. Bill put Swenson off, again saying
he wanted a fresh start and not a rehash of old adventures.[23]

There was always the lucrative magazine market. He wrote for *Life*, *Collier's*, and *Sports Illustrated* on subjects ranging from the suburban do-it-yourself craze to the opening of the Air Force Academy in Colorado. In 1953, Henry Luce sent him to cover the coronation of Queen Elizabeth II from a remote Cornish village. Bill then wrote his way across Europe, driving an MG and carousing with John Huston, William Wyler, Art Buchwald, Humphrey Bogart, Rex Harrison, and Truman Capote. The resulting articles betrayed little of the edgy, outrageous, or sordid aspects of his tour. Instead, they offered a gentle send-up of boorish American tourists colliding with inscrutable foreign customs.[24]

An investigation of juvenile delinquency for *Collier's* in 1954 came closer to vintage Mauldin. Sensationalized press reports, movies, and congressional hearings had cast wayward young people as a national threat almost equal to Communism. Calling American youth the "most publicized, analyzed, speculated-upon, worried about, frowned-upon generation of teen-agers in modern times," Bill traveled across the country to hear what the kids themselves had to say. He interviewed teens on drag strips, in pool halls, and outside of high schools, smoking marijuana with them in Texas and New Orleans and working with them on hot rods in Southern California.

In the end, Bill dismissed the juvenile delinquency crisis as a projection of adult fears and hypocrisies. He judged American teens to be, if anything, more conservative, conformist, and "security-conscious" than his generation, acting "like a bunch of little Republicans sometimes."[25]

But Bill really hit his stride when taking on the excesses of Cold War American culture. With Republican Dwight Eisenhower in the White House and Joseph McCarthy poisoning political discourse, Bill launched a humor column in *The Reporter*, an esteemed journal of liberal opinion. Most of the columns satirized anti-Communist hysteria and the inquisitions, loyalty tests, domestic snooping, and anti-intellectualism that went with it. Americans, he thought, had surrendered their rights, privacy, and independent thinking for the illusion of security. Writing about the FBI in a rare flash of anger, Bill charged that "if we can't win our wars on our feet like men, as in the past, instead of crawling through the telephone cables into citizens' homes, then we've lost moral superiority over the hairy Bolshevik and might as well embrace him as a brother."[26]

Such social and political concerns also shaped the evolution of Willie and Joe, now revived in various screenplays, film outlines, and manuscript drafts. To Bill, the former dogfaces represented dueling impulses of Cold War America. The domesticated, "security-conscious" Willie reacts to the prospect of nuclear annihilation by withdrawing into private life. "He wants to insulate himself against this horrible world we face in the future," Bill explains in notes, adding that Willie likes Ike, grumbles about taxes and labor, and turns his auto garage grease pit into a bomb shelter. Joe, by contrast, is the fatalistic, alienated drifter who refuses to settle down or hold a permanent job. Bill describes him as an "honest bum," cynical about politics but sentimental about people.[27]

Bill tried several times to get his various Willie and Joe stories into production as a television series or movie. He sold one version of the script, in which Willie appears as "Dave" and Joe as "Sam," to NBC for $2,000. A second version went to Tyrone Powers' Copa Productions and a third to director Walter Doniger. None was ever produced.[28]

The novel also remained incomplete, joining "a closet-full of half-assed manuscripts," as Bill put it. In 1953, he signed a contract with W. W. Norton for a book about his European tour titled *Unarmed in Europe*. The material proved too thin, so Norton transferred the contract and advance money to Bill's next project. Titled *Day to Day,* the book was about "the Mauldins coping with life— with a Great Dane who considers himself his master's keeper and with fast-moving poison ivy which threatens to engulf their home." When this, too, fizzled, editor Eric Swenson once again suggested a war memoir. He warned Bill not "to pull off another steal such as the Korean book." He didn't want a reprint of magazine articles bulked up by big type, huge margins, heavy paper, and extra pages for chapter breaks. He wanted, rather, a book that would make a "permanent dent in the world."[29]

As he launched and then abandoned one ambitious task after another, hoping to make that dent, Bill thought of Pop. The nights of heavy drinking and late night poker were another reminder. Bill woke up most mornings now with a hangover. Sometimes, only a whiskey sour or two got him back on his feet and into the studio. Natalie grew concerned. She told Bill that if he ever lost "sovereignty" over his life, it would be to alcohol. Bill took the warning to heart, trembling at the thought of following in Pop's footsteps.[30]

Natalie, meanwhile, struggled with the burden of running a household and raising four small children. While she shared Bill's ambivalence about bourgeois domesticity, Natalie frequently clashed with her husband over household roles and duties. Even the nannies and housekeepers became a source of strain. Natalie had grown up in the company of servants, nurses, and maids. Such privilege brought with it responsibilities and rules that didn't include Bill's leniency and familiarity with the household staff. She was positively embarrassed when he greeted them with an obvious hangover. "You are always to give the feeling you are in *command*," she lectured Bill. "It must be like the army," she continued in unintended irony. "If all the privates don't feel like there is an officer running things they'll do it to suit themselves, and worse, they'll quit altogether."[31]

Despite its bohemian exterior, South Mountain Road adhered to many conventions that ruled other American suburbs of the 1950s, especially with respect to women. "The only thing that was required of a woman was beauty," explains Hesper Anderson. "Talent, even a woman's own success, didn't count for much." For Natalie Mauldin, the Road was often a stifling environment. She'd once entertained literary aspirations more promising than Bill's.

Four pregnancies in six years, coupled with a lack of encouragement from Bill and friends, all but doused these ambitions. In their place grew her natural melancholy.

Hesper Anderson, who was fourteen when the Mauldins moved into the Hargrove house, recalls Natalie as embodying "everything I'd ever dreamed of having—a successful husband, a house I loved, four beautiful babies. I couldn't figure out why she kept having breakdowns."[32]

One came after the birth of their fourth son, Nathaniel, in September of 1953. Natalie spiraled into postpartum depression requiring weeks of inpatient treatment at the Payne Whitney Clinic in New York City. The already chaotic household fell to pieces in her absence. Unpaid bills mounted and expenses soared as Bill enlisted a small army of servants and nurses to tend to the children and get meals on the table. He reluctantly borrowed $5,000 from Natalie's mother, Alice Rossin, who temporarily took over the family finances.[33]

The pressures of breadwinning bore down like never before. Bill took to reeling off the "roll call" of his ten legal dependents (Jean and Natalie; six children: Bruce, Tim, Andy, David, John, and Nat; his grandparents, Uncle Billy and Nana, to whom Bill dutifully sent monthly checks). He pushed harder to secure a television deal, and solicited Omar Bradley's help in pitching a series about the infantry to rival NBC's *Victory at Sea* and CBS's *Air Power.* He also, for the first time since joining the army, sold advertising copy. He promoted only those products he knew intimately: Kent cigarettes, Seagram's gin, and Piper airplanes.[34]

Airplanes were an old passion. As a kid in Phoenix, he'd painted a poster for an aviation school and received one flying lesson in return. His second time in the cockpit had come during the war, when a bomber crew let him fly a B-26 from Naples to Corsica. The experience fascinated him, but not enough to dampen his infantryman's prejudice against the flyboys. After Bill had complained loudly about being strafed by American P-51 Mustangs in northern

Italy, an air force general had taken the cartoonist up in his fighter and proceeded to roll, climb, spin, and dive his way up and down the Po Valley until Bill was covered in his own vomit and bleeding from his nose and ears.[35]

In the summer of 1953, Bill began flying lessons from Bill Bohlke, the flight instructor at nearby Spring Valley airport. Bohlke, said Bill, treated piloting "like a craft to be learned, not some mysterious art." As if discovering the craft focus that had eluded him on South Mountain Road, Bill immersed himself in aviation. Within weeks he was soloing. Nine months later, he had a commercial pilot's license, soon followed by multiengine, instrument, and even helicopter ratings. Bill read everything he could find on aeronautics and became nothing short of an expert on the subject. He enjoyed raising old-timers' hackles by telling them that the throttle doesn't actually control speed, nor the rudder steering. He wrote articles for *Life, Sports Illustrated,* and *Air Facts* magazine about his growing mastery of the skies (see figure 65). By the end of 1956, he'd logged over 100,000 miles in his Piper Tri-Pacer, payment from the manufacturer in exchange for advertising and promotional material.

Friends might dismiss the Piper as "just a great big yo-yo for Bill to play with," but flying provided Bill with a much-needed mechanism for control, as well as escape. Few who traveled with Bill considered it fun. He was as meticulous about piloting as about drawing. He never relaxed or took chances in the cockpit, always seeking a higher level of proficiency, whether it be in maintaining the machine, studying the instruments, reading the weather, or calculating navigation. "As a pilot," Bill said, "you are sovereign in the air." In flying, Bill found a way to sublimate his nomadic instincts into a useful skill set that, he told Eric Swenson, warranted a book.[36]

Now that he had a new craft, he needed only a crusade to justify it. He found his cause on March 14, 1956, when, after a whiskey-fueled meeting with two local Democratic Party officials, Bill Mauldin decided to run for Congress.

FIGURE 65 Always eager for an air adventure he could turn into a salable article, Bill took his sons Andy (left), age eight, and David (right), six, on a tour of the Caribbean basin in the summer of 1957. The resulting three-part account, published in *Sports Illustrated* in January 1958, was Mauldin at his most charming and expert. The journey inspired him to consider a family flight to Moscow. He consulted with Eleanor Roosevelt about getting security clearance but abandoned the plan when he began work at the *St. Louis Post-Dispatch* in April 1958.

*George Moffett*/Sports Illustrated.

BILL'S INITIATION in Democratic Party politics had come on the campaign trail with Adlai Stevenson in the fall of 1952. Pleased at first by Eisenhower's nomination at the Republican National Convention, Bill was aghast when Ike agreed to the Red-baiting Richard Nixon as his running mate. He was also dismayed by Eisenhower's refusal to defend his army colleague General Marshall, whom Senator Joseph McCarthy attacked as being treasonously soft on Communism (see figure 66). ("Sometimes," Bill later wrote of Ike, "when I feel outraged because he lets fools run wild, I take heart in his consistency, remembering that once long ago he let us fools run wild, too.") Along with World War I hero Alvin York and several other former soldiers, Bill founded "Veterans for Stevenson" and traveled around the country giving speeches for the Democratic candidate.[37]

**FIGURE 66** In late 1953, Bill began cartooning again on rare occasions. He would drive his cartoons to the *New York Post* in Manhattan, offering them for free if the editors would print them the next day. Bill did such pro bono work only when piqued by Senator Joseph McCarthy, who was then directing his anti-Communist venom against the United States Army. In this cartoon from February 25, 1954, McCarthy, dressed as a German storm trooper, oversees the surrender of Dwight Eisenhower and high-ranking army brass. Not long after this cartoon appeared, Eisenhower began standing up to McCarthy, hastening his downfall.

After Ike's victory in November, Bill became the national chair of the American Veterans Committee (AVC), a group of 30,000 "lusty liberals" who supported civil liberty, civil rights, and a strong national defense. Considering himself "not much of a team man," Bill liked the AVC because, he said, "it's a veterans' organization opposed to veterans' organizations." Bill spent most of his time issuing press releases denouncing the 3-million-member American Legion for its segregated chapters, undemocratic bylaws, and secret committees that collected dossiers on suspected subversives.[38]

When Bill's work for the AVC ended in early 1956, John Sullivan and Michael Gurda, chair and vice-chair of the Orange County Democratic Party, approached him about running in New York's Twenty-eighth Congressional District. The party was desperate for a candidate. A Democrat had not been elected in the Republican stronghold for over a half century. "They [the Twenty-eighth's residents] were Tories in the Revolution, Copperheads in the Civil War, and Nazi lovers in World War II—a bunch of really raunchy assholes," Bill carped in later years. Most Democratic candidates, however, were hopeless politicians, either high-minded idealists without a campaign strategy or hack attorneys looking to boost their prestige. Bill offered something different: a tough-minded liberal with solid party credentials, a war record, and widespread name recognition. Sullivan and Gurda smoothed the way for Bill's nomination, brushing aside a late challenge by conservative big-money Democrats who backed a local county sheriff.[39]

By mid-March, the nomination was his if he wanted it. His opponent would be the formidable Katharine Delano Price Collier St. George. The gray-haired St. George was an archconservative with the same patrician background but polar opposite political philosophy as her first cousin Franklin Roosevelt. She was the living legacy of her grandfather Warren Delano, who said, "I will not say that all Democrats are horse thieves, but it would seem that all horse thieves are Democrats." At sixty-two, Katharine St. George easily held the seat for ten years.[40]

Bill believed he could make it a race. Ensconced in her luxurious Tuxedo Park apartment, St. George had lost touch with her constituents. Though Republican by tradition, the district contained many small poultry and dairy farmers who were going broke in the face of falling prices and corporate competition. Other family-run businesses were disappearing as well, victims of suburban sprawl and chain stores. A recent flood had caused $4 million in damage to crops and machinery. Katharine St. George had opposed relief and didn't even visit the distressed farms. She was unwilling, Bill judged, to muddy her feet for a vote.[41]

Candidate Mauldin launched his campaign in April at the annual Democratic Dinner. Governor Averell Harriman was the guest of honor. The Rockland County *Journal News* reported that "the fast-breaking Congressional candidate who hails from the Southwest stole the show" with his "salty" twang and "easy down-to-earth Will Rogers kind of political humor." Other newspapers praised Bill's candidacy as a masterstroke that might just unseat Mrs. St. George.

"No Democrat had gotten such fair coverage in that district," Bill said later. It helped that he put reporters from several local dailies on his campaign's payroll. Candidate Mauldin, to no one's surprise, was a hard-nosed hustler who played for keeps. With the party's conservative benefactors holding back their contributions, Bill borrowed money from his mother-in-law, took out a second mortgage on his home, and raised thousands of dollars through small donations (each donor received in return a certificate of membership to the "Long Shot Club").[42]

He spent sixteen hours a day on the campaign trail, crisscrossing a district that stretched across four counties west of the Hudson River. By mid-October, he had put 15,000 miles on his Piper Tri-Pacer and 20,000 on his Willys jeep, nicely customized with secondhand red leather seats. Bill's weekly column appeared in newspapers; his campaign song blared, and his signs and orange-on-black bumper stickers sprouted like mushrooms (see figure 67). Al Capp, Mort Walker, Milton Caniff, Roy Crane, and a half dozen other cartoonists inked panels on Bill's behalf (see figure 68). A few crossed party lines to do so. Celebrities like Burgess Meredith and Mitch Miller organized fund-raisers, prompting one observer to call Bill's campaign an "off-Broadway production."[43]

Refusing to be a mere celebrity candidate, Bill immersed himself in the issues. He constructed an eight-point platform that included support for Israel, a strong military, civil rights in housing and jobs, and an increase in federal aid to public schools and the postal service. The focus of his campaign, however, was on the economic well-being of his rural and small-town neighbors. Bill invoked Willie and Joe often, saying that they now represented the "farmers, industrial workers, and small businessmen," all cast aside by big-business Republicans.

Bill spent most of his time in the hard-hit rural districts, where farm foreclosures had become routine. Bill told the farmers he could help them. As he later put it, he was being "economical with the truth." "The truth was that about all I could do was listen to them. At least, this was more than they'd been getting."[44]

Perhaps his finest campaign moment came on Memorial Day, when Bill agreed for the first and only time to give an address at a cemetery. He was reluctant to speak of these dead, to exploit them for political gain, Bill told the crowd. His own rifle company had suffered 1,000% turnover during the war. One thousand eight hundred men had gone through his 170-man company. Why had *he* survived? "By what right did some stray piece of steel go sailing past OUR heads and hit THEM?" he asked on behalf of all the war's survivors. For those who lived through the war, he said, "Memorial Day is every day." He refused to speak of his comrades as self-sacrificing patriots. In fact, he warned the crowd, their deaths only preserved, for the time being, our liberty:

> Liberty is a living thing, and like all living things it needs nourishment. If you feel something needs saying and don't say it for fear of popular disapproval, you have withered liberty a bit. If you

FIGURE 67 Natalie collapsed under the stress of Bill's campaign, and her formidable mother, Alice Henderson Rossin, stepped in to take over the household and the campaign. With her, left to right, are Bill and Natalie's children: Andy, David, John, and Nat.

*Courtesy of the Mauldin Estate.*

FIGURE 68 In his 1956 campaign, Bill enlisted his friends from the cartooning fraternity, including liberal New Dealer Al Capp, creator of "Li'l Abner."

*© Capp Enterprises, Inc.
Used by permission.*

stop another man from saying what he feels, the living plant of liberty dies just a bit. Liberty is dissension, ladies and gentlemen; it is argument, debate, politics, the right to live and work where and as you wish. Liberty is the right of a man to be the captain of his soul and destiny. . . . If we lose it, their deaths are meaningless. If we keep it, their graves are honored in spirit. It is the least we could do for them.[45]

This speech sheds light on Bill's outrage in the last days of the campaign when Katharine St. George, rattled by her contender, resorted to Red-baiting. For the first time, she raised the issue of Bill's former left-wing associations, detailing his membership in such allegedly subversive organizations as the American Youth for Democracy, the American Civil Liberties Union, and the Freedom from Fear Committee. "We don't need any eggheads to run the government," she said.

A few days later, an attack ad appeared in newspapers accusing Bill of being "unfit for office" and a "tool of un-American subversive groups." Produced by a group calling itself "Veterans for an All-American Congress," the ad cited meetings and dinners Bill had attended years before as part of his work for alleged "Communist-front organizations." Decades later, when he obtained his FBI file through the Freedom of Information Act, Bill realized that the charges in the advertisement had been lifted verbatim from his raw dossier, to which St. George somehow gained access.[46]

The questioning of his patriotism infuriated Bill. "Mud and mink are a poor combination," he quipped the next day. "I don't like to see a mink-draped dowager splatter herself in this way." He insisted he would remain a gentleman and keep his campaign focused on local issues. "Now," he told friends, "I would really like to beat her." Hedging his bets, he filed suit against St. George for libel and slander in the Orange County Supreme Court.[47]

The lawsuit, which he eventually dropped, kept the contest alive in Bill's mind for months after his defeat at the polls. Katharine St. George won by 39,000 votes out of almost 164,000 cast. Bill had given St. George the toughest challenge of her career and had electrified the campaign. The district polled the largest tally in its history, and Bill racked up 20,000 more votes than the previous Democratic candidate. He came to within 252 ballots of upsetting his opponent in the heavily Republican Sullivan County, largely because of his aggressive campaigning there. No Democrat in the Twenty-eighth Congressional District had ever polled better. Bill later said he got as many votes as hands he shook.[48]

The campaign left him exhausted, broke, and through with politics. But he'd gained a new appreciation for politicians. "I still don't trust any of them," he said years later. "However, I now find it really difficult to hate one."[49]

BY EARLY 1957, the Mauldins were looking for a fresh start. Natalie had been hospitalized again with depression during the campaign. She wanted to move back to New Mexico. Bill, too, was ready to leave the rarified world of South Mountain Road. He'd always felt somewhat out of place, rarely participating in high-minded discussions of art and literature. "He wasn't interested," says neighbor Joan Crowell. "He was interested in cars."[50]

The campaign, his debt, and ongoing professional frustrations sharpened his hard-boiled attitude. In June, Bill broke with the Watkins Literary Agency, which, he said, "was doing very little to earn the money it was so meticulously extracting from me." Mike Watkins, Bill contended, "belongs to what I consider the 'precious' school. To this day I am paying dues to Literary Leagues and Authors' Guilds Mike talked me into, when the fact is that ever since art school I have disliked the society of 'creative types.'" Bill signed instead with Helen Strauss, who, as head of the literary division of the William Morris Agency, was probably the most powerful agent in America.[51]

He began work on his war memoir. But in truth, he was tired of writing. He wanted to get back to the drawing table, to be at the top of his craft again. "He was very unhappy," recalled Bill's former colleague on the *Stars and Stripes,* Ralph Martin. "He wasn't fulfilled; he was floating around. . . . He couldn't get a focus; he couldn't get an outlet, doing what he really wanted to do."

Martin tried to help Bill find that outlet. In 1957, at lunch with the editor of *Newsday,* Richard Clurman, Martin suggested Bill for the open position of editorial cartoonist. After getting over his shock that Mauldin would even consider such a post, Clurman called Bill to discuss the job. They met several times, agreed on terms, and all but closed the deal. Bill prepared to commute by plane to Long Island.

Then Martin received a phone call from a dejected Mauldin. Clurman had given the job to the twenty-four-year-old Thomas Darcy. "The Boy Wonder isn't the Boy Wonder anymore," Bill said.

A few weeks later, Martin got another lead. During a magazine interview, the great Daniel Fitzpatrick, éminence grise of editorial cartooning, told Martin that he was soon retiring after fifty years at Joseph Pulitzer Jr.'s *St. Louis Post-Dispatch*. Bill had long admired the liberal *Post-Dispatch* as "one of the truly great papers in America." Indeed, back in 1946, it was the *Post-Dispatch*'s dumping of his syndicated feature that finally awakened Bill to the shrill nature of his cartoons.

Martin told Fitzpatrick that Bill would probably be interested in the job. Like *Newsday*'s Richard Clurman, Fitzpatrick was stunned. He figured Bill would want to stay on the East Coast, where the big syndicates would be sure to sign him up again if he wanted it.

Back in New York, Ralph Martin ran into Bill having lunch with cartoonist Walt Kelly, creator of "Pogo." Bill had known Kelly since they both worked at the *New York Star*. Martin told Bill about his interview with Fitzpatrick.

"Boy, would I love to have that job," Bill said.

"You're kidding!" exclaimed Kelly. "You would actually go and live in St. Louis with that crazy, hot, muggy weather?"

"I would walk there to get that job," Bill responded.

Despite his eagerness, Bill refused to lift the phone and call Fitzpatrick. "He was a funny kind of a guy," Martin explains. "He didn't like to solicit. He wanted people to come to him. He didn't want to be in a position where he's applying for a job."

Fitzpatrick may have felt similarly. In any case, he never called Bill either. Bill finally broke through the impasse in early 1958 by touching down in St. Louis on a trip to the Midwest. He called Fitz from the airport, and the two men discussed the position at length. Fitz told Bill he would be an exclusively in-house cartoonist at first, beholden to the editorial page, with no syndication. Robert Lasch, editor at the *Post-Dispatch*, echoed Fitzpatrick's warning.[52]

Bill responded with a passionate apologia for his craft. "I think the only hope for the salvation of American editorial cartooning is for a little more identity with a community and a little less trying to please three hundred editors," Bill told Lasch. "I really think that as the television business—along with the rest of communications and entertainment—tends to get bigger and blander," he continued, "the editorial page is going to get more and more precious to people."[53]

A second trip to St. Louis in March 1958 closed the deal. The paper would start Bill on a two-month trial. The cover story would be that the cartoonist was only temporarily filling in for a vacationing Fitzpatrick. That way, if the arrangement went sour, both the paper and Bill had a face-saving out. The paper would pay him $18,000 a year plus benefits for six cartoons a week. It was Bill's first salaried job since leaving the army.[54]

Bill moved into the Sheraton-Jefferson Hotel in downtown St. Louis and began work on April 21. Three days later, he wrote to his friend Norton Wolf. "I have cranked out four in four days, which is three more than they (or I) expected, and they are not bad. One was pretty good. Unhappily, [Secretary of State] Dulles has kept his mouth shut, nothing huge has happened in a national way, and I think it would be a mistake to draw local things while still a stranger in town, so I have been general in subject matter. . . . Most amazing of all, I find myself getting up cheerfully at seven and going to bed at eleven. Maybe I was cut out to be bourgeois after all."[55]

The job was a huge adjustment. Bill was free to draw what he pleased, but if the editors didn't like a cartoon, they were equally free not to print it. He soon found he had to tone down the heavy, coarse look of his previous work. "I had done Willie and Joe in a bold brush, and it was too stark a technique for political cartooning," Bill said two years later. "The damn drawings jumped out of the page at you. They were as subtle as a punch in the nose. In the end, I finally realized the cartoon had to recede into the page and complement it."[56]

Gone, for the most part, were the intimate characters, lavish landscapes, and thick black lines that had made Mauldin's wartime and postwar cartoons so distinctive. Instead, Bill worked in pen, crayon, and charcoal, delineating caricatures and visual metaphors in economical shades of gray. "Every line and word must justify itself," Bill said, "otherwise it goes out." He developed no recognizable characters of his own, but relied on sophisticated renditions of leaders like Eisenhower, Nixon, Castro, Khrushchev, and Mao. He was no longer viewing events from the mudsill, nor even from Main Street. Rather, he became a global commentator, alone and detached, a catbird perched at a drawing table (see figure 69).

In July, the *Post-Dispatch* declared Bill a fixture on the editorial page. The Mauldins sold their house in Rockland County and moved to the St. Louis suburb of Frontenac. There Bill revived his austere work routine first established at the Lawson YMCA in Chicago.

The process began at night in bed. Surrounded by newspapers, magazines, a steno notepad, and some pencils, Bill read and sketched at the same time, drafting six or seven roughs on various topics of the moment. The next morning, over a large cup of coffee, Bill would take his sketches and settle into a steaming hot

**"Whew!"**

**FIGURE 69** This depiction of the Cuban Revolution as a cat-and-mouse game, with guerrilla leader Fidel Castro recovering from a near miss, was Bill's first cartoon for the *St. Louis Post-Dispatch*. The cartoon is startlingly neutral on the subject of the Communist insurgency in Cuba. The Cold War blunted Bill's sympathies for Third World underdogs. When Castro seized power in early 1959, Bill noted that "Fidel came down out of the hills like Robin Hood and right away began acting like the Sheriff of Nottingham."

bathtub to "boil my brains." The tub acted as a "filter system, like an automatic coffee maker combined with what shrinks might call free association." He worked a day at a time, seeking one good idea a morning, and he never emerged from the boil without one.[57]

After driving to the office in his Willys jeep, Bill sketched a rough version of his idea and presented it to editor Robert Lasch for approval. Only once was there a problem when Bill drew a cartoon about Pope John XXIII, whom Bill admired for his humility and common touch. "Yeah, I know, I know," says one gardener to another at St. Peter's as the pope walks past, "but you *still* shouldn't have called him *Jack!*"

Though Bill intended the gag as a compliment, Lasch feared a backlash from Catholic readers. Bill backed down. "Mauldin does not consider himself bigger than the *Post-Dispatch*," crowed Lasch.[58]

Once approved, the cartoon went back to the drawing table, where Bill would sketch out a half dozen miniaturized "spots" on typing paper ("with a very blunt pencil so as not to get too involved in detail"). Each spot represented a different approach and composition. He then selected his spot and began the four-hour process of drawing the finished cartoon. Fussy as always, he unplugged the phone and began a running dialogue with himself as he drew. As in the army, his workspace was crowded with photo files and reference books, including a well-thumbed Sears, Roebuck catalog. He remained passionate about authenticity and used a Polaroid camera with a remote button to take pictures of himself in various poses. Capturing precisely the curl of an arm, the twist of a face, or the wrinkles in an overcoat was an ongoing obsession. He forced himself to draw fingernails on his figures, even though readers would never see them on the three-column cartoon. Occasionally he even signed his name "Maudlin" to see if anybody noticed. No one ever did.[59]

At the drafting table, Bill divided his paper into a grid of nine squares and began drawing in pencil from the right-hand bottom corner so as not drag his drawing hand, his left, over his work. He then used a fine-point pen as lightly and loosely as he could to go over the pencil lines, which he later erased. Lithographic pencil, or crayon, added shading. A red sable brush and india ink beefed up lines that were too thin. Finally Bill sprayed the drawing with fixative and delivered it by hand to the engravers. "I would never trust a copy boy with it," he said. After a couple of martinis at a nearby bar, he drove back home to begin reading for the next day's cartoon.

The demanding regimen paid off. Within weeks Bill Mauldin wielded one of the hottest brushes in the business. While curbing his "righteous wrath" on nuclear weapons, civil rights, Third World revolution, and the Washington power game, he nonetheless exhibited a candor rare among commentators of the era (see figure 70). Cartoons had become blander and less offensive since the late 1940s, as syndicates sought ever-larger circulations. The Associated Press's John M. Morris, for example, racked up two hundred newspapers with what *Time* magazine called his "almost ingeniously equivocal" cartoons that avoided all controversy and took aim "only at universally accepted villains."

"They try not to be too offensive," said Bill of his colleagues. "The hell with that. We need more stirrer-uppers." "You've got to be a misanthrope in this business, a real son of a bitch. I'm touchy. I've got raw nerve ends, and I'll jump. If I see a stuffed shirt, I want to punch it. If it's big, hit it. You can't go far wrong."[60]

Bill's gut-fighting approach had its costs. A neighbor in Frontenac, a Republican attorney, secretly sent letters to J. Edgar Hoover about Bill's cartoons and activities. He also let the FBI know about Bill's distress over Natalie's ongoing mental health problems. The informant promised to continue in his efforts to "straighten out" Mauldin.[61]

Bill's cartoons cut to the core of complex issues, relationships, and public personalities (see figure 71). His work took him rapidly to the top of his field. Six months after coming to the *Post-Dispatch*, Bill inked the cartoon that earned him a second Pulitzer Prize (see figure 72). In 1959, he was elected Editorial Cartoonist of the Year

*"Me? I'm the little kid you used to call a gook."*

**FIGURE 70** Although he worked toward a looser, more fluid style, Bill occasionally resorted to the bold brush lines of old in making a point, especially during his early months at the *Post-Dispatch*. Published on July 17, 1958, a few days after radical Arab nationalists staged a bloody coup in Iraq, this cartoon expresses a conviction that America's racial arrogance toward the Third World would eventually come back to haunt it.

by the National Cartoonists Society. Such recognition, along with the Pulitzer, brought him syndication offers again.

Joseph Pulitzer Jr. signed Bill up with the *New York Herald-Tribune* syndicate, on Bill's usual terms. Subscribing newspapers need not carry cartoons they disliked. But they could not alter the drawings or the captions (see figure 73).

As Bill's star rose again, press reports dwelled on his years in the wilderness, what *Time* magazine called his decade of "aimless drifting" after leaving United Features in 1948. Bill protested that he had merely taken a well-earned sabbatical. He jokingly compared himself to the "Lost Generation" of World War I. "They were lost, all right, but they were lost in Paris and having a damn good time of it."[62]

IN JUNE 1962, about to leave on an art-buying tour of Europe, Joseph Pulitzer Jr. got a phone call. In a voice filled with regret, Bill Mauldin told Pulitzer he was leaving the *Post-Dispatch*.

The main issue was money. After four years, Bill was only earning $20,000 annually and another $8,000 to $10,000 from his share of syndication royalties. It was a meager sum for a man who had been on the cover of *Time* magazine for a second time, won the Reuben Award for the best cartoonist in America, and published a fast-selling collection of his cartoons. "The Pulitzers had always a great reputation for openhandedness. I ran into the first tightfisted Pulitzer," Bill said years later.

As Bill's contract ran out, Marshall Field IV of the *Chicago Sun-Times* approached Bill with a more fitting offer: $25,000 a year and a full share of the syndication royalties, estimated to be worth another $25,000 to $30,000. Field offered more aggressive syndication and a reduction of his workload from six cartoons a week to five.

If he joined the tabloid, Field offered a freedom denied to him at the *Post-Dispatch*. His cartoons need not conform to the wishes of the *Sun-Times*. No longer would they require editorial approval. His

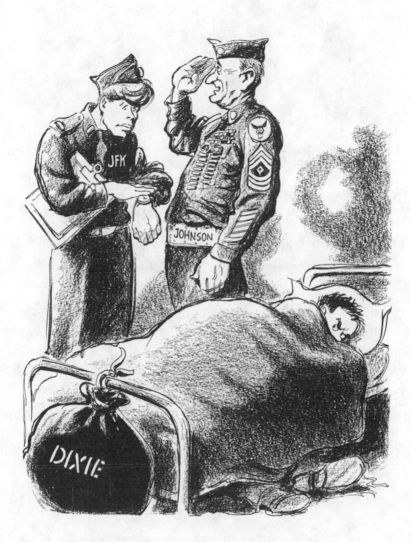

*"All present or accounted for, sir!"*

**FIGURE 71** Bill conceived the relationship between presidential candidate John F. Kennedy and his running mate, Lyndon B. Johnson, in terms he knew so well from the army. Bill wrote: "And so the wise young officer (after all, he'd picked this particular sergeant for his very own) tiptoed out of the barracks and left the grizzled veteran with the recalcitrant goldbrick. The man bucked and kicked, but when the roll was called out yonder he was there."

*"I won the Nobel Prize for Literature.
What was your crime?"*

**FIGURE 72** In the fall of 1958, Russian writer Boris Pasternak learned he had won the Nobel Prize for Literature. Soviet authorities barred him from accepting the award, though he was never arrested or exiled. The episode inspired this Pulitzer Prize–winning cartoon. "It was the first time anybody ever parlayed another man's Nobel into his own Pulitzer," remarked a wag on the *Post-Dispatch*.

"LET THAT ONE GO. HE SAYS HE DON'T WANNA BE MAH EQUAL."

FIGURE 73 Published on March 2, 1960, this cartoon was one of the first to be syndicated under Bill's agreement with the *St. Louis Post-Dispatch*. At least one paper in the deep South canceled its subscription, and readers from all over the country, including a few of Bill's own family members, wrote to the *Post-Dispatch* to complain. The night before, Bill had seen footage on network news of nonviolent lunch-counter demonstrators being beaten with baseball bats.

feature would appear along with signed opinion pieces opposite the editorial page. He would, in fact, be a "columnist who works with an artist's pen," as Bill later put it. Despite his fondness for St. Louis, Bill quickly accepted the offer.[63]

His first day at the *Sun-Times* was unsettling. Exploiting Willie and Joe in its promotion of Mauldin's arrival, the newspaper surprised Bill by sending an army jeep to ferry him down the block to the Sun-Times Building. He was no longer a boy wonder or kid cartoonist, but a sophisticated political commentator, or so he hoped. He wanted to be taken seriously, but here he was, an overgrown child, being cast as a relic from a war long past. "It took me a while to get over that," he said a few years later. "It's not something I'll forget."[64]

Conversely, the respect the paper paid to Bill assuaged his anxiety. By early fall, after moving his family into an apartment overlooking Lake Michigan, Bill persuaded the paper to make him both a correspondent and a commentator. He wanted to get away from the drawing board now and then. "I simply need to see new people and places," he said. "When I stay in an office, I start drawing elephants and donkeys."[65]

He arrived in Oxford, Mississippi, on Saturday, September 29, 1962, two days before African American student James Meredith was scheduled to enroll at the University of Mississippi Law School. Also aboard the rented plane was Hoke Norris, book critic at the *Sun-Times*. The men were looking for local color and expected to be long gone before Meredith arrived. On Sunday afternoon, they noticed the quiet town filling up with "hard-eyed, red-necked, whiskey-soaked young men." Sensing trouble, Bill decided to get out of town.

By evening, however, Oxford's tiny airfield had been overrun by military transports and cargo planes. James Meredith had arrived a day early, and was now surrounded by a phalanx of U.S. marshals. "He looked terribly small and vulnerable," Bill said, "with a

**FIGURE 74** A drawing Bill rushed into publication on October 1, 1962, the day after rioting began in Oxford, Mississippi. Few other images of the event ever appeared in print. One photographer at the scene was shot in the back and killed. Bill never forgot the courage of outnumbered federal marshals, nor the cretinous behavior of the local Mississippi cops, one of whom appears on the left.

*Copyright 1962 by Bill Mauldin. Courtesy of the Mauldin Estate.*

"WHAT DO YOU MEAN, 'NOT SO FAST'?"

*"Up North we sort of nibble 'em to death."*

**FIGURES 75 AND 76** No issue stirred Bill's passions more than civil rights. The African American, Bill said, "is the enlisted man of our society." "It's just that I don't like a man being told he's unequal until he gets a chance to prove his own inequality." Bill drew these two cartoons in the aftermath of the Birmingham movement, when Martin Luther King Jr. and the Southern Christian Leadership Conference overcame water hoses, guard dogs, and prison cells to desegregate the unofficial capital of Dixie. The drawing above left, from May 10, 1963, gives visual expression to King's declaration in the "Letter from Birmingham City Jail" that "there comes a time when the cup of endurance runs over, and men are no longer willing to be plunged into the abyss of despair." Lest liberal white northerners remain smugly blind to their own racism, Bill offered the cartoon above right nine days later.

*Above left: Prints and Photographs Division,*
*Library of Congress, LC-DIG-ppmsca-03251.*

*Copyright 1963 by Bill Mauldin. Courtesy of the Mauldin Estate.*

*Above right: Copyright 1963 by Bill Mauldin. Courtesy of the Mauldin Estate.*

briefcase in his hand." Bill swallowed his fear and joined the procession from the airfield to Ole Miss.

By nightfall, thousands of white protesters bearing clubs, pipes, stones, and guns had laid siege to the campus. Bill and Norris stood among a handful of correspondents near the center of action outside the Greek Revival administration building. The rioters terrorized anyone with a camera or notebook. As sirens, tear gas, and gunshots filled the air, the mob surged forward, overwhelming federal marshals. It was now a matter of hand-to-hand combat.

In the confusion, Bill and Norris slipped back to their hotel, where they filed their stories over the phone. The next morning, they reentered the battle zone. Two people lay dead and several hundred were wounded. Thirty thousand federal troops were en route to quell America's greatest white insurrection since the Civil War (see figure 74).[66]

Bill's reporting from Oxford bolstered his credentials, both as writer and cartoonist. The *Sun-Times* began sending him to New York, Washington, and Europe—wherever statesmen and politicians were making news. He also followed closely the civil rights crusade. By 1963, he had become one of its most vocal and sophisticated supporters (see figures 75 and 76).

For a forty-one-year-old, Bill had lived a lot, arriving at the peak of his power and influence. His syndication topped two hundred papers, about what he'd had during the war. He was the dean of editorial cartooning.

His single most memorable cartoon—indeed, perhaps the most powerful editorial cartoon of the twentieth century—came on his day off, Friday, November 22, 1963. He was attending a Council on Foreign Relations luncheon at Chicago's Palmer House hotel when a woman came in and announced that the president had been shot. The room fell silent. Then someone at Bill's table suggested that they all go home and have a drink.

Instead, Bill headed to the office. His normal 1 p.m. deadline at the *Sun-Times* had come and gone, and in any case, the paper didn't run a Mauldin cartoon on Saturday. But perhaps if he came up with something special in the next hour or so, the editors might sneak a drawing into the next edition.

Bill had not been particularly fond of the eastern, aristocratic John F. Kennedy, despite sharing most of his politics. A few months earlier, he'd traveled to Germany with the White House press corps to cover Kennedy's historic speech at the Berlin Wall. The cheering German crowds had sent a chill down his spine. He could not help but think of another leader who'd basked in adoration in that very square. Kennedy, Bill said, "was inciting them, and he knew it."

Now, however, it was not Kennedy he had in mind so much as the nation he left behind. He thought immediately of Abraham Lincoln, who had died for his support of Emancipation. Bill guessed that Kennedy might have been similarly shot by a right-wing opponent of civil rights. But he had no proof. Kennedy was Catholic. Perhaps he could use a religious symbol, a statue, with tears streaming down its face. No good. Too narrow. Besides, religion always got him in trouble.

At the Sun-Times Building, Bill checked with the managing editor. Was it too late to get a cartoon in the next day's issue? The engravers could probably squeeze it in, the editor told Bill, if they got the drawing within the hour.

With a file photo of the Lincoln Memorial lying next to him, Bill worked faster than ever before. Lincoln's hairline tripped him up. Looking too much like Kennedy's, it might confuse those unfamiliar with the statue. But he had no time to fix it. "If they didn't know the statue," he figured, "they wouldn't get the cartoon anyway." He sprayed his flawed drawing with fixative and ran it to the engravers (see figure 77).

The editors took one look at the drawing and immediately gave it the entire back page. Just under two hours later, the first edition hit the streets. Newsdealers all over Chicago displayed the *Sun-Times* back side up, preferring Bill's cartoon to the blaring headline on the front page. The paper sold out in a matter of hours.

**Figure 77** Bill's Lincoln Memorial cartoon, states Jules Feiffer, exemplifies his "tragic eloquence." "There was a knowledge of tragedy within himself and in his own life, in what he had lived through in the war, before the war, and after the war. He had soul, and it came through in all of the work."

*Copyright 1963 by Bill Mauldin. Courtesy of the Mauldin Estate.*

Over the coming weeks, more than a half million requests poured in for copies of the cartoon. The newspaper began issuing free reprints, and crowds lined up outside the Sun-Times Building to get them. Bill gave the original to Marshall Field IV, a decorated combat sailor in World War II. Not long afterward, Kennedy's press secretary, Pierre Salinger, called to say that Jacqueline Kennedy would like to have the drawing. So Field gave the drawing back to Bill, who whited out the original inscription. Over the top, he wrote: *"For Mrs. Jacqueline Kennedy. Bill Mauldin."*

"I've never been all that sold on it," Bill said about the drawing years later. The hairline still bothered him, as did the public's assumption that Lincoln was crying rather than momentarily buckling under the burden of tragedy and fear. So he wasn't disappointed when the celebrated cartoon did not win the Pulitzer Prize. The award went instead to Paul Conrad of the *Denver Post*.[67]

Chapter Eight

# Fighting On

*(1964–2003)*

*Pleiku, Vietnam. February 7, 1965.* The mortar barrage began while Bill was asleep in his cot, a little after 2 a.m. His first waking thought was that someone had set off fireworks left over from Tet. Then a round hit outside his "hooch," the barracks assigned to him as a guest of the 52d Aviation Battalion.

"Is that what I think it is?" Bill shouted to the battalion commander at the other end.

The commander ordered Bill into the sandbagged bunker behind the hooch, then bolted out the door to take charge of his battalion.

As Bill made his way down earthen steps to the bunker, a soldier appeared in the doorway, silhouetted against the drumming bursts of light outside. In his underwear and bare feet, the man looked like Bill's shadow, except he was covered in blood.

"Help me," the man said, "I've got to lie down."

Bill led the wounded man to his cot and inspected the gash in his abdomen. A mortar had exploded outside the soldier's hooch, killing his two bunkmates, one on either side of him. The lone survivor was turning white.

"I'm pretty sure I'm going to die in a minute," the man said, as if admitting an embarrassing truth. He asked Bill to hold his hand while he said the Lord's Prayer. It was an awkward moment for the agnostic cartoonist, who, if he prayed at all, addressed it "To Whom It May Concern."

In a few minutes, medics appeared looking for wounded. With Bill's help, they carried their patient across Camp Holloway to the dispensary. For the first time, Bill saw the magnitude of the damage. Sixty men were crammed into the open-air pavilion, and more were coming in. Some were screaming, some crying. A few were dying. The floor was slippery with blood. "The whole place looked like a slaughterhouse," Bill scribbled in his notebook later that morning.

After saying goodbye to the now-stabilized soldier, Bill ran back across the compound to grab his sketchbook and camera. The mortars had stopped falling, but the sky glowed over the airstrip. Guerrillas had infiltrated and blown up several parked aircraft. It suddenly occurred to Bill that, dressed in his shorts and bare feet, he might be mistaken for a Vietcong. He made it a point to talk loudly as he ran, littering his speech with obscenities, the mark of a true American soldier.

Bill was the only newsman at Pleiku to record images of the attack. The *Chicago Sun-Times* had sent him to Saigon, but Bill had hitched a helicopter ride on a private mission: to visit his son Bruce, a warrant officer and helicopter pilot with the 52d Aviation Battalion (see figure 78). As luck would have it, the Vietcong chose Bill's second night to launch their first major assault on American ground forces in Vietnam.[1]

Bill took six rolls of film and sketched seven drawings and then helped to load casualties into a cargo plane bound for an evac hospital. From the airstrip, he cheered as a pair of fighter-bombers thundered low overhead. Ordnance hung down from their wings like ripe fruit. They were headed North for revenge.[2]

FIGURE 78 The *Chicago Sun-Times* pulled out all the stops in promoting Bill's trip to Vietnam, making lavish use of Willie and Joe. Bill rushed to Saigon after the attack at Pleiku and managed to get his film and a 2,000-word dispatch to the *Sun-Times* within thirty-six hours. Two hundred seventy-five Field Syndicate newspapers ran the photos and story the next day, and *Time, Newsweek, Life,* and several other national magazines reprinted them. The *Sun-Times* published an editorial boasting of Bill's heroism, and Jacob Burck, the paper's editorial cartoonist, inked a panel of Bill in a helmet hunched over his drawing board. The American Legion awarded him a plaque, and the governor of Illinois cited him for his service to the troops. When asked about what he thought of being back up front, Bill said, "I like it even less than I did in World War II."

Those two sorties previewed a sustained bombing campaign against North Vietnam that would begin three weeks later. Within two months American command for the first time would authorize offensive operations against the Vietcong. By August, draft boards across the country would be calling up young men at a rate of 35,000 a month. After Pleiku, President Lyndon Johnson decided to turn the small war he'd inherited into a big one.

Pleiku was also a turning point for Bill Mauldin. Despite his tough Cold War liberalism, he had long been skeptical about Vietnam. In the early 1950s, he had opposed the idea of sending American troops to bail out the French in their fight against Ho Chi Minh. He remained pessimistic during the Kennedy years, when the president touted, and then abandoned, South Vietnamese dictator Ngo Dinh Diem. In Vietnam, Bill said, the nation faced the "miserable choice of underwriting tyranny or chaos." He sympathized most with the peasants of that country, as well as with the combat soldiers sent there as "advisers." They were the ones destined to suffer if the Cold War should turn hot in Southeast Asia (see figures 79 and 80).[3]

After Pleiku, Bill later admitted, "I got a little fucked up." The war had become personal. His cartoons grew more hawkish (see figures 81 and 82). "Before I went to Vietnam," Bill wrote on the eve of his departure from Saigon, "I wondered how we got into the situation there. Now that I've been there, I still wonder, but the question has become academic. We are there." Bill saw Vietnam as a battleground between the United States and Communist China. "Not an ideal battleground for us," he wrote, "but if we retire from this one, they'll find an even worse one next." President Johnson was pleased with Bill's change of heart (see figure 83).[4]

At the same time, Bill empathized with the "peaceniks"— "not unwashed doves with stringy hair hanging in their guitars," he said, but "the serious ones who are genuinely troubled." He reminded those who complained about draft evaders that during World War II, "the draft board had to drag most of us, whimpering, out of the bushes."[5]

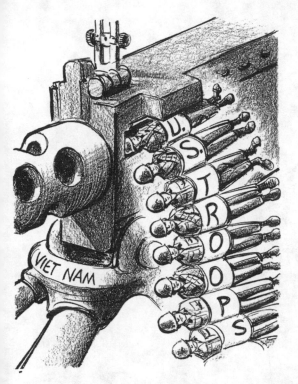

*Live Ammunition*

**FIGURES 79 AND 80** One of Bill
Mauldin's earliest cartoons about
Vietnam, above, turned out to
be his most prescient. Published
on October 19, 1962, after yet
another infusion of troops into
that troubled land, the original
drawing still hangs in the hallway
of the editorial offices at the
*Sun-Times.* The cartoon on the
right, drawn days before he took
off for Vietnam, expresses Bill's
recognition of war's real cost, as
well as his disdain for patriotic
cant and sloganeering, no matter
the source.

*Copyright 1962 (above) and 1965 (right)
by Bill Mauldin.
Courtesy of the Mauldin Estate.*

**"Who's winning—the forces
of freedom or the people's
democracies?"**

"It Leaks."

"Whatever it is,
it isn't paper."

**FIGURES 81 AND 82** Above left, Bill's first after the Pleiku attack. He'd just learned that the enemy mortars were American-made, launched from a supposedly friendly village near the camp. The cartoon on the right, published on April 25, 1965, cheered LBJ's show of force in Vietnam.

*Both cartoons copyright 1965 by Bill Mauldin. Courtesy of the Mauldin Estate.*

FIGURE 83 Bill and the president on a speedboat at the LBJ ranch in 1965. A regular at the ranch after JFK's assassination, Bill enjoyed the president's favor for a while. "He liked me because of where I was from," Bill said. "He had this thing that most of the press was down on him because he was an old shitkicker—well, he knew that I was an old shitkicker too." As Bill turned against the war, LBJ turned against Bill. The trips to the ranch stopped in 1967.

*Courtesy of the Mauldin Estate.*

As with so many other American families, Vietnam divided the Mauldins. Bill especially clashed with his and Natalie's eldest son Andy, who turned eighteen in September of 1966. By then, says Andy, "I had realized that Vietnam was a mistake on a large scale. I became politically radicalized; I grew my hair long. It didn't go over with Dad." Bill disapproved of Andy's radicalism and his reluctance to serve in Vietnam. Andy called his father a reactionary. In weaker moments, Bill growled that a tour of duty in the jungles might do the boy some good.[6]

The drumbeat of bad news about the American war effort in Vietnam took the edge off of Bill's conflict with Andy, as did Bill's appreciation of youthful rebellion. "I can understand Andy," he told students at the University of Wisconsin in early 1967. "What I can't understand is Young Republicans. That, to me, is unnatural."

In the same speech, Bill also spoke skeptically about the war. "We should not kid ourselves about it," he said, "right now, the Viet Cong are more in tune with the aspirations of the Vietnamese people than we are." The Johnson administration's rhetoric about freedom and the right to self-determination would only lead America "deeper and deeper into fictions" about the war and away from the lived reality of rockets, bombs, grenades, and machine guns.[7]

The fictions surrounding Vietnam hit home, oddly, after Bill's trip to another war zone, his fourth as a correspondent. In May 1967, he traveled to Israel anticipating that war would soon break out there. Dug in with the Israeli infantry overlooking the Sinai Peninsula, Bill witnessed the Israelis' surprise invasion of Egypt that launched the Six Day War. He marveled at the Jewish troops' esprit, resourcefulness, and seriousness of purpose. Israel won a lightning victory with true citizen-soldiers, he said, making do with what little they had, reusing even spent machine-gun casings. It was an army devoid of chickenshit. "I never saw one man salute another," Bill wrote, "I never saw one man hold a car door open for another. I never saw anybody treat anybody else as a social inferior." In a war of necessity, when national survival is at stake, Bill knew, there's no time for swagger and no need for jingoism. His admiration for the beleaguered Jewish state was so great, his sons began calling him "Lawrence of Israel" upon his return.[8]

For Bill, the performance of Israel's army in the Six Day War cast the American effort in Vietnam in a harsh light. "The problem in Vietnam is in the nature of the war itself," Bill announced after his return from the Middle East, "and in the fact that for motivation our people are forced to fall back upon tired slogans, dubious assumptions about 'commitments,' and antiquated abstractions such as the 'domino theory.'"[9]

Like many Americans in 1967, Mauldin was just beginning to

come around to the "peacenik" point of view. Few could have guessed just how far he would go.

IF PLEIKU represented the apex of Bill's swing to the right, then the Chicago Democratic National Convention in August 1968 completed his return to the left. As thousands of young people poured into the city to demonstrate against the war, Mayor Richard Daley oversaw what an official commission would later term a "police riot." He forbade all marches, rallies, and demonstrations and mobilized 12,000 police and 7,500 National Guardsmen to disperse crowds that assembled in city parks and outside the convention hall. Egged on by taunting demonstrators, the police lashed out with violence, targeting members of the media along with protesters. They wielded billy clubs and shot teargas canisters with abandon. At the convention hotel, the Conrad Hilton, police pushed people through a plate-glass window, hopped over the sill, and beat them some more. "The cops had one thing on their minds," reported one journalist. "Club and then gas, club and then gas, club and then gas." The lobby of the Hilton turned into a triage center for hundreds of the injured.[10]

Bill waded into the rioting from his base at Riccardo's, a restaurant and bar on Rush Street favored by journalists. With friend Mike Royko and restaurant owner Ric Riccardo, Bill saw the beatings and tasted the tear gas. He watched as cops took off their badges and charged the crowds. As with Vietnam, the Battle of Chicago had become personal. Several colleagues on the *Sun-Times* and the Fields' sister paper, the *Daily News*, ended up in police paddy wagons for trying to record the events.

Bill focused his ire on the mayor, whom he considered the embodiment of bigoted bullying power. He ran Chicago, said Bill, like Mussolini ran Italy. "Just being in the same town with Daley" was enough to radicalize almost anyone. "I figured that if that son of a bitch is on the right, then I wanna be on the left."[11]

The Chicago convention scandal reached beyond the streets into the city's news offices. Daley's control over local media was so great that few Chicagoans ever learned the full extent of police malfeasance. Editors altered, killed, and even later rebutted stories that cast the administration in a negative light. In response, scores of reporters, brought together in part by the *Sun-Times'* Roger Ebert, met at Riccardo's after the convention to plan a protest of their own. Most of the dissident journalists were young, but three respected veterans—Mike Royko, Studs Terkel, and Bill Mauldin—joined them.[12]

The meeting at Riccardo's bore fruit weeks later in the birth of the *Chicago Journalism Review (CJR)*. Issued monthly, usually with a hard-hitting Mauldin cartoon on the cover, the *CJR* served as a watchdog over Chicago's media, reporting on distortions, omissions, and behind-the-scenes manipulations of the news by city officials and business interests (see figures 84 and 85).

Bill's work for the *CJR* drew him into the counterculture in a way that recalled his campaign against army brass in World War II. His cartoons tweaked the establishment, his bosses at the *Sun-Times* in particular. But Bill, as always, had a popular constituency that preserved his bully pulpit.

No longer complementing the editorial page, his drawings, once again, virtually leaped off the paper. Overshadowing the editorials, Bill's work attracted a new generation of readers. Bill Mauldin, says Chicago journalist Michael Miner, "was the biggest reason the *Sun-Times* of those days is remembered as fiercely liberal. In fact its editorial page was wishy-washy and insignificant. Mauldin, however, was an angry, ironic sharpshooter. The editorials endorsed Richard J. Daley and Richard Nixon, but nobody read the editorials. Mauldin savaged them both, and everybody read him."[13]

Perceptive followers of Bill's work had long seen him as holding something back in the 1950s and early 1960s, when the rebel became the satirist. Perennial Mauldin booster Charles Poore of the *New York Times* speculated in 1961 that Bill suffered from

*Chicago Journalism Review*

50¢

**FIGURE 84** In the late 1960s, Bill Mauldin began drawing Mayor Daley as a pint-sized Keystone Cop. "Daley has a mouth that looks like a baby's when the bottle's been taken out of his hand," said Bill. After the Chicago convention, Bill designed an emblem for an anti-Daley art exhibit: a flower growing out from behind barbed wire.

*Copyright 1969 by Bill Mauldin. Courtesy of the Mauldin Estate.*

FIGURE 85 On December 4, 1969, Chicago police raided the Black Panthers' West Side headquarters, killing the Chicago chapter's founder Fred Hampton and another Panther. Police claimed they fired in self-defense. The *CJR* and Bill Mauldin were among the first to publicly question the police version of events. Ballistic evidence later showed that of the one hundred shots fired in the raid, only one came from the Panthers.

*Copyright 1969 by Bill Mauldin. Courtesy of the Mauldin Estate.*

the "Pagliacci syndrome," a profound disaffection masked by the clean, flowing lines of his work. "It always seemed to me," recalled cartoonist Jimmy Johnson, "that Bill was far more radical or progressive than he was allowed to be." Enthralled as a child by Willie and Joe, cartoonist Bill Griffith similarly found Bill's editorial cartoons before 1968 disappointingly respectful and mainstream. "As a kid, growing up in the Fifties, I always wished I'd pick up a *Mad* magazine one month and see Mauldin's work. Too bad it never happened."[14]

While Bill did not turn to alternative cartooning in the late 1960s, he did begin to follow the burgeoning underground comics movement launched by artists like Bill Griffith. He delighted especially in the drug-influenced, id-driven humor of Robert Crumb and Zap Comix. It confounded his middle-aged fans, many of them World War II veterans, when he recommended Crumb's work. Zap has "the same distribution system" as marijuana, he told them. "It's everywhere, but you have to know how to find it."[15]

On the surface, Bill Mauldin still appeared to be a conventional white-collar family man. He and Natalie lived in a large colonial revival house on Chicago's South Side, just down the street from Elijah Muhammad, the founder of the Nation of Islam. As the children grew up and moved away, Natalie, still beset by depression, became increasingly unhappy. Bill, meanwhile, turned to the counterculture.

The most visible transformation in Bill took place in the fall of 1970. Nat Mauldin, the youngest child, left for college in August. When he returned three months later for a visit home with friends, he was stunned by the change. He found his father in his Near North Side studio, perched at his drawing board, a vision of countercultural liberation. His clothes were casual, his hair was long, and for the first time, he sported a full-fledged beard. Rock music played in the background. On the bed, sitting cross-legged, was a gorgeous blonde in a t-shirt, rolling a joint.

"Wow, your dad's pretty cool," said Nat's goggled-eyed friends. Nat, meanwhile, shuddered at the sight and tried to contain his rising hysterics.

Bill even took up the guitar, mainly to combat the arthritis that was beginning to seize his drawing hand. "Nobody could teach him, of course," recalls Nat. "He taught himself and became pretty accomplished at it." He was particularly fond of classical guitarist Andrés Segovia. The choice was apt. A half century earlier, Segovia had done for the guitar what Bill had for cartoons—taken lowbrow entertainment and infused it with high-culture legitimacy.[16]

Bill's new unwashed look was a bit deceiving. While supporting counterculture start-ups like the Poor People's Campaign, feminism, and eventually gay rights, he fiercely resisted being labeled "liberal" or "left-wing." "I think he's somewhere in the stew of Jeffersonian Conservative, Populist, Libertarian. And he'd kill me for getting that wrong, too," says friend Norton Wolf.[17]

To Bill, America was the best country in the world to get ahead, unless you were handicapped, he said, "by being black or something." An avid firearms collector, he opposed gun control. He distrusted bureaucracies, disdained unearned privilege, and derided hypocrisies on the left and the right. He hated war, but was not a pacifist, thinking it too much like Christian Science. "They are right ninety percent of the time," he said. "It's that other ten percent I worry about."[18]

This prickly independence shaped his first major book since *A Sort of a Saga*. He'd begun the sequel to his memoir back in 1957 and sold it then to Harper & Row. But a grinding six-day week at the *Post-Dispatch* had left no time for book work, so Harper settled for two cartoon collections in the 1960s, *What's Got Your Back Up?* (1961) and *I've Decided I Want My Seat Back* (1965). He then resold the memoir to Eric Swenson at W. W. Norton. By 1968, the manuscript had swelled to 150,000 words. He traveled to his mother's house in Arizona for research. She still had the letters he'd written home during the war. Then he spent two years pruning and revising it for greater frankness. When finally published in the fall of 1971, *The Brass Ring* bore the imprint of the counterculture.

In sometimes raw language and earthy humor, *The Brass Ring* tells the story of how Bill infiltrated two downbeat "underground" cartoon characters, Willie and Joe, into *Stars and Stripes*. The book also praises the marginalized Native Americans with whom he served, recounting in moving detail the death of his mentor, Rayson Billey, the Medicine Man. At the center of the story is a puckish, ambitious, jug-eared trickster, who always seemed to land on his feet, even when tossed around by the likes of General Patton (see figure 86).

THE COUNTERCULTURE might have revitalized Bill's writing and cartooning, but it did nothing for his troubled home life. Natalie and Bill fought more than ever, over his drinking, his carousing, and his frequent absences from home. "Their battles were brutal," recalls Nat Mauldin, a teenager during these years. "It was not a fun house to come home to."

The marriage probably should have ended, but Bill and Natalie held to their agreement never to divorce. They settled on a separation of sorts. In the summer of 1970, they sold their South Side house and Natalie moved back to Santa Fe. Bill stayed in Chicago and flew now and then to New Mexico in his airplane.

No ideal husband, Bill still found the separation from Natalie intolerable. For years he'd left home months at a time on assignment, but he could never stand for *her* to leave *him*. In the summer of 1969, Natalie and her sons John and Nat had traveled to Europe and Israel for eight weeks, a period during which Bill felt lost and abandoned. Her departure for Santa Fe sparked a similar crisis. Bill moved into his studio, which became a bachelor pad.[19]

Back in New Mexico, Natalie settled into an airy stucco house outside of town along the Old Santa Fe Trail. The ruts from wagon wheels still marked the surrounding landscape. Bill loved the

**FIGURE 86** *The Brass Ring*'s remarkable account of Bill's meeting with Patton struck a nerve among readers in 1971. The year before, Hollywood had released the movie *Patton*, starring George C. Scott, to great acclaim. The team-written script and Scott's portrayal of the general as a gravelly voiced, larger-than-life tough guy skillfully divided audiences. Right-wingers saw Patton as a strong leader, while left-wingers condemned him as embodying reckless violence and jingoism. Bill cleverly changed the terms of the debate by depicting the general as a small, remote, whiny, almost inconsequential figure. In Bill's confrontation with Patton, after all, the downy-faced tech-sergeant cartoonist had come out on top.

setting, and he flew out often in the twin-engine Beechcraft Baron bought with the proceeds from *The Brass Ring*'s Book-of-the-Month Club selection.[20]

On August 28, 1971, Natalie put a roast in the oven and headed down to the Albuquerque airport, where Bill was due to land. When Bill arrived, Natalie wasn't there. Her car had crashed into an abutment. At the age of forty-six, Natalie Evans Mauldin was dead.

Bill's grief was compounded by a suspicion that his wife had committed suicide. An autopsy later revealed that Natalie had suffered a massive stroke behind the wheel before her car even left the road.[21]

After several weeks in New Mexico, Bill returned to Chicago and picked up his pen, ink brush—and his life—again. As he had after the end of his first marriage, Bill wasted little time pursuing a new relationship.

Bill had met Chris Lund two years earlier, when she worked as a summer intern at the *Daily News,* whose offices were located in the Sun-Times Building. Since then, Chris had graduated from Boston University and gotten a job as an editorial assistant at the paper. Bill's way to his office in the *Daily News* section took him by Chris's desk every morning. Sometimes he stopped to show her a drawing of long-haired hippies. "Does this look right?" he would ask, not acknowledging that his hippie-looking sons were Chris's age.

Chris, at first, had no idea who he was. She knew nothing about *Up Front* or Willie and Joe. Bill liked that about her. She liked Bill because he was a charismatic firebrand whose cartoons defied the staid editorials of the two Field papers.

Of Swedish background, Chris was gorgeous (she was the blonde sitting on Bill's bed smoking a joint), but, more, she was smart, spiritual, and literary. Her prominent liberal Republican family lived north of Chicago, where her father, Paul Lund, was a vice president of AT&T. Raised to think for herself and find her own path, Chris, by the time she met Bill, was immersed in the civil rights and antiwar movements. Like Natalie, she wanted to be a writer.

Twenty-seven years Bill's junior, Chris Lund had the beauty and intelligence to capture Bill Mauldin's attention—and hold it.

In early 1972, Bill and Chris announced their engagement. "To think I was so worried about you going to live on a commune in California!" Chris's mother groused. "At least there you would have been with people your own age."[22]

Their July wedding marked a shift in Bill's base of operations. He and Chris now lived almost exclusively in Santa Fe. He still traveled a lot, though not so much on assignment anymore. Instead, he flew about the country and the world collecting awards, lecturing (at $1,800 per appearance), and, in 1974 and 1975, teaching cartooning at Yale. Rarely did he return to Chicago to check in at the *Sun-Times*. "I'm living away, sending stuff in, and being as independent as a hog on ice," he told a reporter.[23]

On one such trip in May 1975, Bill and Chris attended a dinner party at the house of Field Enterprises executive Dick Trezevant. Just down the street, friends and family of Mayor Daley were celebrating the upcoming wedding of Daley's son. At the Trezevants', the doorman called up. "Tell Mr. Mauldin," he said, "there's finally something for him to take a picture of with that camera he's always carrying around."

Bill, Chris, Trezevant, and friend Jon Gordon stepped onto the sidewalk to see cars from the Daley party double-parked up and down the street. The police were there, doing nothing. Bill began to photograph license plate numbers. It was an intern's job, says Neil Steinberg, a columnist for the *Sun-Times*. "Mauldin did it because he hated the arrogance of power, the casual disregard for laws we mortals must obey."[24]

As one version of the story has it, the driver of one car gave Bill the finger. Bill smiled and snapped his picture. The enraged man got out of the car, charged over to Bill, ripped the camera off the cartoonist's neck, smashed it into his face, and kicked him in the groin. Dick Trezevant picked up Bill's camera, turned around, and took a picture of Bill, nose broken and face bloodied, next to an

**FIGURE 87** Dick Trezevant's photo of Chris and Bill, taken immediately after the scuffle, appeared in the *Chicago Sun-Times* the next day.

*As published in the Chicago Sun-Times. Photographer Dick Trezevant. Copyright 1975 by Chicago Sun-Times, Inc. Reprinted with permission.*

astonished Chris (see figure 87). The police sauntered over and began interrogating Bill about why he was taking pictures. The assailant, meanwhile, left the scene in a taxi.

The next day, Trezevant's photograph of Mauldin appeared in the city's newspapers, making him a local cause célèbre. "The beating of Mauldin, who is a friend of mine," wrote Mike Royko four days later, "was one of the finest events to occur in Chicago in many years. The sound of his nose breaking was sweet music. . . . All those nameless people who can be freely punched in the nose, pushed around, kicked, stomped, walked on—thousands of them all over the city. But this had to be Bill Mauldin."

Bill pressed charges against Thomas D. Flanagan, an attorney and friend of the mayor. Flanagan first denied being at the scene, then accused Mauldin of attacking *him*. Despite the strong testimony of

witnesses—one police captain, whom Bill swore wasn't there, testified on behalf of the accused—the judge acquitted Flanagan, reading rapidly from a ruling written before the trial had ended. That
was how the justice system worked in Daley's Chicago. Royko's wry
sense of triumph had been premature.[25]

After the trial, Bill and Chris returned to Santa Fe. His street-
fighting days were over.


MAY-DECEMBER RELATIONSHIPS, Bill soon discovered, had
problems of their own. Not only did he sometimes feel "like an old
lech," especially around Chris's young friends, he also had trouble
taking his wife seriously when she announced a desire to have children. "I found it hard to think of her as an adult," he said.

The issue almost drove them to divorce. They even signed the
papers, but didn't file them. Instead, they went to marriage counsel-
ing. Bill laughed at the counselor's blinding insight: "It turns out,"
he said, "I'm too old for her!"

Finally, after many months, Bill surrendered. "He realized that
not having a child would take a certain warmth out of me that he
loved," explained Chris. When Chris got pregnant, Bill went to
Lamaze classes with other couples less than half his age and was
there in the delivery room when his wife gave birth.

"It's got no pecker! It's got no pecker!" shouted Bill, dancing
down the hallway in joy. He had assumed he could only father
boys.[26]

Kaja, his baby daughter, did what Bill had always feared: she
charmed him. "When I get into parenthood I get very involved,"
he explained. He wanted to be equally involved in writing the book
on flying, but Kaja sidetracked the project. Bill swelled with pride
at his virility. Eventually he would teach Kaja to identify herself as
"Girl One, Litter Three."[27]

Shortly before Kaja's birth, Bill managed to complete a book
he'd worked on for four years, a rollicking illustrated history of the

Revolutionary War titled *Mud & Guts*. It would be his last book of original cartoons and text. When the National Park Service had commissioned the work back in 1974 for the Bicentennial, he expected simply to "put Willie and Joe under cocked hats." Instead, Bill threw himself into the project, reading widely about the Revolution and traveling to battle sites on the East Coast. The Bicentennial came and went, and Bill was still researching. Most readers found it well worth the wait.

The book's heavy line drawings puncture heroic notions of the Founding Fathers, especially George Washington, depicted as a priggish martinet. The war was won and the nation was founded, Bill makes clear, from the bottom-up by "rabble with rifles" (see figure 88).[28]

The flashing black lines of *Mud & Guts* again turned up in Bill's daily political cartoons, though without so much shading. The reason for his change in style had nothing to do with aesthetics or ideology, but, rather, with the limitations of telefacsimile technology. Living in Santa Fe, Bill couldn't trust the mails to get drawings to Chicago within his deadlines, so he bought a fifty-pound Telecopier machine. It had, Bill said, "approximately the reproductive capability of a Sicilian copy camera dug from the rubble." The resolution was so poor that his delicate shadings and thin lines were lost in transmission. Bill put aside his crayon and relied on his brush again for several years, until discovering Federal Express in 1983. For the first time, Bill had sacrificed craftsmanship for the comforts and conveniences of home.[29]

Home held plenty of attractions, besides his family. He spent more time than ever with his cherished machines. He'd become an accomplished photographer, though he preferred tinkering with his elaborate camera equipment to actually using it. He converted a spare bedroom into a darkroom. His garage became a machine shop, complete with three metal lathes. (When Chris asked him what the machines were for, he responded, "they can make parts for themselves.") No Mauldin backyard was complete without vehicles

*"I'm a disgrace to what uniform, sir?"*

FIGURE 88 The Spirit of '76, Bill declared, "was best embodied in unlettered, unshaven, sardonic riflemen, whose aim was to get the unpleasantness over and head back to a wilderness full of uncut logs and uncooked game. I had the honor of knowing some of their descendants a couple of centuries later. The offspring weren't much of an improvement, cosmetically speaking, but their attitudes were still healthy—to my way of thinking. I trust they haven't become an endangered species."

*Copyright 1978 by Bill Mauldin. Courtesy of the Mauldin Estate.*

to work on. In addition to his old Willys jeep, Bill had a 1967 Clark Cortez motor home (which served as a traveling darkroom), a 1971 Chevy pickup, and at least two other cars, along with a lawn tractor older than Chris. "It's just something to keep my hands busy," he explained to a visiting reporter. "Machinery demands less of me than people."[30]

In laid-back Santa Fe, his sweat-stained cowboy hat with a Navajo hatband fit right in, as did his various pets, which he had a habit of taking in. But his work regimen remained grueling by any standard. In addition to cartooning, he wrote a 500-word column several days a week for the Field Newspaper Syndicate. Drawn from his day-to-day life in New Mexico, most of his columns involved Kaja, his cats, his machines, and his growing list of pet peeves, from postage stamps that tasted bad and failed to stick to the ubiquity of televised sports.

In addition, he developed remarkable one-minute animated "cartoon-a-torials" for the CBS news affiliate in Chicago. Bill's friend Norton Wolf, acting as his agent, tried to market them to a national network but found no takers. Bill also collaborated briefly with underground filmmaker Ralph Bakshi (director of the X-rated *Fritz the Cat*) on an animated Willie and Joe television series. Bill pulled out of the deal at the last minute when network executives refused his demand to write the pilot episodes himself. Similarly, Bill scuttled a plan to merchandise his World War II cartoons in limited-edition lithographs and plaques. Someone had carelessly left a rag on one of his lithographic stones. Bill flew into a rage, then quit the whole project. He wasn't yet ready, as he would later put it, to "play out the string" of his career.[31]

He did, however, think about his legacy, which, he said, amounted to nothing but "a ton of drawings."[32] In 1975, he donated his papers and 1,700 of his cartoons to the Library of Congress. (Afterward, he fought a court battle to get his full tax deduction for it.) Four years later, he gave over 200 of his most famous World War II drawings to the 45th Infantry Division Museum in Oklahoma City. The museum created a Bill Mauldin Room to house the collection and lured him to the dedication during the 45th's reunion weekend.

Bill normally steered clear of reunions and commemorations. "He disliked VFW and American Legion types. They were always inviting him to events," recalls friend Jet Zarkadas. "He ran in the other direction when he saw them coming. He didn't like glorifying war." Neither could Bill stand to hear middle-aged veterans tell lies about combat heroics. The more somber memorials, conversely, were "too harrowing" for him. They brought back gruesome memories. "I'm protecting my own psyche, I guess," he said, explaining his aversion to such events.[33]

Steeling himself, Bill traveled to Oklahoma City in September 1979 for his first reunion with the old outfit. Nothing could have prepared him for it. Out of a crowd of veterans stepped a hobbled old man in an army jacket and Australian campaign hat. He was a Choctaw Indian with an unmistakable arched nose—Rayson Billey, the Medicine Man.

Bill stared in disbelief at the man whose bullet-ridden body he surely had seen on the ground in Sicily. Had he really seen him there, or had he just heard of it?

"Billey," Bill finally stammered, "where have you been? . . . You're dead."

"I know," Billey replied. "I read your book."

The wry, stocky sergeant whom Bill had made into Willie had allowed thirty-six years to pass with everybody thinking him dead. In fact, Billey had seen his own name on a list of "Honored Dead" in an official history somewhere. After the war, he'd returned with three Purple Hearts and other medals—some of them awarded "posthumously"—to the tiny town of Keota, Oklahoma. For twenty years he worked at a munitions factory, but his body, especially his knees, so shattered in Sicily, Salerno, and Anzio, finally gave out. By the mid-1960s, he could no longer work, so he retired to his small house with no telephone to fish, read, paint, play piano, and try to drown out his memories of war.[34]

"You NEVER get rid of it," Billey said. "There's no way. I've seen many psychiatrists."

They stayed up late drinking whiskey and swapping stories. Then, long past midnight, Billey, who had killed two Germans with his bare hands during the war and many another with only a knife, staggered back to his motel room, stripped the canvas braces from his knees, and collapsed in bed.

"My legs don't work like they used to," he mumbled before falling asleep. "But my hand is quicker than an eye."[35]

BILL CUT BACK his cartooning to three days a week in 1983. A younger, edgier generation of cartoonists had taken over the field. Coming of age professionally during Vietnam and Watergate, Pat Oliphant, Jeff MacNelly, Garry Trudeau, and others looked to Mauldin as a spiritual forefather of sorts, someone who'd kept the craft alive during the moribund fifties and early sixties. Bill would publish one last cartoon collection in 1985, *Let's Declare Ourselves Winners . . . and Get the Hell Out,* but the center of gravity had shifted. "You see it at the cartoonist conventions," remarked one cartoonist in 1984. "Those over forty surround Bill Mauldin. Those under forty surround Jeff MacNelly."[36]

The less Bill cartooned, the more he was remembered for his wartime work. His public speeches had once focused almost exclusively on the personalities and issues of the day: LBJ, Nixon, Vietnam, Watergate. By the early 1980s, however, veterans began packing his speaking events. They would sit restively through the cartoonist's discussion of Reagan, the Ayatollah, and El Salvador in order to get to the question-and-answer session. "They want war stories," observed a reporter in Baltimore. "One can feel it; it becomes ominous."

Most of the stories came not from Bill, but from audience members themselves. Veterans would stand up, identify their former units, their campaigns, and the comrades they had left behind. The room would hum with dozens of other stories shared in hushed tones, almost as if Bill were not there. "It seems as though Mauldin not so much gives a lecture, or leads a discussion, as sits at the room's peak serving as a lightning rod," noted one reporter. "In many ways, he belongs to those he wrote about," the journalist concluded. "He is the property of our veterans' corps—a natural resource, only limitedly free to do as he pleases."[37]

After turning sixty, Bill had somehow been recalled into active duty as a spokesman for the veteran, a role he had always accepted with ambivalence. "Willie and Joe are my creatures," he told Studs Terkel in 1983. "Or am I their creature?" "Because he became a folk hero at such a young age, there were people who thought they owned a piece of him," explains Bill's friend and attorney Jon Gordon. "He kind of bristled at that. His feeling was, 'I want to live my own life.'"[38]

That life largely involved family. In 1987, he and Chris had a son, Sam, who bore a stunning resemblance to his father. Bill was sixty-five years old. He grew nostalgic about his childhood home in Mountain Park, where his brother still lived on the family apple farm. Each autumn, Bill felt an urge to visit. "We need to go see ol' Sid," he would say, though the brothers could hardly spend an hour together without fighting.

Bill also talked more about building a house in the Arizona desert, on the quarter section Pop had homesteaded during the Depression. He would fly to the undeveloped parcel in his Baron, touching down on the airstrip he'd built, and emerge from the cockpit almost giddy with energy. "His personality would change entirely," explains Andy Mauldin. "Here was the man coming home to the child he used to be. . . . It was his paradise."[39]

Held increasingly captive by Willie and Joe, Bill found no takers for an illustrated manuscript about his various pets, titled *Animals That Have Owned Me*. Publishers didn't like books that mixed cats and dogs. "He's also been out of sight for so long," one editor explained in a rejection letter, "only oldsters like me remember him."[40]

Bill's relationship to the *Sun-Times* cooled. It had been many years since his cartoons had dealt with Chicago's foibles, and only occasionally did he travel to Washington, Europe, or other hot spots on assignment. He'd managed to steer clear of upheavals at the *Sun-Times*, where circulation and profits were in decline. In 1984, Rupert Murdoch bought the tabloid, added a strong dose of sensationalism to it, and sold it to a partnership headed by a New York investment bank two years later. The paper continued to struggle. By 1989, the *Sun-Times* seemed on the verge of folding, as had its sister paper, the *Daily News,* a decade earlier. A new management team sought to save the newspaper by cutting staff and focusing more tightly on local coverage.

In 1990, when the new editor in chief, Dennis A. Britton, called, Bill wasn't surprised. He had Chris listen in from the bedroom phone, so as to witness his professional execution.

Britton spoke of cost-cutting measures and then broke the news that the *Sun-Times* would not renew the cartoonist's contract when it ran out at year's end. With the money it paid Bill for three cartoons a week, the paper could hire a full-time reporter.[41]

It was not, however, in Bill's temperament to go gently. Despite his vow in 1973 never to cover another war, Bill accepted ABC News reporter Sam Donaldson's invitation to visit troops mobilized in the Persian Gulf for Operation Desert Shield. Three months earlier, during the summer of 1990, Saddam Hussein had invaded neighboring Kuwait. President George H. W. Bush had responded immediately with a buildup of American forces in Saudi Arabia. By the time Bill arrived in the Saudi capital in November, a half million American troops were already there.

Bill positively sparkled as he circulated among the soldiers, most of them too young to know of him. With his baseball hat pushed back over unwieldy salt-and-pepper hair, he traded jokes and listened attentively as they groused about a lack of liquor, women, and other amusements. They felt exploited, like "an army for hire," one said, shipped overseas to defend Saudi sheiks. Bill sketched the men as they practiced assaults; he even drove an Abrams tank for a while, rotating the turret and leaving billows of sand in his wake. He was most impressed, however, with the upside-down traffic cones the soldiers used as funnels to fill sandbags. Those would have been useful back in Italy.

The war became personal for Bill, as had all of his wars. "I love these guys," he told Donaldson at the end of his trip. "I feel like they're all my kids and my grandkids, every one of them. I really do. . . . I want to see them come home in one piece, or if they're going to come home sewn up in bags, I hope it is for a proper, useful cause, not something frivolous."

Bill couldn't hide his disdain for the way President Bush (who purposely excluded Bill from his Thanksgiving celebration with the troops) seemed to be rushing these youngsters into combat. Peaceful means, like economic sanctions, were still available. "Some wars I approve of . . . and some wars I don't approve of," he later said, "and I most emphatically do not approve of this one."[42]

The trip affected Bill deeply. He even recalled Willie and Joe from retirement and drew them in desert camouflage, complete with the new American square-cut helmets that reminded Bill of the Wehrmacht's.

But none of it mattered to the *Sun-Times*. Indeed, the paper made little of Bill's presence in the Persian Gulf, barely mentioning his appearance on ABC's *PrimeTime Live*.

At the end of 1990, two weeks before the U.S. bombing campaign in Iraq was to begin, Bill Mauldin retired from the *Chicago Sun-Times*. There was no announcement, no retirement party. That was the way Bill wanted it. He continued to cartoon for his syndicate. It wasn't much money, but it took the edge off a humiliating indignity.

ON OCTOBER 28, 1991, just before his seventieth birthday, Bill decided to affix a snowplow to his olive drab Willys jeep. Using an engine hoist, he lifted the jeep's front end while he worked on getting the plow in place. Bill's large arthritic left hand was wrapped between the plow and the jeep's bumper when the hoist slipped slightly, jerking the vehicle downward onto Bill's drawing hand. The jeep crushed his ring and middle fingers, slicing off their fleshy pads. Bill and Chris raced to the emergency room, where a hand surgeon, who happened to be around that day, repaired the damage.

Bill fully intended to return to syndicated cartooning, but the hand was slow to recover. The very jeep that had been the symbol of Bill's success and independence put an end to his long cartooning career. Bill never quite saw the irony (see figure 89).[43]

To rehabilitate his hand and help his arthritis, Bill traveled almost every day to the nearby Shidoni art foundry, where he sculpted from clay. He worked alone, meticulously, mastering the process whereby his clay creations were cast into bronze (see figure 90).[44]

He also began drawing again.

When President Bush warned that the media shouldn't focus on the casualties resulting from Desert Storm, Bill penned a cartoon, coupled with a blistering opinion piece, and sent it to the *Santa Fe New Mexican*. "They're coming out with this line that we're supposed to support our troops," he complained to the editor there. "Sure, I'll support our troops. I'm very pro-troop, but that doesn't mean I'll support our leaders in this thing. Our leaders have led us into something very awful here."[45]

Bill also resisted the gauzy nostalgia about World War II that accompanied many fiftieth anniversary commemorations. With the publication of a special edition of *Up Front* and the reprinting of *Bill Mauldin's Army*, Willie and Joe enjoyed a revival, but Bill wasn't entirely pleased with how they were used. Most of the commemorative books, articles, and television programs, he believed, romanticized the war and its soldiers. "He didn't share a lot of people's glorification of the war," says Jon Gordon. "He felt that a lot of people misinterpreted who he was and what he really stood

**FIGURE 89** Bill and his jeep in December 1995, four years after his accident.

*AP Images/Murrae Haynes.*

**FIGURE 90** Bill Mauldin's favorite cartoon was always this image of a cavalry sergeant putting his broken jeep out of its misery. "To me, a captionless cartoon is like a home run to a batter." When he began sculpting, he chose this as his first subject. The Shidoni Foundry cast twelve limited-edition bronzes. After Bill's death, a coalition of New Mexico veterans raised $27,000 to have this one created. Dedicated on Memorial Day, 2003, it is now on display at the New Mexico Veterans Memorial Park in Santa Fe.

*Photographer: Josh Stephenson.*
*Copyright:* The Albuquerque Journal. *Reprinted with permission.*

for." When Tom Brokaw said that the real Willies and Joes were the "Greatest Generation," Bill responded that "they were human beings, they had their weaknesses and their flaws and their good sides and bad sides. The one thing they had in common was they were a little too young to die."[46]

Although still feisty after his jeep accident, Bill grew increasingly infirm. In 1993, while repairing a retractable landing gear on his Beechcraft Baron, Bill got stuck in the gear housing. Overweight and stiff from arthritis, he called out for an hour before someone happened by to help him out. Obsessive about safety, Bill decided on the spot that he could no longer pilot the plane. He sold the Baron and stood on the tarmac holding back tears as the new owner flew the machine away. "It was one of the many straws that broke the camel's back," remarks Nat Mauldin.[47]

Bill's family began to notice changes in his personality. Actually, they were more like distortions or exaggerations of preexisting traits. Always of a peppery disposition, Bill became anxious and irritable much of the time. His wary regard of others slipped over into paranoia; and his sharp wit turned downright nasty, especially toward Chris.

He became possessive of his wife, not wanting her out of his sight, even for a trip to the store. (She would eventually refer to her rare excursions from home as "out-of-house experiences.") He undermined her parenting and sabotaged her writing. He was terrified of being abandoned. At the same time, he resented his vulnerability and his increasing dependence upon Chris. Forcing a turn of the tables, he orchestrated the appearance of *her* dependence upon *him*. It was as if, needing to do battle but having no editors, executives, or officers within range, Bill targeted his wife, the only available adversary.

As Bill's friends and family struggled to understand his abusive behavior, they couldn't help but think of the stories Bill so often told about his childhood, especially about his mother Katrina. She would storm out of the house, as if leaving forever, while Billy cried and pleaded with her to stay. Then, days later, she would return, kiss Billy, place a crown on his head, and sit him upon his Morris chair throne. It was his favorite make-believe role.

In 1994, Bill was working on the plumbing and had shut off the water to the house. On finishing, he tried a spigot and became frustrated when no water came out. Chris told him he needed to turn the water back on outside. Bill flew into a rage.

"Goddammit, Chris," he shouted, "would you quit trying to use your brain for anything but keeping your ears apart!?"

"That's when I first realized," Chris later said, "that he was slipping his clutch."

He traveled to Washington, D.C., soon afterward and gave a terrific talk about his wartime cartoons at the National Press Club. Perhaps, Chris hoped, he was turning a corner. But then, at another event in Seattle, he bombed. "He just couldn't do it," she explains. "He just couldn't bring it together the way he always had before."[48]

Drinking compounded the problem. His relationship with alcohol had always been complex, almost like a game. He would drink heavily for months, then quit for months, only to resume it again. "He could turn it on and off like a spigot," Nat says. "Dad had two speeds: a quart of vodka a day or total abstinence." A counselor later observed that Bill played his drinking off his other emotional problems. When he felt the demons rise, he fought them off with their equal, alcohol. Then, when the drinking became a demon, he demonstrated his control by quitting and waiting for its counterparts to return.[49]

Chris began divorce proceedings in the summer of 1996 and kicked him out of the house for good on Labor Day weekend. Andy loaded up his dad's possessions and drove him to Tucson, Arizona, where Bill moved into his mother's old house. His children came to visit and tried to help, but he was drinking now almost nonstop. He would not accept help, especially from those closest to him. Bill's greatest strength, his feisty independence, had become his Achilles' heel.

Speaking on behalf of the family, Nat called from his home in Los Angeles to inform his father that they would no longer suffer his abuse and would not visit until the drinking stopped.

"The day you call and say, 'I need help,'" Nat told his dad, "I'll be there in six hours."

When that day came, in the fall of 1997, Nat and his brother John made it to Tucson in four. Bill had called in the morning, frightened. He'd stumbled home from a restaurant the night before and had hurt himself. Within the day, the two brothers got their father packed up and checked into the Sierra Tucson, an elite inpatient treatment center specializing in addictions and behavioral disorders.

Bill endured the detoxification regimen without complaint. Then, after two months, it was time for therapeutic work, when patients examine the underlying causes of their behavior. That was when Bill resisted. A therapist told Andy that Bill was one of the toughest cases he had ever seen. The patient was cunning, charming, and expert in deflecting attention away from his vulnerabilities. "He really was a kind of tortured man," observes Andy.

Just what, precisely, was the source of the pain?

"That," says Nat, "is the Rosebud question."

Bill kicked hard enough to get himself released from the center. Before he left, a doctor told him and the children of Bill's advanced Alzheimer's. His health would probably deteriorate rapidly, and the paranoia, mood swings, and confusion would only get worse.

Still, Bill refused to enter an assisted-living complex and returned to his mother's house.

Within two weeks Bill's first wife Jean, the woman he'd divorced over fifty years earlier and whom Bill had always considered his betrayer, appeared on his doorstep and became Bill's partner and caregiver.[50]

According to Jean, Bill had called her in Southern California. He'd fallen out of a truck and hurt himself. "I figured I could assess the situation," she explained. So she traveled out to Tucson to Bill's house. "I ended up staying. He definitely needed help."[51]

Jean took over Bill's life, regulating his eating, drinking, and excursions from home. Bill fought with her as hard as he could, but his invectives failed to drive her away. "He treated her like shit," says Andy, "and she toughed it out."[52]

Jean occasionally accompanied Bill to events where he was the guest of honor. One such tribute took place in 1999 at the National Cartoonists Society convention in San Antonio. Bill stood at the podium while the audience encouraged him to tell war stories. Bill launched into an anecdote, soon lost his train of thought, and stared helplessly at the crowd. Charles Schulz leapt to Bill's aid, asking his cartoonist hero if it would be okay if he finished Bill's story for him. It was Schulz's final tribute to the man he had idolized since World War II, when he had served as an infantry squad leader in France (see figure 91).[53]

In late 2000, Jean drove Bill to Santa Fe to visit his twenty-two-year-old daughter Kaja. Several months before, Kaja had been diagnosed with a rare form of non-Hodgkins lymphoma. "It was unbearable, just unbearable," recalls Jet Zarkadas, who witnessed the reunion. "*She* was so fragile, and *he* was so fragile . . . it was unbearable." Kaja tried to get her father to tell some stories into a tape recorder. There wasn't much he could remember, but he was fully aware of his daughter's illness and pain. And he would remain aware over five months later, when, grief-stricken, he returned to Santa Fe for Kaja's funeral.[54]

NOT LONG AFTER Kaja's death, Jean and Bill moved to Southern California, but not to Jean's house. It had been destroyed by a fire that had also killed Bill and Jean's adult grandson Willie.

**FIGURE 91** World War II wrenched twenty-year-old Charles Schulz from his sheltered life in St. Paul, Minnesota, and placed him in the 20th Armored Division. Never before had he been away from home or even seen a gun. Now he was a machine-gun squad leader in Europe. Gripped by loneliness, desperation, and "the fear that it was never going to end," Schulz found solace in Willie and Joe. In 1969, the old machine gunner began to pay tribute to Bill in his own cartoons. Almost every Veterans Day thereafter, Snoopy put on his garrison cap and went to quaff root beers with Bill Mauldin. When the two cartoonists finally met in 1986, Bill asked Schulz about his annual tribute. Schulz responded simply that he had been an infantryman in France. "That's all he needed to say," explained Bill. In 1998, Schulz included one of Mauldin's old drawings of Willie and Joe in the panel. It was the only time in fifty years that someone else's work appeared in a Peanuts comic strip.

*Peanuts: © United Features Syndicate, Inc.*

The couple stayed in a series of hotels. On a summer morning while Jean was out, Bill eased into a hot bath, as he had done for decades. He liked the water steamy. It stimulated his imagination. This time, however, the bath was too hot. Desensitized perhaps by his Alzheimer's, Bill didn't notice his scalding skin. The damage increased by the minute, reaching deep below the epidermis and destroying his sebaceous glands, nerve endings, muscle fibers, and subcutaneous tissue. By the time Jean found him, Bill had third-degree burns down his back and buttocks.

A specialist at the University of California at Irvine's Regional Burn Center told the family that Bill had only a fifty-fifty chance of surviving the injuries.

He did survive, barely, after weeks of fighting. "When you saw him, it was shocking," says Nat. "Getting through that, indeed, took everything he had."

When he'd stabilized enough to enter Park Superior nursing home in Newport Beach, Bill had all but lost his ability to speak. When not having his burns dressed, his food delivered, or his mail read to him, he passed most waking hours staring out the window.

After a lifetime surviving by his wits and shrugging off constraints, Bill Mauldin was finally beholden to the mercy of others. It was an old story, stretching back to Job and Oedipus Rex. "His life, in the end, could have been written by the Bard himself," says Jet Zarkadas.[55]

A FINAL IRONY of Bill's life was the submersion of his identity into his legend. Born almost sixty years earlier, the legend had dogged him through his days like a shadow.

For decades he had not opened fan mail. Now, his sons and the staff at Park Superior spent hours each day reading select cards and letters from grateful veterans, widows, children, and grandchildren.

And the old soldiers began to come. Bill had always kept them at arm's length, sometimes brusquely. Now, they arrived day in and day out to sit by his bed for a while.

Those World War II veterans mattered most to Bill at the end. He didn't always recognize friends or family. He remembered nothing about his marriages or career. But he seemed to know *them*. They were the source of his sovereignty, the ones who'd exalted him to an office no government or institution could grant.

UNLIKE THE LEGEND, Bill Mauldin the man was dying. Each round of infections required stronger antibiotics and more invasive procedures to clear his lungs. The treatments grew more punishing as Bill weakened. Finally, in early 2003, a physician approached Nat, who had the power of attorney, and asked him to imagine his father floating above the bed and looking down on himself. What would he say?

Nat burst out laughing at the memory of a line his dad had so often used about those who lingered after their minds and bodies had failed: "Why doesn't someone just hit him in the back of the head with a shovel?"

Nat decided to let his father go. He would approve no more drainage tubes or other extraordinary lifesaving measures.

When the next round of respiratory infection hit several days later, the family gathered around, held his crippled hand, and told him they loved him. They were still there on January 22, 2003, when Bill took his last labored breath. He had made it almost three months past his eighty-first birthday.[56]

Sometime before his scalding, Bill had expressed a wish, or at least a willingness, to be buried at Arlington National Cemetery. The arrangements surprised at least one of his sons. "The last I'd heard," said David Mauldin, "he wanted to crash his airplane into a swimming pool."[57]

THE GRAVESIDE CEREMONY took place on January 29. Sodden clouds slung low, spitting rain and sleet. Even the gleaming rows of white marble headstones could not assuage the gloom. "It would make sense for him to die in the middle of winter, in terrible weather with lots of mud," observed David. The family and honor guard gathered under a canvas shelter. A few dozen others stood amid small patches of icy snow.

An army chaplain delivered a brief eulogy. Then, from a stand of distant gravestones, a bugler from the U.S. Army Band played "Taps." A seven-man team from the 3rd Infantry Regiment fired three shots in the air with their M14 rifles. The honor guard carefully folded the flag covering Bill's casket thirteen times, then handed the tricornered package to the Sergeant Major of the Army, Jack L. Tilley.

Tilley's presence was appropriate. As the senior enlisted man in the United States Army, Tilley served as official spokesperson for noncommissioned personnel, reporting their concerns directly to the Chief of Staff. Created during the Vietnam War, it was an office that owed its existence to prior, unofficial spokespersons like Bill Mauldin.

Sergeant Major of the Army Tilley marched over to sixteen-year-old Sam Mauldin and presented him with the flag "on behalf of a grateful nation and the United States Army."[58]

More tributes were paid by Bill's other, less hallowed fraternity. Newspapers around the country ran various likenesses of Willie and Joe grieving for the "dogface cartoonist" or greeting him in heaven (see figure 92).

Ever the sentimentalist, despite a gruff exterior, Bill probably would have smiled at this mawkish display, but he would have howled at the copyright infringement.

*"Here's to that dogface cartoonist."*

**FIGURE 92** Unlike most of the cartoon tributes, this one from J. D. Crowe of the *Mobile Register* was offered in the understated spirit of Bill's World War II cartoons. "It was my intent to come up with something fittingly reverent in its irreverency," says Crowe. Bill usually drank cognac before heading to the front. He also knew the significance of soldiers' standing with their hands in their pockets, a practice forbidden by General Patton. Bill was delighted when *Stars and Stripes* printed a front-page photograph of Patton standing next to General Dwight Eisenhower. In the photo, a scowling Patton stands erect next to a beaming Ike, whose hands are carelessly resting in his pants pockets.

*J. D. Crowe/artizans.com.*

# Acknowledgments

A life complete is a crime scene forever withholding its mysteries from even the most dogged and ingenious investigator. The biographer soldiers on out of fanaticism, obsession, or the delusion that somehow *he* will find the key that unlocks the life. In my pursuit of Bill Mauldin, I've had many enablers, and I'd like to thank some of them here.

First are those at key libraries, archives, and museums: Sarah Willett Duke at the Library of Congress's Prints and Photographs Division; Mike Gonzales at the 45th Infantry Division Museum; Patrick Rand at the Sacramento Mountains Historical Museum; Shirley Rabon and Dawn T. Santiago at the Tularosa Basin Historical Society Museum; Jean Ashton at Columbia University's Rare Book and Manuscript Library; and the staffs at the Harry Ransom Humanities Research Center at the University of Texas at Austin (whose fellowship generously funded my research there), the Alamogordo Public Library, the Museum of New Mexico, Mount

Lebanon Public Library, the National Museum of American History's Archives Center, and Penn State University libraries.

Still better than archives were those who crossed paths with Bill Mauldin. I am grateful for the insights of René Auberjonois, Bernard Bellush, Marvin Bunker, Joan Crowell, Nat Gertler, Tiny Harris, Mike Haymes, Ralph Martin, Stanley Meltzoff, Michael Miner, Michel Monteaux, Diana Schilling, Jean Schulz, Mark Simon, Neil Steinberg, Frederick Voss (who also generously shared his own research materials with me), and Jim Washburn. Cartoonists J. D. Crowe, Bill Griffith, Jimmy Johnson, Tim Menees, Pat Oliphant, and Mike Peters also offered important insights. Joan Lipton, Norton Wolf, and Jet Zarkadas shared especially poignant reflections and comments on my manuscript. Norton gave me his own small Mauldin archive and, through his intelligent, often hilarious correspondence, deepened my understanding of his old friend's genius.

This book would not have been possible without the generosity and cooperation of the Mauldin Estate and family. Sons Andy, David, John, and Nat patiently answered all my questions, no matter how misguided. They reviewed drafts, sent research materials, and offered warm encouragement all along the way, never asking for anything in return. Their refusal to "authorize" or otherwise steer my inquiry is a tribute to their father's freethinking ideals. Jonathan Gordon, the attorney for the Mauldin Estate, gave similar help and support, as did Chris Lund and Tish Frank. I only hope this book repays a portion of my debt to them.

Several other people read all or parts of this manuscript and saved me from embarrassing errors. Bernice DePastino, John Donoghue, Drew Haberberger, Stephen Oates, Paul Paolicelli, Eric Rauchway, Vince Rause, Stephanie Ross, and Louis Warren made the book better, though they cannot be blamed for errors that remain.

What can one say about Jacques de Spoelberch? How often do such measures of grace, warmth, diligence, and expertise combine in one person? Jacques was with this book from the beginning and read my every thought on the matter, before and after placing it at

W. W. Norton. In a fit of gratitude, I tried to pay him more money, which he gently refused by instructing me to review my contract.

I'm most grateful to Jacques for finding Ed Barber, my editor. Ed spent a great deal of ink, not to mention time and intellectual energy, tightening the prose and vastly improving the finished product. Thank you.

As always, I owe the biggest debt to my family, for whom Bill Mauldin was like a rowdy houseguest overstaying his welcome. My daughters Ellie and Libbie, and nieces Rosaleigh and Annabel, became neighborhood experts on Bill Mauldin, and often wondered why I was so fascinated with someone who smoked cigarettes at age three and drove a brakeless Model T down a mountain at age ten. My wife Stephanie Ross understood. May each day bring new ways to express my gratitude.

# Notes

## Prologue: "He Was Our Champion"

1. PBS, *The Battle of the Bulge,* http://www.pbs.org/wgbh/amex/bulge/film more/fd.html.

2. Jay Gruenfeld, *Purple Hearts and Ancient Trees: A Forester's Life Adventures in Business, Wilderness, and War* (Seattle: Peanut Butter Publishing, 1997), 100–2; Chelsea J. Carter, "To Bill, From Willie and Joe," *Chicago Sun-Times,* Dec. 29, 2002; "Willie and Joe's Creator in New Battle," *Los Angeles Times,* Sept. 15, 2002.

3. Bill Mauldin, *Up Front* (New York: World Publishing, 1945), 8.

4. "To Bill, From Willie and Joe."

5. Gordon Dillow, "Calling All WWII Vets for a Vital Mission," *Orange County Register,* July 30, 2002.

6. Jim Washburn, "Bill Mauldin's Enduring Cartoons," *OC Weekly,* Oct. 3, 2002.

7. "Cartoonist Championed Average GI," *Rocky Mountain News,* Sept. 19, 2002; Bob Greene, "Somewhere, Willie and Joe Are Proud and Grateful," *Chicago Tribune,* Aug. 25, 2002.

8. "To Bill, From Willie and Joe."

Chapter One: **Roughing It**

1. Karen Evans, "Bill Mauldin: Cartoonist on a High Roll," *New Mexico Magazine* 75 (Nov. 1997), 32; Bill Mauldin, *A Sort of a Saga* (New York: W. W. Norton, 1949), 55–58, 60.

2. Bill Mauldin, *The Brass Ring* (New York: W. W. Norton, 1971), 15.

3. *Sort of a Saga,* 30–31.

4. *Brass Ring,* 14, 18; *Sort of a Saga,* 25, 52, 208.

5. Steve McDowell, "Pulitzer Prize-Winning Cartoonist Bill Mauldin," *El Palacio* 98 (Winter 1993), 12.

6. Susan L. Woodford, "Merriam's Life Zones," http://www.runet.edu/~swoodwar/CLASSES/GEOG235/lifezone/merriam.html.

7. *Sort of a Saga,* 27.

8. Carole Larson, *Forgotten Frontier: The Story of Southeastern New Mexico* (Albuquerque: University of New Mexico Press, 1993), 13–14.

9. Ibid., xii, 25; "'Uncle Billy' Mauldin Came to Southwest for Visit 70 Years Ago and He's Still Here," *El Paso Times,* Mar. 16, 1952; Mrs. Tom Charles, "Mauldin, Uncle Billy," typescript, Mar. 12, 1952, Sacramento Mountains Historical Society, Cloudcroft, N.M.

10. "Mauldin Family [Tentative]: First Generation," http://freepages.genealogy .rootsweb.com/~oldpend/mauldin/maug01.htm#169737; "'Uncle Billy' Mauldin Came to Southwest"; "Mauldin, Uncle Billy."

11. Sidney Mauldin, Jim Abbott and Henry Nutting's interview, Feb. 27, 2003, Oral History Series, Tularosa Basin Historical Society, Alamogordo, N.M. (hereafter cited as TBHS); "'Uncle Billy' Mauldin Came to Southwest"; "Mauldin, Uncle Billy."

12. *Sort of a Saga,* 20–33.

13. "Pulitzer Prize-Winning Cartoonist," 12.

14. *Sort of a Saga,* 44–45; *Brass Ring,* 27.

15. Sidney Mauldin, interview; Christine Lund, author correspondence, Feb. 14, 2005.

16. Sidney Mauldin, interview; Mark Twain, *The Innocents Abroad; Roughing It,* ed. Guy Cardwell (New York: Library of America, 1984), 544.

17. *Brass Ring,* 25–28.

18. Sidney Mauldin, interview; Christine Lund, author's interview, May 8, 2004; Andy Mauldin, author's interview, May 7, 2004; Nat Mauldin, author's interview, July 25, 2004.

19. *Brass Ring,* 14, 27; *Sort of a Saga,* 127–28; Christine Lund, author's interview; David Mauldin, author's interview, May 7, 2004; Nat Mauldin, author's interview.

20. "Cartoonist on a High Roll," 32; *Sort of a Saga,* 11–19, 67–103.

21.  *Sort of a Saga,* 129–30.

22.  *Sort of a Saga,* 196–97; *Brass Ring,* 13; Sidney Mauldin, interview.

23.  *Brass Ring,* 15–18; "Pulitzer Prize-Winning Cartoonist," 12.

24.  *Sort of a Saga,* 245–59; *Brass Ring,* 27.

25.  Tiny Harris, author's interview, June 25, 2004.

26.  Robert C. Harvey, *Children of the Yellow Kid: The Evolution of the American Comic Strip* (Seattle: Frye Art Museum, 1998), 17–32, 69–112; Richard Marschall, *America's Great Comic-Strip Artists: From the Yellow Kids to Peanuts* (New York: Stewart, Tabori & Chang, 1989), 19–39, 183–93.

27.  *Brass Ring,* 25–29.

28.  Robert C. Harvey, "A Flourish of Trumpets: Roy Crane and the Adventure Strip," http://www.adventurestrips.com/washtubbs/washtubbs_harvey_crane .html.

29.  *Brass Ring,* 28–41, 44.

30.  Errol Lincoln Uys, *Riding the Rails: Teenagers on the Move in the Great Depression* (New York: TV Books, 1999), 11, 23.

31.  *Brass Ring,* 45–46, 53–56.

32.  Jonathan Gordon, author's interview, June 8, 2004.

33.  *Brass Ring,* 19, 50–52.

34.  Andy Mauldin, author's interview; David Mauldin, author's interview.

35.  *Brass Ring,* 47, 57, 273; E. W. Montgomery to Bill Mauldin, Aug. 16, 1943, Box 5, William Henry Mauldin Papers, Library of Congress, Washington, D.C. (hereafter cited as WHM).

36.  *Brass Ring,* 74.

37.  Ibid., 57, 67; "Cartoonist on a High Roll," 34.

38.  *Brass Ring,* 60–62.

39.  "Humor Is Ultimate Sanity for Bill Mauldin," *Alamogordo Daily News,* n.d., clipping files, Bill Mauldin, TBHS; Harvey, *Children of the Yellow Kid,* 69–112; Marschall, *America's Great Comic-Strip Artists,* 183–93.

40.  *Brass Ring,* 62–69, 273.

41.  "Bill, Willie & Joe," *Time,* June 18, 1945, 17.

42.  *Brass Ring,* 56, 75, 78–79; "Pulitzer Prize-Winning Cartoonist," 12.

43.  *Brass Ring,* 18.

44.  Ibid., 80; "Mauldin, William H., Enlisted Record and Report of Separation, Honorable Discharge," Box 17, WHM.

45.  Flint Whitlock, *The Rock of Anzio: From Sicily to Dachau: A History of the U.S. 45th Infantry Division* (New York: Westview Press, 1998), 20–21.

46.  *Brass Ring,* 82–85; Whitlock, *The Rock of Anzio,* 1, 19; George A. Fisher, *The Story of the 180th Infantry Regiment* (San Angelo, Tex.: Newsfoto Publishing, 1947), chap. 1.

*Chapter Two:* **Manuevering**

1. Bill Mauldin, *The Brass Ring* (New York: W. W. Norton, 1971), 85–86.
2. Paul Fussell, *Wartime: Understanding and Behavior in the Second World War* (New York: Oxford University Press, 1989), 80.
3. *Brass Ring,* 86–88.
4. Ibid., 90–93, 102; V. Jack Frye, "History of the *45th Division News*" (master's thesis, University of Oklahoma, 1968); Walter Munford Harrison, *Log of the 45th* (Oklahoma City: Harrison, 1941).
5. *Brass Ring,* 90–91.
6. *Arizona Highways,* Sept. 1941, 44; July 1941, 44.
7. Cartoon drawing no. 1273, n.d., William Henry Mauldin Papers, Library of Congress, Prints and Photographs Division, Washington, D.C. (hereafter cited as WHM).
8. *Brass Ring,* 91–93; Bill Mauldin, "Notes on KP and/or The Egghead," *New York Times Magazine,* Dec. 8, 1957, 35.
9. *Brass Ring,* 94.
10. Ibid., 96; Charles T. Jones, "'Willie and Joe': Cartoonist 'Astonished' to Find Inspiration Alive," Dec. 31, 1999, http://www.inkboy.net/resume/WillieAndJoe/willie&joe.htm.
11. Flint Whitlock, *The Rock of Anzio: From Sicily to Dachau: A History of the U.S. 45th Infantry Division* (New York: Westview Press, 1998), 20–21; George A. Fisher, *The Story of the 180th Infantry Regiment* (San Angelo, Tex.: Newsfoto Publishing, 1947), chaps. 1 and 2.
12. *Brass Ring,* 97–98.
13. Ibid., 101–2.
14. Cartoon drawings nos. 1262–73, n.d., WHM.
15. *Oklahoma City Times,* Oct. 15, 1941.
16. *Brass Ring,* 108.
17. Ibid., 99, 104.
18. Robert C. Harvey, *Children of the Yellow Kid: The Evolution of the American Comic Strip* (Seattle: Frye Art Museum, 1998), 86–91, 100–7.
19. *Oklahoma City Times,* June 19 and 26, 1941.
20. *Rock of Anzio,* 23–24.
21. Rick Atkinson, *An Army at Dawn: The War in North Africa, 1942–1943* (New York: Henry Holt, 2002), 8; Michael C. C. Adams, *The Best War Ever: America and World War II* (Baltimore: Johns Hopkins University Press, 1994), 71, 76; *Brass Ring,* 102–4.
22. *Best War Ever,* 72; *Wartime,* 4; *Brass Ring,* 102.

23. *Brass Ring,* 104–8; Sgt. Don Robinson, *News of the 45th,* illustrated by Sgt. Bill Mauldin (Norman: University of Oklahoma Press, 1944), 21–28.

24. *Oklahoma City Times,* Sept. 13, 1941.

25. *Brass Ring,* 109.

26. *Army at Dawn,* 10; *Rock of Anzio,* 23–24.

27. *Brass Ring,* 113.

28. "Bill, Willie, and Joe," *Time,* June 18, 1945, 17–18; Frederick C. Painton, "Up Front with Bill Mauldin," *Saturday Evening Post,* Mar. 17, 1945, 69; *Brass Ring,* 113.

29. *Brass Ring,* 114; *News of the 45th,* 30–31.

30. *Brass Ring,* 114–18, 122, 130.

31. *Rock of Anzio,* 26–27; *Brass Ring,* 116, 122–23; Russell Hall to Bill Mauldin, Feb. 2, 1944, Box 6, WHM.

32. Annie Davis Weeks, "Yank, The Army Weekly," in *Close to Glory: The Untold Stories of WWII by the GIs Who Saw and Reported the War,* edited by Art Weithas (Austin, Tex.: Eakins Press, 1991), xxi–xxiii; Art Weithas, "*Yank* Milestones," in *Close to Glory,* 2–4; George Baker, "The Words of George Baker," 1946, http://sadsack.net/GBAutobiography.htm; *Brass Ring,* 123.

33. *Rock of Anzio,* 27.

34. John Keegan, *The Second World War* (New York: Viking, 1989), 316–17; Carlo D'Este, *World War II in the Mediterranean, 1942–1945* (Chapel Hill, N.C.: Algonquin Books, 1990), 1–4; *An Army at Dawn,* 11–16.

35. *Rock of Anzio,* 27–28; Bill Mauldin, "A Salute for 'General Bill,'" *Oklahoma City Times,* Oct. 25, 1942; *Brass Ring,* 122–30.

36. Guy Nelson, *Thunderbird: A History of the 45th Infantry Division* (Oklahoma City, Okla.: 45th Infantry Division Association, 1970), 23; *Rock of Anzio,* 31–34; *An Army at Dawn,* 280–89; *Second World War,* 318–19.

37. "Bill, Willie, and Joe," 18; "Up Front with Bill Mauldin," 69; contract between Bill Mauldin and Army Times Publishing Company, May 23, 1943, Box 2, WHM; Bill Mauldin to Mel Ryder, Dec. 3, 1944, Box 2, WHM.

38. *Rock of Anzio,* 32.

39. *News of the 45th,* 48; *Brass Ring,* 133.

Chapter Three: **Going In**

1. Pierre Teilhard de Chardin, *The Making of a Mind: Letters from a Soldier-Priest, 1914–1919,* trans. René Hague (New York: Harper & Row, 1961), 205.

2. Bill Mauldin, *The Brass Ring* (New York: W. W. Norton, 1971), 133–35.

3. Michael C. C. Adams, *The Best War Ever: America and World War II* (Baltimore: Johns Hopkins University Press, 1994), 100; Gerald F. Linderman, *The World Within War: America's Combat Experience in World War II* (Cambridge, Mass.: Harvard University Press, 1997), 188–89; *Brass Ring,* 133.

4. *Brass Ring,* 135–37; *Daily Oklahoman,* Aug. 1, 1943.

5. Flint Whitlock, *The Rock of Anzio: From Sicily to Dachau: A History of the U.S. 45th Infantry Division* (New York: Westview Press, 1998), 32.

6. *Brass Ring,* 137, 140.

7. Rick Atkinson, *An Army at Dawn: The War in North Africa, 1942–1943* (New York: Henry Holt, 2002), 462–63.

8. *Brass Ring,* 140–42.

9. Ibid., 143–47; *Rock of Anzio,* 38–42.

10. *Rock of Anzio,* 39; Robert Leckie, *Delivered from Evil: The First Complete One-Volume History* (New York: Harper & Row, 1987), 524.

11. *Rock of Anzio,* 44–46.

12. Ibid., 44–47; *Brass Ring,* 147–56; Sgt. Don Robinson, *News of the 45th,* illustrated by Sgt. Bill Mauldin (Norman: University of Oklahoma Press, 1944), 73–77.

13. *45th Division News,* July 17 and 19, 1943, 45th Infantry Division Museum, Oklahoma City, Okla.

14. *Brass Ring,* 158–60; *News of the 45th,* 82–85.

15. Eric Severeid, *Not So Wild a Dream* (New York: Atheneum, 1976 [1946]), 388; Bill Mauldin, *Bill Mauldin's Army* (Novato, Calif.: Presidio Press, 1983 [1951]), 97.

16. *Brass Ring,* 160–66; *News of the 45th,* 86–88.

17. *Brass Ring,* 164–65; *News of the 45th,* 88–93; V. Jack Frye, "The History of the Forty-fifth Division News" (master's thesis, University of Oklahoma Graduate College, 1968), 56–58.

18. *Rock of Anzio,* 54–59. Eric Ethier, "Patton's Race to Messina," Apr. 2001 http://historynet.com/ah/blpattontomessina/index1.html.

19. *Daily Oklahoman,* Oct. 17, 1943.

20. *Brass Ring,* 168–69.

21. Charles T. Jones, "'Willie and Joe': Cartoonist 'Astonished' to Find Inspiration Alive," Dec. 31, 1999, http://www.inkboy.net/resume/WillieAndJoe/willie&joe.htm; Paul Fussell, *Wartime: Understanding and Behavior in the Second World War* (New York: Oxford University Press, 1989), 35–38.

22. *Rock of Anzio,* 61–62; *Brass Ring,* 170–72; "Bill, Willie & Joe," *Time,* June 18, 1945, 18; Will Lang and Tom Durrance, "Mauldin," *Life,* Feb. 5, 1945, 50; *Industrie Riunite Editoriali Siciliane* to Bill Mauldin, receipt, Sept. 16, 1943; Don Robinson to Bill Mauldin, receipt, Sept. 5, 1943, Box 11, William Henry Maul-

din Papers, Library of Congress, Prints and Photographs Division, Washington, D.C. (hereafter cited as WHM).

23. *Brass Ring,* 196; Art Weithas, "*Yank* Milestones," in *Close to Glory: The Untold Stories of WWII by the GIs Who Saw and Reported the War,* edited by Art Weithas (Austin, Tex.: Eakins Press, 1991), 2–3, 7; Herbert Mitgang, *Newsmen in Khaki: Tales of a World War II Soldier Correspondent* (Lanham, Md.: Taylor Trade Publishing, 2004), x–xi, 29.

24. Mitgang, *Newsmen in Khaki,* 66, 72; Ralph Martin, author's interview, July 27, 2005.

25. Frank James Price, *Troy H. Middleton: A Biography* (Baton Rouge: Louisiana State University Press, 1974), 142, 159–60; "Bill, Willie & Joe," 16–17.

26. *Brass Ring,* 170–73; Bill Mauldin, *Up Front* (New York: World Publishing, 1945), 125–26.

27. *Brass Ring,* 173–76; *Rock of Anzio,* 68–98; Carlo D'Este, *Fatal Decision: Anzio and the Battle for Rome* (New York: HarperCollins, 1991), 38.

28. John Ellis, *Brute Force: Allied Strategy and Tactics in the Second World War* (New York: Viking, 1990), 292.

29. John Keegan, *The Second World War* (New York: Viking, 1989), 354.

30. *Fatal Decision,* 33.

31. Ibid., 46.

32. John Huston, *An Open Book* (New York: Alfred A. Knopf, 1980), 107.

33. *Brass Ring,* 185.

34. *Rock of Anzio,* 104–10; *Up Front,* 98.

35. *Best War Ever,* 104.

36. Ibid., 110.

37. *Delivered from Evil,* 630.

38. *Rock of Anzio,* 115.

39. *Delivered from Evil,* 631; *Rock of Anzio,* 115, 118.

40. "Mauldin," 50.

41. *Brass Ring,* 188.

42. *Wartime,* 37–38.

43. *Best War Ever,* 104.

44. *45th Division News,* Dec. 4, 1943.

## Chapter Four: Doing Battle

1. Ernest Hemingway, foreword to *Treasury for the Free World,* edited by Ben Raeburn (New York: Arco Publishing, 1946), quoted in Robert W. Trogdon, ed., *Ernest Hemingway: A Literary Reference* (New York: Carroll & Graff, 2002), 262.

2. Bill Mauldin, *The Brass Ring* (New York: W. W. Norton, 1971), 200–1; Frederick C. Painton, "Up Front with Bill Mauldin," *Saturday Evening Post,* Mar. 17, 1945, 71.

3. *Brass Ring,* 195–96; *45th Division News,* Oct. 28 and Dec. 25, 1943.

4. Ed Vebell, author's interview, May 15, 2004.

5. *Stars and Stripes,* Mediterranean edition, Nov. 29, 1943.

6. *Stars and Stripes,* Mediterranean edition, Dec. 18, 1943.

7. David Lamb, "Bill, Willie, and Joe," *MHQ: The Quarterly Journal of Military History,* vol. 1, no. 4 (Summer 1989): 40.

8. *Stars and Stripes,* Mediterranean edition, Dec. 18, 1943.

9. Bill Mauldin, *Up Front* (New York: World Publishing, 1945), 16.

10. James Tobin, *Ernie Pyle's War: America's Eyewitness to World War II* (Lawrence: University Press of Kansas, 1997).

11. *New York World-Telegraph,* Jan. 15, 1944.

12. "Speaking of Pictures . . . : A Soldier Draws Italian War Cartoons," *Life,* Jan.17, 1944, 8–10.

13. George Carlin to Ernie Pyle, telegram, Jan. 15, 1944, Box 6; Melvin Ryder to Bill Mauldin, telegram, Feb. 1944, Box 2, William Henry Mauldin Papers, Library of Congress, Manuscripts Division, Washington, D.C. (hereafter cited as WHM).

14. Russell Hall to Bill Mauldin, Feb. 2 and 26, 1944, Box 6, WHM.

15. Bill Mauldin, *Back Home* (New York: William Sloane Associates, 1947), 32; *Brass Ring,* 203; Ernie Pyle to George Carlin, telegram, Feb. 1944, Box 5, WHM.

16. Anne Watkins to Bill Mauldin, Mar. 20 and May 16, 1944; George Carlin to Melvin Ryder, Mar. 8, 1944, Box 7, WHM.

17. George Carlin to Bill Mauldin, telegram, Feb. 3, 1944, Box 7, WHM; *Brass Ring,* 203.

18. *Brass Ring,* 203.

19. Matthew Parker, *Monte Cassino: The Hardest-Fought Battle of World War II* (New York: Doubleday, 2004), 205–6; Norman Lewis, *Naples '44* (New York: Pantheon, 1978), 72, 86; *Brass Ring,* 192–93; Stephen E. Ambrose, *Citizen Soldiers: The U.S. Army from the Normandy Beaches to the Bulge to the Surrender of Germany* (New York: Simon & Schuster, 1998), 333.

20. Ernie Pyle to Lt. Col. Kenneth Clark, Public Relations Officer, Fifth Army, Apr. 3, 1944, Box 5, WHM.

21. *Brass Ring,* 192; *Stars and Stripes,* Mediterranean edition, Dec. 22, 1943.

22. Michael C. C. Adams, *The Best War Ever: America and World War II* (Baltimore: Johns Hopkins University Press, 1994), 100; Paul Fussell, *Wartime: Understanding and Behavior in the Second World War* (New York: Oxford University Press, 1989),

145; *45th Division News,* Dec. 11, 1943, 45th Infantry Division Museum, Oklahoma City, Okla.

23. Ibid., 195–202; Will Lang and Tom Durrance, "Mauldin," *Life,* Feb. 5, 1945, 49–50; "Up Front with Bill Mauldin," 71; *Up Front,* 28–29.

24. *Brass Ring,* 195.

25. *Up Front,* 80; *Monte Cassino,* 52.

26. *Up Front,* 28–29.

27. George H. Roeder Jr., *The Censored War: American Visual Experience During World War II* (New Haven, Conn.: Yale University Press, 1993), 10–12; *Brass Ring,* 137.

28. *Censored War,* 12–15.

29. *Brass Ring,* 233.

30. *Wartime,* 153–61; Gerald F. Linderman, *The World Within War: America's Combat Experience in World War II* (Cambridge, Mass.: Harvard University Press, 1997), 311–15; *Ernie Pyle's War,* 118.

31. *Wartime,* 161.

32. *World Within War,* 45.

33. Mark Skinner Watson, *Chief of Staff: Prewar Plans and Preparations* (Washington, D.C.: Center of Military History, United States Army, 1991 [1950]), 362.

34. *Brass Ring,* 185.

35. *Best War Ever,* 60, 70, 79–81; *World Within War,* 1.

36. *Best War Ever,* 82, 86–87; Robert Leckie, *Delivered from Evil: The First Complete One-Volume History* (New York: Harper & Row, 1987), 624.

37. *Best War Ever,* 87–88, 129–31.

38. *Up Front,* 5.

39. *Monte Cassino,* 39, 60.

40. *Up Front,* 139–42.

41. Flint Whitlock, *The Rock of Anzio: From Sicily to Dachau: A History of the U.S. 45th Infantry Division* (New York: Westview Press, 1998), 123.

42. *Monte Cassino,* 102–16; Carlo D'Este, *World War II in the Mediterranean, 1942–1945* (Chapel Hill, N.C.: Algonquin Books, 1990), 126.

43. *Brass Ring,* 216.

44. *45th Division News,* Feb. 22, 1944.

45. *Brass Ring,* 201.

46. Stanley Meltzoff, author's interview, Jan. 23, 2006.

47. John Horne Burns, *The Gallery* (New York: Harper & Brothers, 1947), 1.

48. *Monte Cassino,* 205.

49. *Brass Ring,* 204.

50. *Up Front,* 73.

51. *Wartime,* 101; Ed Vebell, author's interview; Stanley Meltzoff, author's interview.

52. *Brass Ring,* 204; Ed Vebell, author's interview; Stanley Meltzoff, author's interview; *Gallery,* 265.

53. Ed Vebell, author's interview.

54. *Brass Ring,* 205.

55. Ibid., 211–15; "Mauldin," 50; "Up Front with Bill Mauldin," 71.

56. Herbert Lyons, "Bill Mauldin's Book," *New Republic,* June 18, 1945, 848.

57. Bill Mauldin, "How GI Joe Was Born," *Life,* Mar. 27, 1944, 12.

58. "A Soldier Draws Italian War Cartoons"; Will Lang to Bill Mauldin, Feb. 15, 1944, Box 4, WHM.

59. *Ernie Pyle's War,* 138; *Up Front,* 15.


### Willie and Joe: A War Gallery

1.   Gerald F. Linderman, *The World Within War: America's Combat Experience in World War II* (Cambridge, Mass.: Harvard University Press, 1997), 330.

2.   Charles T. Jones, "'Willie and Joe': Cartoonist 'Astonished' to Find Inspiration Alive," Dec. 31, 1999, http://www.inkboy.net/resume/WillieAndJoe/willie&joe.htm.

3.   Bill Mauldin, *Back Home* (New York: William Sloane Associates, 1947), 265; idem, *Up Front* (New York: World Publishing, 1945), 32.

4.   Norman Mailer quoted in Paul Fussell, *Wartime: Understanding and Behavior in the Second World War* (New York: Oxford University Press, 1989), 252–53.


### Chapter Five: Breaking Out

1. Wynford Vaughan-Thomas, *Anzio* (New York: Holt, Rinehart & Winston, 1961), 222–23; Flint Whitlock, *The Rock of Anzio: From Sicily to Dachau: A History of the U.S. 45th Infantry Division* (New York: Westview Press, 1998), 287–88.

2. *Rock of Anzio,* 278, 303–6, 309–10; Matthew Parker, *Monte Cassino: The Hardest-Fought Battle of World War II* (New York: Doubleday, 2004), 276.

3. Bill Mauldin, *The Brass Ring* (New York: W. W. Norton, 1971), 221–22.

4. Will Lang and Tom Durrance, "Mauldin," *Life,* Feb. 5, 1945, 49–50; "Up Front with Bill Mauldin," 50; Frederick C. Painton, "Up Front with Bill Mauldin," *Saturday Evening Post,* Mar. 17, 1945, 71.

5. Jonathon Gordon, author's interview, June 8, 2004; Herbert Mitgang to author, June 1, 2004.

6. Ernie Pyle to Bill Mauldin, June 30, 1944, Box 5, William Henry Mauldin Papers, Library of Congress, Washington, D.C. (hereafter cited as WHM).

7. Ann Watkins to Bill Mauldin, Aug. 24, 1944, Box 7, WHM; George Carlin to Bill Mauldin, Sept. 23, 1944, Box 6, WHM.

8. "Mauldin," 52; "Up Front with Bill Mauldin," 22.

9. Ann Watkins to Bill Mauldin, Aug. 24, 1944, Box 7, WHM.

10. "Hey, Joe, Shave," *Stars and Stripes,* Mediterranean edition, July 12, 1944; ibid., July 28 and 29, 1944.

11. Bill Mauldin to Melvin Ryder, Dec. 3, 1944, Box 2, WHM; George Carlin to Bill Mauldin, Nov. 9, 1944, Box 6, WHM.

12. "Neville for White," *Time*, Aug. 7, 1944; "Thought Control," *Time*, July 17, 1944; Charles G. Bolte, "The War Fronts," *The Nation*, June 22, 1944, 90; Egbert White, "A Free Press in a Citizen's Army," *Journal of Educational Sociology*, vol. 19, no. 4 (Dec. 1945): 245–48.

13. Robert Neville, "Travel Orders of *Stars and Stripes* Artist," July 31, 1944, Box 6, WHM.

14. *Brass Ring*, 225; Bill Mauldin, *Up Front* (New York: World Publishing, 1945), 201; Sylvia Jukes Morris, *Rage for Fame: The Ascent of Clare Boothe Luce* (New York: Random House, 1997).

15. *Brass Ring*, 225–27.

16. *Stars and Stripes*, Mediterranean edition, Sept. 25, 1944.

17. *Brass Ring*, 228.

18. George Carlin to Roy Howard, Sept. 23, 1944 , Box 6, WHM.

19. *Up Front*, 211.

20. Ibid., 206–7; Carlin to Howard, Sept. 23, 1944; *Editor & Publisher*, Oct. 14, 1944, 39.

21. Bill Sloane to Margot Johnson, June 13, 1944; Sloane to Johnson, Aug. 9, 1944, Box 7, WHM.

22. Contract between William Mauldin and Henry Holt, Sept. 25, 1944, Box 4, WHM; Ed Vebell, author's interview, May 15, 2004.

23. *Up Front*, 211–27; Carlo D'Este, *World War II in the Mediterranean, 1942–1945* (Chapel Hill, N.C.: Algonquin Books, 1990), 189.

24. *Brass Ring*, 235–39.

25. Ibid., 241–45; *Up Front*, 138.

26. *Stars and Stripes,* Sept. 14, 1944.

27. Stephen E. Ambrose, *Citizen Soldiers: The U.S. Army from the Normandy Beaches to the Bulge to the Surrender of Germany, June 7, 1944 to May 7, 1945* (New York: Simon & Schuster, 1997), 336–38; *Brass Ring*, 245.

28. *Brass Ring*, 245–48; Harry C. Butcher, *My Three Years with Eisenhower: The*

*Personal Diary of Captain Harry C. Butcher, USNR, Naval Aide to General Eisenhower, 1942–1945* (New York: Simon & Schuster, 1946), 773–75.

29.  Herbert Mitgang, *Newsmen in Khaki: Tales of a World War II Soldier Correspondent* (Lanham, Md.: Taylor Trade Publishing, 2004), 58–59.

30.  *Brass Ring,* 245–55; *My Three Years with Eisenhower,* 774; Ralph Martin, author's interview, July 27, 2005.

31.  *Brass Ring,* 255; Stanley Hirshson, *General Patton: A Soldier's Life* (New York: HarperCollins, 2002), 606–7.

32.  *Brass Ring,* 256–58; *General Patton,* 607.

33.  *Brass Ring,* 259–64.

34.  "G.I. Mauldin v. G. Patton," *Time,* Mar. 26, 1945; *My Three Years with Eisenhower,* 801.

35.  Ann Watkins to Bill Mauldin, Mar. 6 and 14, 1945, Box 7, WHM; Watkins to Mauldin, Mar. 15, 1945, and Mauldin to Watkins, Apr. 1, 1945, Box 67, Watkins Loomis, Inc., Records, Rare Book and Manuscript Library, Columbia University, New York (hereafter cited as WL).

36.  *Brass Ring,* 266–70.

37.  *New York Times,* May 8, 1945; "'Up Front' Cartoons Win Pulitzer Prize for Mauldin," *Stars and Stripes,* Mediterranean edition, May 9, 1945; *Brass Ring,* 271.

38.  "Mauldin on GI," *Stars and Stripes,* Mediterranean edition, Jan. 11, 1945; David Lamb, "Bill, Willie, and Joe," *MHQ: The Quarterly Journal of Military History,* vol. 1, no. 4 (Summer 1989): 40; John Koffend, "Hit It If It's Big," *Time,* July 21, 1961, 52; *Brass Ring,* 273.

39.  *Brass Ring,* 272.

40.  Ibid., 241.

41.  Bill Mauldin, "All That Glitters Is Not Gold," *The Reporter,* Dec. 8, 1953, 42.

42.  *Brass Ring,* 272.

### Chapter Six: Coming Home

1.  Bill Mauldin, *Back Home* (New York: William Sloane Associates, 1947), 1–6.

2.  Ibid., 33; Bill Mauldin to Ann Watkins, May 30, 1945, Box 67, Watkins-Loomis, Inc., Records, Rare Book and Manuscript Library, Columbia University, New York (hereafter cited as WL).

3.  Mauldin to Watkins, May 30, 1945, WL.

4.  *Back Home,* 6–8.

5.  "Mauldin Arrives Here," *New York Times,* June 11, 1945.

6.  *Back Home,* 4, 9–10.

7.  Mauldin to Watkins, May 30, 1945, WL.

8. *Back Home,* 10.

9. "Mauldin Insists the Soldiers' Newspaper Is 'the One Thing That Should Be Left Free,'" *New York Times,* June 12, 1945; "Sgt. Bill Mauldin Returns from War," *New York World-Telegram,* June 11, 1945.

10. *Back Home,* 9–13; Bill Mauldin, "Ex-GI," *Collier's,* Oct. 20, 1945, 23.

11. Mauldin to Watkins, Mar. 12, 1945, WL.

12. Bill Mauldin, *Up Front* (New York: World Publishing, 1945), 143–44.

13. Sterling North, review of *Up Front, New York Post,* June 21, 1945; John Senior, "Not Funny," *The Nation,* July 7, 1945, n.p. (digital archive).

14. Charles Poore, "Books of the Times," *New York Times,* Nov. 22, 1945; "Willie and Joe Still Telling Best Unadorned War Story," *New York Times,* Dec. 2, 1951.

15. *Back Home,* 33; Bert Allenberg to Ann Watkins, telegram, June 15, 1945, Box 67, WL.

16. "Latest Figures on Estimated Sale of Bill Mauldin's *Up Front,*" June 19, 1945; Ann Watkins to Bill Mauldin, memo, June 1945, Box 67, WL.

17. Eleanor Roosevelt, "My Day," June 21, 1945, Eleanor Roosevelt Papers, My Day Project, http://www.gwu.edu/~erpapers/documents/myday/displaydoc.cfm?_y=1945&_f=md000056.

18. Frederick C. Painton, "Up Front with Bill Mauldin," *Saturday Evening Post,* Mar. 17, 1945, 69; *Back Home,* 35–39.

19. "Mauldin Meets Son," *Life,* July 8, 1945, 30; *New York Herald-Tribune,* June 27, 1945.

20. *New York World-Telegram,* Aug. 27, 1945.

21. Bill Mauldin to Ann Watkins, Aug. 16, 1945, Box 67, WL; transcript of telephone conversation, Bill Mauldin and Jean Mauldin, Oct. 1945, Box 67, WL.

22. "Ex-GI," 38.

23. Ibid., 22–23, 38; *Back Home,* 138–40; Mauldin to Watkins, Aug. 16, 1945, WL.

24. "Ex-GI," 22–23, 38; *Back Home,* 24–29.

25. *New York World-Telegram,* Aug. 23, 1945.

26. "Mauldin Reconverts," *Time,* Sept. 24, 1945, 61.

27. Bill Mauldin, untitled manuscript, 1946, Box 67, WL.

28. Andy Mauldin, author's interview; Tish Frank, author's interview; "Mauldin Sues for Divorce," *New York Times,* Oct. 23, 1945; "Complaint for Divorce," William H. Mauldin vs. Norma Jean Mauldin, Oct. 22, 1945, Superior Court of the State of California, Los Angeles County, County Archives Center, Los Angeles, Ca.

29. "Mauldin Reconverts," 61.

30. *New York World-Telegram,* Sept. 10, 1945; Nat Mauldin, author's interview;

Bill Mauldin, draft manuscript of *Back Home,* 37, Box 10, William Henry Mauldin Papers, Library of Congress, Washington, D.C. (hereafter cited as WHM); "Mauldin Reconverts," 61; Gerald W. Johnson, review of "What's Got Your Back Up?" clipping, n.d., Box 7, WHM; *Back Home,* 39.

31. Edward Weeks, review of *Back Home, Atlantic Monthly,* n.d., clippings file, Box 19, Mauldin Cartoon Collection, 1946–87, National Museum of American History Archives Center, Smithsonian Institution, Washington, D.C.

32. Studs Terkel, *"The Good War": An Oral History of World War II* (New York: Ballantine, 1984), 362. On the cultural front, see Michael Denning, *The Cultural Front: The Laboring of American Culture in the Twentieth Century* (New York: Verso, 1996).

33. Ronald Reagan to Bill Mauldin, June 27, 1945, Box 6, WHM; Bill Mauldin, "Bill Mauldin Goes to Legion Convention," *Life,* Dec. 3, 1945, 38–39; Bill Mauldin, "Poppa Knows Best," *Atlantic Monthly,* Apr. 1947, 29–36.

34. Ralph Martin, author's interview; Norton Wolf, author's interview; Herbert Mitgang, *Newsmen in Khaki: Tales of a World War II Soldier Correspondent* (Lanham, Md.: Taylor Trade Publishing, 2004), 14, 54, 56; "Black, Brown, and Yellow," *Stars and Stripes* (Mediterranean edition), Mar. 25, 1945.

35. *New York Herald-Tribune* forum speech, Oct. 31, 1945, Box 8, WHM; *Bill Mauldin Says* (New York: Writers' Board, 1945).

36. Natalie Evans to Alice Corbin Henderson, Nov. 28, 1945, Alice Corbin Henderson Collection, Box 48, Harry T. Ransom Center, University of Texas at Austin (hereafter cited as ACH).

37. Affidavit, William H. Mauldin vs. Norma Jean Mauldin, Jan. 4, 1946; "Interlocutory Judgment of Divorce," June 13, 1946, Superior Court of the State of California, County Archives Center.

38. *Back Home,* 113; Bill Mauldin to Ann Watkins, Mar. 19, 1945, Box 67, WL.

39. John Lardner and Ring Lardner Jr., *Up Front,* movie script, Sept. 21, 1945, Box 14, WHM.

40. Phil Berg to Anne Watkins, Nov. 30, 1945, Box 67, WL; *Back Home,* 115.

41. *Back Home,* 115–29.

42. Orson Welles, "Voice of the G.I.," *New York Post,* Sept. 4, 1945; Nat Mauldin, author's interview.

43. *Back Home,* 264–65; "In War and Peace," *Time,* Sept. 26, 1960, 49; Natalie Evans to Alice Corbin Henderson, Feb. 13, 1946, ACH.

44. *Back Home,* 276–77; Richard Samuel West, "Mauldin: From Willie and Joe to Ronnie," *Target,* vol. 3, no. 10 (Winter 1984): 8.

45. *Back Home,* 267; Frederick S. Voss, "Mauldin Dons His Mufti," conference paper, "Caricature and Cartoon in Twentieth-Century America: A Joint Conference of the Library of Congress and the National Portrait Gallery," May 15, 1998, National Portrait Gallery, Washington, D.C.

46. *Daily Worker,* Jan. 4, 1946; Bill Mauldin, draft manuscript of *Back Home,* 37, Box 10, WHM; *Back Home,* 272–80.

47. *Back Home,* 171, 176, 252.

48. "Education of a GI," *Time,* July 7, 1947, 62; *Back Home,* 231.

49. *Back Home,* 252.

50. Ibid., 310–11.

51. John Lardner, review of *Back Home, New York Times,* Nov. 2, 1947.

52. Clifton Fadiman, quoted in "A Quick Preview of *Back Home* by Bill Mauldin: A Report by John P. Marquand," n.p., n.d., author's collection.

53. Jean Macy, undated memo, Box 67, WL; Joe Alex Morris to Mike Watkins, Aug. 8, 1947; *Saturday Evening Post* to Mike Watkins, Aug. 27, 1947, Box 67, WL; E. J. Kahn, profile of Bill Mauldin, *'48: The Magazine of the Year* (Feb. 1948), 66.

54. Christopher Morley, quoted in "A Quick Preview of *Back Home*"; "Lost . . . the New Look," *New York Times,* Dec. 7, 1947; Kahn, profile of Bill Mauldin, 70; Atkinson quoted in Mike Watkins to Bill Mauldin, Oct. 28, 1947, Box 67, WL.

55. Kahn, profile of Bill Mauldin, 70; Alice Henderson Rossin to Alice Corbin Henderson, Jan. 9, 1946, Box 49, ACH.

56. *New York Herald-Tribune,* Apr. 8, 1948.

57. "People Who Read and Write," *New York Times,* May 2, 1948; "A *Star* Is Born," *Time,* June 28, 1948, 39; Norton Wolf, personal correspondence, Jan. 29, 2006.

58. "First Draft of Bill Mauldin Agreement," Oct. 7, 1948, Box 67, WL.

59. Mark R. Grandstaff, "Making the Military American: Advertising, Reform, and the Demise of an Antistanding Military Tradition, 1945–1955," *Journal of Military History,* vol. 60, no. 2 (Apr. 1996), 306–8; "Mauldin Attacks Army Distinctions," *New York Times,* Mar. 29, 1946; "Mauldin Says Army Believes Only Officers Are Gentlemen," *New York Herald-Tribune,* Mar. 29, 1946.

60. "Sarge's Wife in a Tizzy Over That New House," *New York Post,* Feb. 4, 1949.

61. D. K. Brown to J. Edgar Hoover, teletype, Jan. 13, 1949; J. Edgar Hoover to D. K. Brown, teletype, Jan. 14, 1949, file of Mauldin, William H., Federal Bureau of Investigation, Department of Justice, Washington, D.C.

62. Norton Wolf, author's correspondence, July 4, 2006.

63. Mike Watkins to Bert Allenberg, May 2, 1949, Box 67, WL; Meyer Berger, "The Early Meanderings of Mauldin," *New York Times,* Oct. 30, 1949; *Saturday Review* quoted on dust jacket of *A Sort of a Saga,* by Bill Mauldin (New York: W. W. Norton, 1973); Charles Poore, review of *A Sort of a Saga, New York Times,* Oct. 29, 1949; Lewis Gannett, review of *A Sort of a Saga, New York Herald-Tribune,* Oct. 25, 1949.

64. Hesper Anderson, *South Mountain Road: A Daughter's Journey of Discovery* (New

York: Simon & Schuster, 2000), 18–19; untitled newspaper clipping, n.d., Box 15, WHM.

### Chapter Seven: Starting Over

1. Lillian Ross, *Picture: John Huston, MGM, and the Making of The Red Badge of Courage* (London: Andre Deutsch, 1953 [1952]), 52; "Controversial Little Cuss," *New Yorker,* Dec. 26, 1953, 16.
2. Jean G. Parker, notes of telephone conversation with Bill Mauldin, Mar. 23, 1950, Box 69, Watkins-Loomis, Inc., Records, Rare Book and Manuscript Library, Columbia University, New York (hereafter cited as WL); "Of Local Origin," *New York Times,* Apr. 3, 1950; "Warners Feuding with Talent Unit," *New York Times,* Apr. 27, 1950; Stewart Stern and Alfred Hayes, *Teresa,* temporary shooting script, "with holograph changes by Bill Mauldin," 1950, Box 14, William Henry Mauldin Papers, Library of Congress, Manuscripts Division, Washington, D.C. (hereafter cited as WHM); "Bill Mauldin to Appear in Film," *New York Times,* May 7, 1950; Bill Mauldin to Mike Watkins, May 7, 1950, Box 69, WL.
3. John Huston, *An Open Book* (New York: Alfred A. Knopf, 1980), 109–11, 119–20; Mike Watkins, notes of telephone conversation with Bill Mauldin, June 27 and 28, 1950, Box 69, WL;
4. *Picture,* 6; Lawrence Grobel, *The Hustons* (New York: Charles Scribner's Sons, 1989), 354.
5. Watkins, notes of telephone conversation, WL.
6. *The Hustons,* 356; Bill Mauldin, "Bill Mauldin's Tribute to Audie Murphy," *Life,* June 11, 1971, 77.
7. "Bill Mauldin's Tribute to Audie Murphy."
8. Mike Watkins, notes of telephone conversation with Bert Allenberg, Bert Allenberg to Mike Watkins, Sept. 21, 1949, Box 68, WL; Watkins to Allenberg, June 19, 1950, Box 69, WL; "New Films," *Newsweek,* Apr. 2, 1951, 85.
9. *Picture,* 102, 176–203; *The Hustons,* 364–65.
10. "Controversial Little Cuss," 16.
11. "New Films," *Newsweek,* Apr. 2, 1951, 85.
12. Mike Watkins, notes of telephone conversation with Bill Mauldin, May 7, 10, and 29, 1951, Box 69, WL.
13. Herbert Mitgang, *Dangerous Dossiers: Exposing the Secret War Against America's Greatest Authors* (New York: Ballantine Books, 1989), 199–200; V. P. Keay to A. H. Belmont, memo, Nov. 28, 1951; "William Henry Mauldin, aka Bill Maul-

din," Nov. 28, 1951, file of Mauldin, William H., Federal Bureau of Investigation, Department of Justice, Washington, D.C.

14. Bill Mauldin, *Bill Mauldin in Korea* (New York: W. W. Norton, 1952), 15, 37–38, 44.

15. Ibid., 48.

16. Ibid., 41, 67–79, 113–15.

17. Ibid., 160–70.

18. Ibid., 10.

19. Beatrice A. Barron to Natalie Mauldin, Feb. 19 and 28, 1952; Apr. 11, 21, and 30, 1952, Box 7, WHM; Martin Blumenson, "The Latter-Day Willie," *Saturday Review of Literature,* Nov. 22, 1952, 49.

20. Universal Pictures Company, Inc., to Bill Mauldin, Apr. 12, 1952, Box 7, WHM; Mike Watkins to Bert Allenberg, Oct. 10, 1952, Box 69, WL.

21. Hesper Anderson, *South Mountain Road: A Daughter's Journey of Discovery* (New York: Simon & Schuster, 2002), 14, 73; René Auberjonois, author's interview, July 20, 2006.

22. Bill Mauldin, untitled newspaper clipping, 1951, Box 69, WL.

23. Mike Watkins, notes of tleephone conversation with Bill Mauldin, Nov. 30, 1953, Box 69, WL; Eric Swenson to Bill Mauldin, Mar. 3, 1953, Box 5, WHM.

24. Bill Mauldin, "Ox-Roasting Ceremony in Remote Cornish Village," *Life,* June 15, 1953, 36–37; Bill Mauldin, "Europe on Less than $28,411," *Life,* Aug. 17, 1953, 69–70, 72, 75–76, 78, 81–82, 84; Bill Mauldin to Natalie Mauldin, June 18, 19, and 21, 1953; July 2, 1953, Box 1, WHM.

25. Bill Mauldin, "Bill Mauldin Asks Today's Teenagers—'What Gives?'" *Collier's,* Jan. 21, 1955, 46–53; "Bill Mauldin Asks Today's Teenagers—'What Gives?'" draft, 1955, Box 8, WHM.

26. Bill Mauldin, "The Era of the Cop," *Reporter,* Dec. 22, 1953, 40.

27. Notes for "Sam Bean," television script, Box 9, WHM; Bill Mauldin to Mike Watkins, Dec. 12, 1955, Box 7, WHM; "Sam Bean," television script, Box 70, WL.

28. Arthur B. Cuddihy Jr. to Mike Watkins, Apr. 6, 1954; Mike Watkins to Arthur B. Cuddihy Jr., Apr. 7, 1954, Box 70, WL; "Memorandum to William Mauldin—Re: Proposed 'Willy and Joe' Television Deal"; Pincus Berner to Reece Halsey, Dec. 1, 1954, Box 17, WHM; Bill Mauldin to Mike Watkins, Dec. 12, 1955, Box 7, WHM; Bill Mauldin to Sam Weisborg, Dec. 18, 1957, Box 5, WHM; Walter Doniger to Bill Mauldin, Nov. 17, 1961, Box 3, WHM.

29. Bill Mauldin to Eric Swenson and George Brockway (never sent), Feb. 19, 1958, Box 5, WHM; Bill Mauldin to Eric Swenson, Mar. 24, 1955, Box 7, WHM; "*Day to Day* by Bill Mauldin," promotional copy, undated, Box 5, WHM.

30. Natalie Mauldin to Bill Mauldin, undated correspondence, Box 1, WHM.

31. Ibid.

32. *South Mountain Road*, 15, 26–27, 73.

33. Bill Mauldin to Alice Rossin, May 5, 1954; Frank G. Bossong to Bill Mauldin, Mar. 4, 1954; Bill Mauldin to Corn Exchange Bank Trust Co., Jan. 13, 1954, Box 15, WHM.

34. Bill Mauldin to Andrew E. Rice, Nov. 28, 1953, Box 2, WHM; Peggy Caufield to Paul Gitlin, Jan. 16, 1957, Box 70, WL; "Advertising Copy" file, Box 9, WHM; Bill Mauldin to Omar Bradley, undated correspondence, Box 2, WHM.

35. Bill Mauldin, *The Brass Ring* (New York: W. W. Norton, 1971), 206–7, 233–34.

36. Barbara Witchell, "Bill Mauldin," magazine clipping, n.d., Box 15, WHM; "Crazy Like an Eagle," *Sports Illustrated,* Nov. 8, 1954, 36–37; "Hit It If It's Big," *Time,* July 21, 1961, 53; Bill Mauldin, *Up High with Bill Mauldin* (Lockhaven, Pa.: Piper Aircraft Corp., 1956), 3, 32.

37. "Bill Mauldin Abandons Ike for the Stevenson Campaign," *Cincinnati Enquirer,* clipping, n.d.; "Vets for Stevenson Pick Chairmen Here," *Chicago Daily News,* clipping, n.d., Box 15, WHM; Bill Mauldin, "The Eisenhower I'll Always Remember," *Reporter,* Sept. 23, 1954, 45.

38. "Controversial Little Cuss," 15; Bill Mauldin, AVC press release, Jan. 29, 1954; "Mauldin Hits Legion Stand," *AVC Bulletin,* Feb. 1954, clipping, Box 2, WHM; "Dispute Widened Over 'Red' Hunts," *New York Times,* June 30, 1954.

39. Bill Mauldin, untitled manuscript, n.d., Box 17; Donald R. Katz, "Drawing Fire," *Rolling Stone,* Nov. 4, 1956, 56; "Won't Wage Naive Campaign, Mauldin Spokesman Says," newspaper clipping, n.d., campaign scrapbook, Box 18, WHM.

40. "Picking a Tartar," *Time*, Mar. 26, 1956, 24.

41. "Mauldin Warms Up to Work in Campaign Talk at Hillcrest," May 31, 1956, newspaper clipping, n.d., campaign scrapbook.

42. "Mauldin Cops Spotlight at Party Dinner," *Rockland County Journal News,* Apr. 9, 1956, campaign scrapbook; Bill Mauldin, untitled manuscript, Jan. 4, 1977, Box 18, WHM; Ray Galant, "Mauldin Has Try at Political War," *Army Times,* July 28, 1956, campaign scrapbook.

43. "Two State GOP Congressmen in Lively Races," *New York Times,* Oct. 18, 1956; "A Lively Political Tilt in Our Own Backyard," *Binghamton Press,* Oct. 20, 1956, campaign scrapbook.

44. "Bill Mauldin's Platform," Box 15, WHM; "Mauldin's Cartoons Appear in *Collier's*—On Stands Today," *Sullivan County Democrat,* Sept. 13, 1956, campaign scrapbook; untitled manuscript, Jan. 4, 1977.

45. "Famous Veteran Speaks Here," *Sullivan County Democrat,* May 31, 1956, campaign scrapbook.

46. "St. George Hits Rival on Left Wing Links," *Newburgh News,* Oct. 26, 1956; "Americans Beware!," *Middletown Daily Record,* Oct. 29, 1956, campaign scrapbook; *Dangerous Dossiers,* 200.

47. "'Mud and Mink Don't Mix,' Mauldin Charges Panic," *Rockland Independent,* Oct. 30, 1956; clipping, *Rockland County Journal News,* Nov. 1, 1956, campaign scrapbook.

48. "Mrs. St. George Wins by 39,000 Votes in Four Counties," *Rockland County Journal News,* Nov. 7, 1956, campaign scrapbook; "Drawing Fire," 56.

49. Untitled manuscript, Jan. 4, 1977.

50. Joan Crowell, author's interview, July 17, 2006.

51. Bill Mauldin to Mike Watkins, May 14, 1958, Box 5, WHM; Bill Mauldin to Eric Swenson and George Brockway (never sent), Feb. 19, 1958.

52. Ralph Martin, author's interview, July 27, 2004; Bill Mauldin, *Back Home* (New York: William Sloane Associates, 1947), 272.

53. Bill Mauldin to Robert Lasch, Feb. 24 and 26, 1958, Box 6, WHM.

54. Bill Mauldin to Joseph Pulitzer Jr., Mar. 29, 1958; Bill Mauldin to Robert Lasch, Mar. 31, 1958, Box 4, WHM; Natalie Mauldin to Alice Rossin, Apr. 4, 1958, Box 1, WHM.

55. Bill Mauldin to Norton Wolf, Apr. 24, 1958, private correspondence of Norton Wolf.

56. "In War and Peace," *Time,* Sept. 26, 1960, 49.

57. Bill Mauldin, untitled manuscript, n.d., 9, personal collection of Norton Wolf.

58. "Hit It If It's Big," *Time,* July 21, 1961, 50; Steve McDowell, "Pulitzer Prize-Winning Cartoonist Bill Mauldin," *El Palacio,* vol. 98, no. 4 (Winter 1993): 56.

59. Jack Star, "Bill Mauldin: The Idea Factory," *Look,* July 30, 1963, 71–73.

60. "Hit It If It's Big," 50–53.

61. CD DeLoach to Mr. Mohr, Sept. 12, 1960, file of Mauldin, FBI.

62. Ibid., 52; Richard Samuel West, "Mauldin: From Willie and Joe to Ronnie," *Target,* vol. 3, no. 10 (Winter 1984), 9.

63. "New Job for Mauldin," *Time,* June 15, 1962, 42; "The Three-Step," *Newsweek,* June 18, 1962, 82; "Mauldin: From Willie and Joe to Ronnie," 10; "Bill Mauldin: The Idea Factory," 73.

64. Bob Greene, "Bill Mauldin and Willie and Joe," *Audience,* vol. 2, no. 4 (1972): 27.

65. untitled manuscript, n.d., 10, personal collection of Norton Wolf.

66. Bill Mauldin, *I've Decided I Want My Seat Back* (New York: Harper & Row, 1965), 27–29.

67. "Bill Mauldin and Willie and Joe," 29; "Drawing Fire," 58; *I've Decided I Want My Seat Back,* 75; Pat Oliphant, author's interview, May 9, 2004.

*Chapter Eight:* **Fighting On**

1. Bill Mauldin, *I've Decided I Want My Seat Back* (New York: Harper & Row, 1965), 118–23; untitled newscript, *Los Angeles Times,* n.d., Box 2, William Henry Mauldin Papers, Library of Congress, Manuscripts Division, Washington, D.C. (hereafter cited as WHM); Bill Mauldin, Vietnam Sketchbook, Mauldin Cartoon Collection, 1946–87, Box 18, Archives Center, National Museum of American History, Smithsonian Institution, Washington, D.C.; Bill Mauldin, "Vivid Picture of the Attack on Pleiku," *Life,* Feb. 19, 1965, 32–33.
2. "Back Up Front," *Newsweek,* Feb. 22, 1965, 56; Bill Mauldin, "Evolution of a Dove," *New Republic,* Feb. 10, 1973, 18–19.
3. *I've Decided I Want My Seat Back,* 9.
4. Donald R. Katz, "Drawing Fire," *Rolling Stone,* Nov. 4, 1956, 89; Bill Mauldin, Vietnam notebook, Box 9, WHM.
5. Bill Mauldin, "Think Charitably of the Peaceniks," *Chicago Sun-Times* clipping, Nov. 1965, Box 6, WHM.
6. Andy Mauldin, author's interview, May 7, 2004.
7. "Revolution '67," *Daily Cardinal,* Feb. 15, 1967, Box 15, WHM.
8. "Bill Mauldin Sees Birth of War," *Chicago Sun-Times,* June 6, 1967; Bill Mauldin, untitled manuscript, n.d., Box 8, WHM; Gilbert A. Harrison, "Compelled to Irritate," *New Republic,* Dec. 25, 1971, 27.
9. Bill Mauldin, "Not a Litterbug Among Them," *New Republic,* June 24, 1967, 6.
10. William Chafe, *The Unfinished Journey: America Since World War II,* 4th ed. (New York: Oxford University Press, 1999), 374–75.
11. "Drawing Fire," 89; Nat Mauldin, author's interview, Aug. 19, 2006.
12. Steve Macek, "The *Chicago Journalism Review* and the Radical Movements of the Sixties," Union for Democratic Communications conference, Boca Raton, Fla., May 20, 2006, Ministry of Truth podcast, http://www.podcastdirectory .com/podcasts/2152.
13. Michael Miner, "Drawing on the Past," *Chicago Reader,* June 15, 2001, http:// www.chicagoreader.com/hottype/2001/010615_1.html.
14. Gerald W. Johnson, "Wartime, Peacetime, He's Fine," untitled newspaper clipping, Box 7, WHM; "Books of the Times," *New York Times,* Nov. 9, 1961; Jimmy Johnson, author's interview; Bill Griffith, personal correspondence, July 3, 2004.
15. Bob Greene, "Bill Mauldin and Willie and Joe," *Audience,* vol. 2, no. 4 (1972), 33.
16. Nat Mauldin, author's interview.
17. Norton Wolf, personal correspondence, May 20, 2004.
18. "Drawing Fire," 89; Chris Lund, author's interview, May 8, 2004.

19.  Nat Mauldin, author's interview.

20.  "Drawing Fire," 54.

21.  "It Happened in Santa Fe," *Albuquerque Tribune,* clipping, n.d., Bill Mauldin clipping file, Alamogordo Public Library, Alamogordo, N.M.; Bill and Chris Mauldin, "A Famed Cartoonist and His Wife Weather the Storms 'Twixt May and December," *People,* Nov. 22, 1982, 81.

22.  "A Famed Cartoonist and His Wife," 81–82; Chris Lund, author's interview.

23.  "Drawing Fire," 54.

24.  Neil Steinberg, "Bill Mauldin's Battles Were Worth the Fight," *Chicago Sun-Times,* Jan. 24, 2003.

25.  "Chicago Cartoonist Beaten Outside Daley Party," *New York Times,* May 25, 1975; quoted in "Drawing Fire," 60.

26.  "A Famed Cartoonist and His Wife," 82; Jet Zarkadas, author's interview, Aug. 29, 2006; Jet Zarkadas, author's correspondence, Oct. 9, 2006.

27.  David Lamb, "Bill, Willie, and Joe," *MHQ: The Quarterly Journal of Military History,* vol. 1, no. 4 (Summer 1989), 38.

28.  Bill Mauldin, *Mud & Guts: A Look at the Common Soldier of the American Revolution* (Washington, D.C.: Division of Publications, National Park Service, U.S. Department of the Interior, 1978), iv.

29.  Bill Mauldin, *Let's Declare Ourselves Winners . . . and Get the Hell Out* (Novato, Calif.: Presidio Press, 1985), vii.

30.  "Drawing Fire," 58.

31.  Norton Wolf, author's interview, May 27, 2004.

32.  "Bill Mauldin and Willie and Joe," 33.

33.  Jet Zarkadas, author's interview; "Willie, Joe Spawned Career," *Tulsa World,* Aug. 22, 1993.

34.  "Soldier's Cartoonist Bill Mauldin, 81, Dies," *Tulsa World,* Jan. 23, 2003.

35.  Charles T. Jones, "'Willie and Joe': Cartoonist 'Astonished' to Find Inspiration Alive," Dec. 31, 1999, http://www.inkboy.net/resume/WillieAndJoe/willie&joe.htm.

36.  "Political Cartoonists: Their Acid Pens May Wound, but Seldom Maim," *Sacramento Bee,* Oct. 28, 1984.

37.  Leonard J. Kerpelman, "Bill Mauldin . . . Up Front," *Army Times,* June 14, 1982, 43–44.

38.  Studs Terkel, *"The Good War": An Oral History of World War II* (New York: Ballantine Books, 1985), 360; "GI Cartoonist Drew It Like It Was in Foxholes," *Los Angeles Times,* Jan. 23, 2003.

39.  Chris Lund, author's interview; Andy Mauldin, author's interview.

40.  M. S. Wyeth Jr. to Gloria Loomis, Dec. 2, 1986, private correspondence of Norton Wolf.

41. Chris Lund, author's interview.

42. "Button Pusher Dogfaces Willie and Joe Won't Join in Gulf War," *Long Beach Press-Telegram,* Feb. 16, 1991; *PrimeTime Live* (ABC News), Nov. 22, 1990.

43. Steve McDowell, "Pulitzer Prize-Winning Cartoonist Bill Mauldin," *El Palacio,* vol. 98, no. 4 (Winter 1993), 59.

44. "Bronze Mettle," *Albuquerque Journal,* Apr. 6, 2003.

45. David Roybal, "We Ignore Painful Realities of War at Our Peril," *Santa Fe New Mexican,* Mar. 30, 2003.

46. "GI Cartoonist Drew It Like It Was in Foxholes"; "Bill Mauldin, World War II Cartoonist, Dies," *Army Times,* Jan. 22, 2003.

47. Nat Mauldin, author's interview.

48. Chris Lund, author's interview.

49. Nat Mauldin, author's interview.

50. Ibid.; Andy Mauldin, author's interview.

51. Neil Steinberg, "Bill Mauldin's Battles Were Worth the Fight," *Chicago Sun-Times,* Jan. 24, 2003.

52. Andy Mauldin, author's interview.

53. Chip Beck, "With a Little Help from His Friends," http://editorialcartoonists .com/news/article.cfm/275.

54. Jet Zarkadas, author's interview.

55. Nat Mauldin, author's interview; Jet Zarkadas, author's interview.

56. Nat Mauldin, author's interview.

57. Michael Miner, "Mauldin on the Attack," *Chicago Reader,* Jan. 31, 2003.

58. "Cartoonist Mauldin Is Laid to Rest at Arlington," *Stars and Stripes* (Pacific edition), Jan. 31, 2003.

# Permissions

# Index

Page numbers in *italics* refer to illustrations.